**PRENTICE HALL MATHEMATICS**

# COURSE 3

# Study Guide & Practice Workbook

PEARSON

Prentice
Hall

**Boston, Massachusetts**
**Upper Saddle River, New Jersey**

**Pearson Prentice Hall™** is a trademark of Pearson Education, Inc.
**Pearson®** is a registered trademark of Pearson plc.
**Prentice Hall®** is a registered trademark of Pearson Education, Inc.

ISBN: 0-13-125457-X
18   V031   12 11

# Study Guide & Practice Workbook

## Contents

**Answers appear in the back of each Grab & Go File.**

# Contents (cont.)

# Reteaching 1-1

**Algebraic Expressions and the Order of Operations**

A *variable* represents a number. An *algebraic expression* is formed from numbers, variables, and operations.

To evaluate an algebraic expression, substitute a number for each variable. Then follow the order of operations.

|  | | Evaluate $4(n + 2)$ for $n = 3$. | Evaluate $n + 12 \div (3 \times m)$ for $n = 4$ and $m = 2$. |
|---|---|---|---|
| ① | Substitute for each variable. | $4(3 + 2)$ | $4 + 12 \div (3 \times 2)$ |
| ② | Work inside grouping symbols. | $= 4(5)$ | $= 4 + 2 \div 6$ |
| ③ | Multiply and divide from left to right. | $= 20$ | $= 4 + 2$ |
| ④ | Add and subtract from left to right. | | $= 6$ |

**Evaluate each expression for $g = 4$, $k = 2$, and $t = 9$.**

**1.** $4t$

**2.** $3k$

**3.** $g + 4$

**4.** $5t + 7$

**5.** $4(g - 1)$

**6.** $15k + 6$

**7.** $3t - g$

**8.** $gt \div k$

**9.** $27 \div t \times k$

**10.** $g + 12 - 3 \times k$

**11.** $32 \div g \times k$

**12.** $(2t + 2) \div g$

**13.** $(20 \div g) \times k$

**14.** $4g + t - k$

**15.** $3(3g - t)$

**16.** $2g + 2 \times 3$

**17.** $kt - 3$

**18.** $10 + 4k \div 8$

**19.** The formula for the perimeter of a rectangle is $P = 2l + 2w$. If $l = 2$ in. and $w = 4$ in., what operation(s) would you do first?

_____

# Practice 1-1

**Algebraic Expressions and the Order of Operations**

**Write an algebraic expression for each word phrase.**

1. 5 less than
   a number _____

2. 15 more than the absolute
   value of a number _____

3. the product of a
   number and −8 _____

4. 5 more than a number,
   divided by 9 _____

5. 3 more than the product
   of 8 and a number _____

6. 3 less than the absolute
   value of a number, times 4 _____

**Write an algebraic expression for each situation. Explain what the variable represents.**

7. the amount of money Waldo has if he has
   $10 more than Jon

   _____

   _____

8. the amount of money that Mika has if she
   has some quarters

   _____

   _____

9. how much weight Kirk can lift if he lifts
   30 lb more than his brother

   _____

   _____

10. how fast Rya runs if she runs 5 mi/h slower
    than Danae

    _____

    _____

**Write a word phrase that can be represented by each variable expression.**

11. $n \div (4)$

    _____

12. $n + 4$

    _____

13. $3n$

    _____

14. $n - 8$

    _____

**Evaluate each expression for $n = 2$, $x = 6$, and $y = 4$.**

15. $11x + 7$ _____

16. $29y - 15$ _____

17. $6(n + 8)$ _____

18. $(24 \div x) + 18$ _____

19. $(x + n) \div y$ _____

20. $xn + y$ _____

21. $(6 \cdot 8 + y) \cdot n$ _____

22. $6(8 + y) \cdot n$ _____

23. $6 \cdot 8 + y \cdot n$ _____

24. $y + n \cdot n$ _____

25. $12 \div x + xy$ _____

26. $(2n + 2y) \div 2x$ _____

27. $n + x(y + 1)$ _____

28. $y \div n \cdot 3x$ _____

29. $4 + x \div n + 2$ _____

30. $4n + x(y + 1)$ _____

# Reteaching 1-2

**Problem Solving: Use a Problem-Solving Plan**

You can use a problem-solving plan to organize information and solve problems. Use these three steps to solve problems.

① Read and understand the problem.

② Plan how to solve the problem, and then solve it.

③ Look back and check to see if your answer makes sense.

Sarah is 2 years older than her sister Lacey.
If the sum of their ages is 14, how old is each girl?

**Read and Understand**  What are you asked to find? *the ages of Sarah and Lacey*

**Plan and Solve**  You can use the *Try, Test, and Revise* strategy and *Make a Table*.

Pick two ages that are 2 years apart and add. If the sum is too low, try again. If the sum is too high, decrease your number. Keep a record of the results.

|  | Sarah's Age | Lacey's Age | Total |  |
|---|---|---|---|---|
| first try → | 4 | 2 | 6 | ← too low |
| second try → | 6 | 4 | 10 | ← too low |
| third try → | 9 | 7 | 16 | ← too high |
| fourth try → | 8 | 6 | 14 | ← Solved! |

Sarah is 8 and Lacey is 6.

**Look Back and Check**  Is Sarah 2 years older than Lacey? *yes*
Is the sum of their ages 14? *yes*

---

**Use the problem-solving plan to solve each problem.**

1. Joe is 5 years older than Bijan. If the sum of their ages is 25, how old is each boy?

2. A chicken dinner costs $2.50 more than a spaghetti dinner. If the cost of both is $18.40, how much does each meal cost?

3. Elaine sold twice as many T-shirts as Kim. How many did each girl sell if the total number of T-shirts sold was 27?

4. There are 5 more rows of corn than rows of peas in the garden. How many rows of each are there if there are 19 rows in all?

5. Becki thinks of a number. If she multiplies her number by 8, adds 10, and then divides by 5, the result is 26. What is Becki's number?

6. Martina went shopping. She spent one-fifth of what she had in her wallet and then one-fifth of what remained. In all she spent $36. How much did she start with?

# Practice 1-2

**Problem Solving: Use a Problem-Solving Plan**

**Use the problem-solving plan to solve each problem.**

1. Philip drove 1,096 miles in two days. He drove 240 miles more on the second day than he drove on the first day. How many miles did he drive each day?

   _____

2. Bea raised some cows and some turkeys. She raised a total of 28 cows and turkeys. There were 96 legs in all. How many cows and how many turkeys did Bea raise?

   _____

3. Two integers have a difference of −11 and a sum of −3. What are the integers?

   _____

4. Tickets for a benefit dinner were on sale for three weeks. Twice as many tickets were sold during the third week as were sold during the first two weeks combined. If a total of 1,095 tickets were sold, how many were sold the third week?

   _____

**Choose a problem-solving method to solve each problem. Show all your work.**

5. Priya ordered twice as many blankets as she did quilts for the department store where she works. The order was for 126 items. How many blankets and how many quilts did Priya order?

   _____

6. Kent is three years older than his sister Debbie. The sum of their ages is 105. Find their ages.

   _____

7. A bowling league has 16 teams. During a single-elimination tournament, the winner of each match goes on to the next round. How many matches does the winning team need to play?

   _____

8. In the addition problems below, each letter represents the same digit in both problems. Replace each letter with a different digit, 1 through 9, so that both addition problems are true. (There are two possible answers.)

   $$
   \begin{array}{r} A\,B\,C \\ +\,D\,E\,F \\ \hline G\,H\,I \end{array}
   \qquad
   \begin{array}{r} A\,D\,G \\ +\,B\,E\,H \\ \hline C\,F\,I \end{array}
   $$

# Reteaching 1-3

*Integers* are the set of whole numbers and their opposites. Negative integers are to the left of zero on a number line. Positive integers are to the right of zero on a number line.

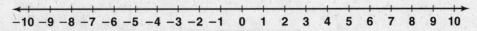

−5 is to the left of −2.    −7 is to the left of 4.    6 is to the right of 3.
−5 is less than −2.    −7 < 4    6 is greater than 3.
−5 < −2    6 > 3

The *absolute value* of a number is its distance from zero on a number line.
The absolute value of 5 is written as $|5|$

−3 is 3 units from 0.    2 is 2 units from 0.    0 is 0 units from 0.
$|-3| = 3$    $|2| = 2$    $|0| = 0$

---

**Write the integers missing from each number line.**

1.
 __ **−6** __ **−4** __ __ **−1** **0** **1** __ **3** __ __ __ **7**

2.
 __ **−60** **−55** __ __ **−35** __ **−25** __ __ **−10** __ **0** __ **10** __

**Compare. Write <, >, or =.**

3. 6 ☐ 0          4. −8 ☐ −5          5. −2 ☐ 2

6. 12 ☐ 5         7. 3 ☐ −2          8. −4 ☐ −6

9. −5 ☐ 5         10. −5 ☐ −10        11. 0 ☐ 0

12. 8 ☐ −1        13. −4 ☐ 0          14. 4 ☐ −2

**Find each absolute value.**

15. $|3|$          16. $|-2|$          17. $|10|$

_____          _____          _____

18. $|-4|$         19. $|4|$           20. $|0|$

_____          _____          _____

21. $|-1|$         22. $|-18|$         23. $|50|$

_____          _____          _____

# Practice 1-3

Integers and Absolute Value

**Write an integer to represent each situation.**

1. The top of the world's lowest known active volcano is 160 ft below sea level.

   _____

2. The football team gained three yards on a play.

   _____

3. Jenni owes her friend $20.

   _____

4. The temperature yesterday was five degrees above zero.

   _____

**Use the information in the graph at the right for questions 5–8.**

5. The highest outdoor temperature ever recorded in Nevada, 122°F, was recorded on June 23, 1954. Was it ever that hot in Idaho? Explain.

   _____

   _____

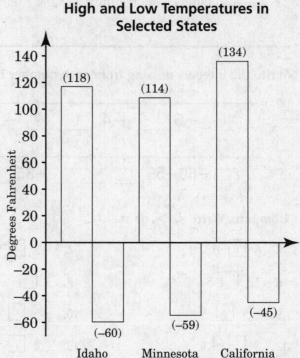

**High and Low Temperatures in Selected States**

6. Which state had a recorded high temperature of 134°F?

   _____

7. The lowest temperature ever recorded in Maine, −48°F, was recorded on January 17, 1925. Was it ever that cold in Minnesota? Explain.

   _____

   _____

8. Which state on the graph had a recorded low temperature of 60°F below zero?

   _____

**Compare. Write >, <, or =.**

9. $-12$ ☐ $10$        10. $9$ ☐ $-12$        11. $|4|$ ☐ $|-9|$        12. $|26|$ ☐ $|-26|$

13. $|42|$ ☐ $|-93|$        14. $53$ ☐ $-21$        15. $|6|$ ☐ $0$        16. $|9|$ ☐ $|-13|$

**Order the integers in each set from least to greatest.**

17. $0, -5, 5, -15, 15, 25, -25$

   _____

18. $6, -4, -8, 3, 1, -2, 7$

   _____

19. $27, -10, -6, -18, 3, 9, -8$

   _____

20. $-3, -7, 7, 4, -9, -4, -1$

   _____

# Reteaching 1-4

**Adding and Subtracting Integers**

A number line can help you add integers. For positive integers, move to the right. For negative integers, move to the left.

*Example* Add $5 + (-3)$:

First, move 5 spaces to the right.
Then move 3 spaces to the left.

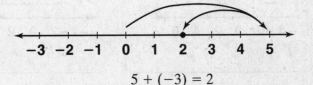

$$5 + (-3) = 2$$

- To add integers with the same sign, add absolute values and use the same sign.

  $3 + 5 = 8$ $\qquad -2 + -4 = -6$

- To add integers with different signs, subtract absolute values and use the sign of the integer with the greater absolute value.

  $-7 + 3 = ?$
  $|-7| - |3| = 7 - 3 = 4$
  Use the sign of $-7$.
  So, $-7 + 3 = -4$.

- To subtract an integer, add its opposite.

  $\begin{aligned}3 - (-2) &= 3 + 2 \\ &= 5\end{aligned}$ The opposite of $-2$ is 2.

  $\begin{aligned}3 - 4 &= 3 + (-4) \\ &= -1\end{aligned}$ The opposite of 4 is $-4$.

  $\begin{aligned}-4 - (-5) &= -4 + 5 \\ &= 1\end{aligned}$ The opposite of $-5$ is 5.

**Simplify each expression.**

1. $8 + (-4) =$ _____

2. $8 + 4 =$ _____

3. $-8 + 4 =$ _____

4. $-3 + (-3) =$ _____

5. $6 + (-2) =$ _____

6. $11 + (-16) =$ _____

7. $-7 + 11 =$ _____

8. $-4 + 16 =$ _____

9. $8 + (-12) =$ _____

10. $-9 + (-10) =$ _____

11. $23 + (-3) =$ _____

12. $-5 + 2 =$ _____

13. $9 - (-3) =$ _____

14. $18 - 14 =$ _____

15. $-6 - 7 =$ _____

16. $-3 - (-3) =$ _____

17. $-4 - 16 =$ _____

18. $8 - (-9) =$ _____

19. $-3 - 12 =$ _____

20. $6 - (-2) =$ _____

21. $10 - (-16) =$ _____

22. $-9 - (-10) =$ _____

23. $2 - (-3) =$ _____

24. $-5 - 2 =$ _____

25. $12 - 32 =$ _____

26. $42 - (-15) =$ _____

27. $-16 - 23 =$ _____

28. You owe your teacher $26 for the class trip. You give her a payment of $11. How much do you still owe?

_____

29. A golf ball is 6 inches under water. While trying to retrieve it, the golfer accidentally kicks it so that it descends another 9 inches. How far under the surface of the water is the golf ball?

_____

# Practice 1-4

**Adding and Subtracting Integers**

**Write the addition equation that is suggested by each model.**

1.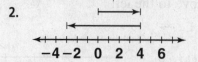

   _____

2.

   _____

3.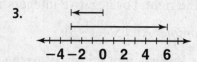

   _____

**Write an algebraic expression to find the sum for each situation.**

4. The varsity football team gained 7 yd on one play and then lost 4 yd. _____

5. The airplane descended 140 ft and then rose 112 ft. _____

6. The squirrel climbed 18 in. up a tree, slipped back 4 in., and then climbed up 12 in. more. _____

7. The temperature was 72°F at noon. At midnight a cold front moved in, dropping the temperature 12°F. _____

**Simplify each expression.**

8. $8 + (7)$ _____
9. $9 + (-4)$ _____
10. $-6 + (-8)$ _____
11. $8 + (-14)$ _____

12. $9 + (-17)$ _____
13. $-15 + (-11)$ _____
14. $-23 + 18$ _____
15. $-19 + 16$ _____

16. $27 + 34$ _____
17. $-8 + (-17)$ _____
18. $19 + (-8)$ _____
19. $23 + (-31)$ _____

20. $-14 - 33$ _____
21. $-32 - (-18)$ _____
22. $-15 - (-26)$ _____
23. $32 - (-16)$ _____

24. $-19 - (-12)$ _____
25. $-16 - (-21)$ _____
26. $27 - 19$ _____
27. $-14 - 27$ _____

**Evaluate each expression for $x = 5$, $y = -6$, and $z = -7$.**

28. $x + y$ _____
29. $15 - z$ _____
30. $y - z$ _____
31. $x + y - z$ _____

32. $y - 15 + x$ _____
33. $32 - z + x$ _____
34. $|x| - |y|$ _____
35. $z + |x|$ _____

36. Jill and Joe are playing a game. The chart at the right shows the points gained or lost on each round.

    a. Who has the most points after the fifth round?

    _____

    b. To win, a player must have 20 points. How many points does each player need to win?

    _____

| Round | Jill | Joe |
|-------|------|-----|
| 1 | 10 | 12 |
| 2 | −2 | 3 |
| 3 | 6 | −8 |
| 4 | 4 | 0 |
| 5 | −2 | 7 |

# Reteaching 1-5

**Multiplying and Dividing Integers**

- If two integers have the same sign, the product is positive.

  $8 \cdot 7 = 56$ $\qquad$ $(-8) \cdot (-7) = 56$

- If two integers have opposite signs, the product is negative.

  $(-8) \cdot 7 = -56$ $\qquad$ $8 \cdot (-7) = -56$

- If two integers have the same sign, the quotient is positive.

  $8 \div 2 = 4$ $\qquad$ $(-8) \div (-2) = 4$

- If two integers have opposite signs, the quotient is negative.

  $(-8) \div 2 = -4$ $\qquad$ $8 \div (-2) = -4$

---

**Determine the sign of the product.**

**1.** $-9 \cdot 3 = \boxed{\phantom{x}} 27$

**2.** $80 \cdot (-2) = \boxed{\phantom{x}} 160$

**3.** $-23 \cdot (-20) = \boxed{\phantom{x}} 460$

**4.** $7 \cdot (-5) = \boxed{\phantom{x}} 35$

**5.** $-6 \cdot (-8) = \boxed{\phantom{x}} 48$

**6.** $64 \cdot 5 = \boxed{\phantom{x}} 320$

**Determine the sign of the quotient.**

**7.** $24 \div (-3) = \boxed{\phantom{x}} 8$

**8.** $-(24) \div (-2) = \boxed{\phantom{x}} 12$

**9.** $-25 \div 5 = \boxed{\phantom{x}} 5$

**10.** $-27 \div (-9) = \boxed{\phantom{x}} 3$

**11.** $160 \div 4 = \boxed{\phantom{x}} 40$

**12.** $90 \div (-30) = \boxed{\phantom{x}} 3$

**Simplify each expression.**

**13.** $12 \cdot (-3)$

**14.** $-9 \cdot (-9)$

**15.** $9 \cdot (-1)$

**16.** $(-8) \cdot (-4)$

**17.** $5 \cdot 70$

**18.** $(-8) \cdot (-3)$

**19.** $-10 \cdot (-5)$

**20.** $-9 \cdot 8$

**21.** $4 \cdot 7$

**22.** $14 \cdot (-3)$

**23.** $-16 \cdot (-3)$

**24.** $5 \cdot (-25)$

**25.** $\dfrac{30}{5}$

**26.** $\dfrac{-72}{-8}$

**27.** $\dfrac{45}{-9}$

**28.** $-2 \div (-2)$

**29.** $6 \div (-1)$

**30.** $40 \div 2$

**31.** $48 \div (-12)$

**32.** $-99 \div (-9)$

**33.** $-21 \div 3$

**34.** $-33 \div 3$

**35.** $100 \div (-5)$

**36.** $75 \div (-3)$

# Practice 1-5

**Multiplying and Dividing Integers**

**Find each product or quotient.**

**1.** $-4 \cdot 8$

_____

**2.** $-7 \cdot (-9)$

_____

**3.** $-5 \cdot (-11)$

_____

**4.** $20 \cdot (-3)$

_____

**5.** $2(-3)(-3)$

_____

**6.** $(-4)(-4)(-4)$

_____

**7.** $(-3)(4)(-5)$

_____

**8.** $(5)(2)(-20)$

_____

**9.** $-63 \div 7$

_____

**10.** $81 \div (-9)$

_____

**11.** $-77 \div 7$

_____

**12.** $96 \div (-12)$

_____

**13.** $-54 \div (-6)$

_____

**14.** $-120 \div 10$

_____

**15.** $-1,000 \div (-100)$

_____

**16.** $540 \div (-90)$

_____

**17.** The value of Jim's telephone calling card decreases 15 cents for every minute he uses it. Yesterday he used the card to make a 6-minute call. How much did the value of the card change?

_____

**18.** One day the temperature in Lone Grove, Oklahoma fell 3 degrees per hour for 5 consecutive hours. Give the total change in temperature.

_____

**19.** The population of New Orleans, Lousiana, decreased from about 558,000 in 1980 to 497,000 in 1990. On average, about how much did the population change *each year*?

_____

**You want to find a route from Start to Finish. Evaluate the expression in each square. You can only move to the right or down, and you can only move to a square that has an answer greater than the expression in your current square. Draw a line through the route you will take.**

**Start**

| | | | | | |
|---|---|---|---|---|---|
| $-9(26)$ | $-29 - 146$ | $-25 + (-100)$ | $-9(40)$ | $8(7)$ | $23 + (-9)$ |
| $-10(27)$ | $-800 - 92$ | $200 \div (-2)$ | $-40 + 12$ | $-600 \div 6$ | $21(16)$ |
| $-26 - 19$ | $-90 - 15$ | $400 \div (-2)$ | $17 - 19$ | $-4(8)$ | $200 \div 4$ |
| $-17 - (-24)$ | $17(11)$ | $500 \div (-4)$ | $5(0)$ | $8 - (-27)$ | $47 + 1$ |

**Finish**

# Reteaching 1-6

- The *median* of this set of data is the middle value when the scores are ordered.

  23 25 25 26 26 **26 26** 26 27 27 28 29

  Since there are two middle scores, add them and divide by 2.

  $\frac{26 + 26}{2} = 26$

**Number of Pages Read by Members of the Science Fiction Book Club**

| 25 | 26 | 28 | 25 |
|----|----|----|----|
| 26 | 27 | 27 | 26 |
| 26 | 29 | 26 | 23 |

- The *mean* is the sum of the scores divided by the number of scores.

  25 + 26 + 28 + 25 + 26 + 27 + 27 + 26 + 26 + 29 + 26 + 23 = 314

  $\frac{314}{12} = 26.166667$ or about 26.2 pages

- The *mode* is the score that occurs the most. The mode is 26 pages.

---

**Find the mean, median, and mode of each set of data.**

1. movies seen:  3  3  1  4  0  4  2  5  7  4  1  2

   _____

2. miles hiked:  5  10  9  12  8  4  5  7  5  13  11

   _____

3. yards earned:  0  0  −8  4  15  −9  1  −1  6  7  −10  2

   _____

4. cost of tickets:
   $3.25  $2.50  $4.00  $4.00  $3.50  $2.00  $4.00  $3.00  $2.50
   $3.00  $4.00

   _____

**Which would you report to your parents—mean, median, or mode? Give your reason.**

5. test scores:  89  84  79  80  81  55

   _____

   _____

6. friends' allowances:  $10  $15  $12  $15  $8

   _____

   _____

# Practice 1-6

**Using Integers with Mean, Median, and Mode**

**Find the mean, median, and mode of each data set.**

1. hours of piano practice

   _____

2. days of snow per month

   _____

3. number of students per class

   _____

4. ratings given by students to a new movie

   _____

5. points scored in five basketball games

   _____

6. account balance for one month

   _____

**Hours Mr. Capelli's students practice**

2  1  2  0  1  2  2  1  2  2

**Monthly snow days in Central City**

8  10  5  1  0  0  0  0  0  1  3  12

**Class size in Westmont Middle School**

32  26  30  35  25  24  35  30  29  25

**Student ratings of a movie**

10  9  10  8  9  7  5  3  8  9  9  10  9  9  7

**Points scored by Westmont JV**

72  67  83  92  54

**Monthly balance for the last five months**

$129   −$136   −$201   $146   −$154

**Is the mean, median, or mode the best measure of central tendency for each type of data? Explain.**

7. most popular movie in the past month

   _____

8. favorite hobby

   _____

9. class size in a school

   _____

10. ages of members in a club

    _____

**Each person has taken four tests and has one more test to take. Find the score that each person must make to change the mean or median as shown.**

11. Barry has scores of 93, 84, 86, and 75. He wants to raise the mean to 86.

    _____

12. Liz has scores of 87, 75, 82, and 93. She wants to raise the median to 87.

    _____

13. Jim has scores of 60, 73, 82, and 75. He wants to raise the mean to 75.

    _____

14. Andrea has scores of 84, 73, 92, and 88. She wants the median to be 86.

    _____

# Reteaching 1-7

Follow the order of operations when evaluating expressions with exponents.

*Example 1* Evaluate $-(3 + 1)^2 + 5 \cdot 3^2$

①  Work inside grouping symbols first.     $-(3 + 1)^2 + 5 \cdot 3^2 = -(4)^2 + 5 \cdot 3^2$

②  Work with exponents.                                          $= -16 + 5(9)$

• To evaluate a power, write the factors and multiply.

$5^4 = 5 \cdot 5 \cdot 5 \cdot 5$     $(-2)^4 = (-2) \cdot (-2) \cdot (-2) \cdot (-2)$     $-2^4 = -(2 \cdot 2 \cdot 2 \cdot 2)$

$\qquad = 625 \qquad\qquad\qquad = 16 \qquad\qquad\qquad\qquad = -16$

③  Multiply and divide from left to right.          $= -16 + 45$

④  Add and subtract from left to right.                $= 29$

To evaluate a variable expression with exponents, substitute a number
for the variable and then evaluate as above.

*Example 2* Evaluate $-2a^3$ for $a = 3$.

$\qquad -2a^3 = (-2)(3)^3$

$\qquad\qquad = (-2)(27)$

$\qquad\qquad = -54$

---

**Write using exponents.**

1.  $7 \cdot 7 \cdot 7 = $ _____

2.  $(-6) \cdot (-6) \cdot (-6) \cdot (-6) \cdot (-6) = $ _____

3.  $10 \cdot 10 \cdot 10 \cdot 10 = $ _____

4.  $1 \cdot 1 \cdot 1 \cdot 1 \cdot 1 \cdot 1 = $ _____

5.  $(-8) \cdot (-8) \cdot (-8) \cdot (-8) \cdot (-8) = $ _____

6.  $2 \cdot 2 \cdot 2 \cdot 2 \cdot 2 \cdot 2 \cdot 2 = $ _____

**Simplify each expression.**

7.  $3^2 + 7 \cdot 9$ _____

8.  $9 \cdot 3 - 2^3$ _____

9.  $2 + (10 - 3)^2$ _____

10.  $6 - 3^2 \cdot 4$ _____

**Evaluate each expression for the given values of the variables.**

11.  $m^2 - 6; m = 4$ _____

12.  $4c^3; c = 2$ _____

13.  $-2k^2 + 3; k = -5$ _____

14.  $2d^2 \div 6; d = 3$ _____

15.  $-2n^2 - 4; n = 4$ _____

16.  $3ab^2; a = -4, b = 2$ _____

# Practice 1-7

**Write using exponents.**

1. $8 \cdot 8 \cdot 8 \cdot 8 \cdot 8$

2. $(-2)(-2)(-2)(-2)$

3. $x \cdot x \cdot x \cdot x \cdot x \cdot x$

_____  _____  _____

4. $(-3m)(-3m)(-3m)$

5. $4 \cdot t \cdot t \cdot t$

6. $(5v)(5v)(5v)(5v)(5v)$

_____  _____  _____

**Write each expression as a product of the same factor.**

7. $a^2$ _____

8. $19^3$ _____

9. $-6^2$ _____

10. $-x^3$ _____

11. $(-5)^4$ _____

12. $4^3$ _____

13. $-(10)^2$ _____

14. $20^1$ _____

**Simplify each expression.**

15. $(-4)^2 + 10 \cdot 2$ _____

16. $-4^2 + 10 \cdot 2$ _____

17. $(5 \cdot 3)^2 + 8$ _____

18. $5 \cdot 3^2 + 8$ _____

19. $9 + (7 - 4)^2$ _____

20. $-9 + 7 - 4^2$ _____

21. $(-6)^2 + 3^3 - 7$

22. $-6^2 + 3^3 - 7$

23. $2^3 + (8 - 5) \cdot 4 - 5^2$

_____  _____  _____

24. $(2^3 + 8) - 5 \cdot 4 - 5^2$

25. $2^3 \cdot 3 - 5 \cdot 5^2 + 8$

26. $2^3 \cdot 3 - 5(5^2 + 8)$

_____  _____  _____

**Evaluate each expression for the given value.**

27. $4x^2$ for $x = 3$

28. $(5b)^2$ for $b = 2$

29. $-6x^2$ for $x = 3$

30. $(-3g)^2$ for $g = 2$

_____  _____  _____  _____

**Estimate the value of each expression.**

31. $7 + 3q; q = 7.6$

32. $j^2 + 6; j = 4.7$

33. $2m^2 - 3m; m = 1.6$

_____  _____  _____

34. $y^2 - 19y + 16; y = 2.5$

35. $x^2 + 7x - 19; x = 4.21$

36. $v^2 + v; v = 9.8$

_____  _____  _____

37. Suppose you own a card shop. You buy one line of cards at a rate of
4 cards for $5. You plan to sell the cards at a rate of 3 cards for $5.
How many cards must you sell in order to make a profit of $100.

_____

# Reteaching 1-8

Properties of numbers can help you find sums, differences, and products mentally.

Use the *Commutative Property* and the *Associative Property* to group opposites, to group negative numbers, or to make multiples of 10.

- Group opposites.

  $(-8) + (-15) + 8$
  $= (-8) + 8 + (-15)$
  $= 0 + (-15)$
  $= -15$

- Group negatives.

  $-13 + 25 + (-18) + 9$
  $= -13 + (-18) + 25 + 9$
  $= -31 + 34$
  $= 3$

- Make multiples of 10.

  $6 + (-28) + 54$
  $= 6 + 54 + (-28)$
  $= 60 + (-28)$
  $= 32$

Use the *Distributive Property* to rewrite one factor as the sum or difference of two numbers.

$3(5.9)$    ⟨ **Think: 5.9 = 6 − 0.1** ⟩

$4(8.2)$    ⟨ **Think: 8.2 = 8 + 0.2** ⟩

$3(5.9) = 3(6 - 0.1)$
$\quad\quad = 3(6) - 3(0.1)$
$\quad\quad = 18 - 0.3$
$\quad\quad = 17.7$

$4(8.2) = 4(8 + 0.2)$
$\quad\quad = 32 + 0.8$
$\quad\quad = 32.8$

---

**Use mental math to simplify each expression.**

1. $-8 + 16 + (-2)$ _____

2. $-4 + 3 + (-26) + 7$ _____

3. $49 + 12 + 31$ _____

4. $5 + (-8) + 25 + 8$ _____

5. $55 + (-6) + 15 + 6$ _____

6. $(4)(-12)(5)$ _____

7. $20 \cdot 18 \cdot 5$ _____

8. $(-2)(9)(-5)$ _____

9. $-8(5 \cdot 7)$ _____

10. $4(36 \cdot 25)$ _____

11. $-81 + 4 + (-19)$ _____

12. $-28 + 32 + (-46) + 28$ _____

**Use mental math and the distributive property to simplify.**

13. $8(3.9)$

14. $6(21)$

_____

_____

15. $4(7.2)$

16. $5(38)$

_____

_____

17. $6(10.1)$

18. $7(42)$

_____

_____

# Practice 1-8

**Use mental math to simplify each expression.**

**1.** $8 + (-2) + 7 + (-5)$

**2.** $-7 + 9 + 11 + (-13)$

**3.** $17 + (-9) + 18 + (-11)$

**4.** $65 + 23 + 35$

**5.** $220 + 343 + 80$

**6.** $230 + 170 + 18 + (-5)$

**7.** $(-5)(38)(-20)$

**8.** $2 \cdot 83 \cdot (-5)$

**9.** $-5 \cdot (2 \cdot 38)$

**10.** $4 \cdot (25 \cdot 27)$

**11.** $(50)(86)(20)$

**12.** $-4 \cdot (36 \cdot 5)$

**Use mental math and the Distributive Property to simplify.**

**13.** $25(-99)$ _____

**14.** $19(-6)$ _____

**15.** $6 \cdot \$2.99$ _____

**16.** $102 \cdot \$21$ _____

**17.** $19 \cdot 21$ _____

**18.** $26 \cdot 97$ _____

**19.** $21 \cdot (-11)$ _____

**20.** $9 \cdot \$4.98$ _____

**21.** $103 \cdot \$32$ _____

**Determine whether each equation is true or false.**

**22.** $9 \cdot 8 + 6 = 9 \cdot 6 + 8$

**23.** $-7(11 - 4) = 7(15)$

**24.** $12 \cdot 7 = 10 \cdot 7 + 2 \cdot 7$

**25.** $15 + (-17) = -17 + 15$

**26.** $93 \cdot (-8) = -93 \cdot 8$

**27.** $53 + (-19) = -53 + 19$

**The table to the right shows changes in daily temperature over a 5-day period.**

**28.** Which two-day period had the greatest change in temperature?

_____

**29.** On Sunday the temperature was 20°F. What was the temperature at the end of the day on Friday?

_____

| Day | Change in Temperature |
|-----|----------------------|
| Mon | $-12°F$ |
| Tues | $+6°F$ |
| Wed | $-4°F$ |
| Thurs | $-9°F$ |
| Fri | $+8°F$ |

# Reteaching 2-1

To solve one-step equations:

①  Use opposite, or inverse, operations to isolate the variable.

②  Simplify.

③  Check by substituting your answer for the variable.

Solve and check each equation.

$x + 7 = 34$

$x + 7 - 7 = 34 - 7$  ← Subtract 7 from each side.

$x = 27$  ← Simplify.

Check:  $x + 7 = 34$

$27 + 7 \stackrel{?}{=} 34$

$34 = 34$ ✔

$\frac{w}{5} = 20$

$5 \cdot \frac{w}{5} = 5 \cdot 20$  ← Multiply each side by 5.

$w = 100$  ← Simplify.

Check:  $\frac{w}{5} = 20$

$\frac{100}{5} \stackrel{?}{=} 20$

$20 = 20$ ✔

---

**Show your steps to solve each equation. Then check.**

**1.**  $n + 5 = 11$

$n + 5 - \boxed{\phantom{0}} = 11 - \boxed{\phantom{0}}$

$n = \boxed{\phantom{0}}$

Check:  $n + 5 = 11$

$\boxed{\phantom{0}} + 5 \stackrel{?}{=} 11$

$\boxed{\phantom{0}} = 11$

**2.**  $13 + b = 27$

$13 + b - \boxed{\phantom{0}} = 27 - \boxed{\phantom{0}}$

$b = \boxed{\phantom{0}}$

Check:  $13 + b = 27$

$13 + \boxed{\phantom{0}} \stackrel{?}{=} 27$

$\boxed{\phantom{0}} = 27$

**3.**  $y - 18 = 24$

_____

_____

Check: _____

_____

_____

**4.**  $3x = 18$

$\frac{3x}{\boxed{\phantom{0}}} = \frac{18}{\boxed{\phantom{0}}}$

$x = 6$

Check: $3x = 18$

$3 \cdot \boxed{\phantom{0}} \stackrel{?}{=} 18$

$\boxed{\phantom{0}} = 18$

**5.**  $\frac{y}{-5} = -13$

$\frac{y}{-5} \cdot \boxed{\phantom{0}} = -13 \cdot \boxed{\phantom{0}}$

$y = \boxed{\phantom{0}}$

Check: $\frac{y}{-5} = -13$

$\frac{\boxed{\phantom{0}}}{-5} \stackrel{?}{=} -13$

$\boxed{\phantom{0}} = -13$

**6.**  $y \cdot 8 = 24$

_____

_____

Check: $y \cdot 8 = 24$

_____

_____

**7.**  $6 = f + 12$

$f = $ _____

**8.**  $-18 = s + (-23)$

$s = $ _____

**9.**  $w + 4 = \frac{1}{2}$

$w = $ _____

**10.**  $-16 = -8x$

$x = $ _____

**11.**  $\frac{b}{0.4} = 1.6$

$b = $ _____

**12.**  $7.5 = 1.5c$

$c = $ _____

# Practice 2-1

**Solve each equation. Check the solution.**

**1.** $x - 6 = -18$

_____

**2.** $-14 = 8 + j$

_____

**3.** $4.19 + w = 19.72$

_____

**4.** $b + \frac{1}{6} = \frac{7}{8}$

_____

**5.** $9 + k = 27$

_____

**6.** $14 + t = -17$

_____

**7.** $v - 2.59 = 26$

_____

**8.** $r + 9 = 15$

_____

**9.** $n - 19 = 26$

_____

**10.** $14 = -3 + s$

_____

**11.** $9 = d - 4.3$

_____

**12.** $g - \frac{1}{4} = \frac{5}{8}$

_____

**13.** $\frac{a}{-6} = 2$

_____

**14.** $18 = \frac{v}{-1.8}$

_____

**15.** $46 = 2.3m$

_____

**16.** $-114 = -6k$

_____

**17.** $0 = \frac{b}{19}$

_____

**18.** $136 = 8y$

_____

**19.** $0.6j = -1.44$

_____

**20.** $\frac{q}{7.4} = 8.3$

_____

**21.** $28b = -131.6$

_____

**22.** $\frac{n}{-9} = -107$

_____

**23.** $37c = -777$

_____

**24.** $\frac{n}{-1.28} = 4.96$

_____

**Write and solve an equation for each situation.**

**25.** Yesterday Josh sold some boxes of greeting cards. Today he sold seven boxes. If he sold 25 boxes in all, how many did he sell yesterday?

_____

**26.** Skylar bought seven books at $12.95 each. How much did Skylar spend?

_____

**27.** After Simon donated four books to the school library, he had 28 books left. How many books did Simon have to start with?

_____

**28.** Eugenio has five payments left to make on his computer. If each payment is $157.90, how much does he still owe?

_____

Name _____ Class _____ Date _____

# Reteaching 2-2

Michael bought 4 books for the same price at a fair. Admission to the fair was \$5.
How much was each book if Michael spent a total of \$17 at the fair?

Follow these steps to solve the two-step equation:          $4b + 5 = 17$

① Add or subtract on each side.          $4b + 5 - 5 = 17 - 5$

$$4b = 12$$

② Multiply or divide to isolate the variable.          $\dfrac{4b}{4} = \dfrac{12}{4}$

$b = 3$     ← Each book cost \$3.

③ Check by substituting your answer for the variable.     Check: $4b + 5 = 17$

$$4 \cdot 3 + 5 \stackrel{?}{=} 17$$

$$17 = 17 \text{ ✔}$$

---

**Show your steps to solve each equation. Then check.**

**1.**          $2k + 5 = 25$

$2k + 5 - \boxed{\phantom{0}} = 25 - \boxed{\phantom{0}}$

$\dfrac{2k}{\boxed{\phantom{0}}} = \dfrac{20}{\boxed{\phantom{0}}}$

$k = \boxed{\phantom{0}}$

Check: $2k + 5 = 25$

$2 \cdot \boxed{\phantom{0}} + 5 \stackrel{?}{=} 25$

$\boxed{\phantom{0}} = 25$

**2.**          $\dfrac{p}{2} - 2 = 2$

$\dfrac{p}{2} - 2 + \boxed{\phantom{0}} = 2 + \boxed{\phantom{0}}$

$\dfrac{p}{2} \cdot \boxed{\phantom{0}} = 4 \cdot \boxed{\phantom{0}}$

$p = \boxed{\phantom{0}}$

Check: $\dfrac{p}{2} - 2 = 2$

$\dfrac{\boxed{\phantom{0}}}{2} - 2 \stackrel{?}{=} 2$

$\boxed{\phantom{0}} = 2$

**3.** $7y - 17 = -38$

_____

_____

_____

Check: _____

_____

_____

**Solve each equation.**

**4.** $\dfrac{x}{-2} + 6 = 4$

$x = $ _____

**5.** $14j - 7 = 91$

$j = $ _____

**6.** $240a - 3 = 5$

$a = $ _____

**7.** $2.4 + 3s = -0.6$

$s = $ _____

**8.** $2 + \dfrac{n}{-5} = 4$

$n = $ _____

**9.** $140 = -4 - 12e$

$e = $ _____

# Practice 2-2

**Solving Two-Step Equations**

**Solve each equation.**

**1.** $4r + 6 = 14$

_____

**2.** $9y - 11 = 7$

_____

**3.** $\frac{m}{4} + 6 = 3$

_____

**4.** $\frac{k}{-9} + 6 = -4$

_____

**5.** $-5b - 6 = -11$

_____

**6.** $\frac{v}{-7} + 8 = 19$

_____

**7.** $3.4t + 19.36 = -10.22$

_____

**8.** $\frac{n}{-1.6} + 7.9 = 8.4$

_____

**9.** $4.6b + 26.8 = 50.72$

_____

**10.** $\frac{a}{-8.06} + 7.02 = 18.4$

_____

**11.** $-2.06d + 18 = -10.84$

_____

**12.** $\frac{e}{-95} + 6 = 4$

_____

**13.** $-9i - 17 = -26$

_____

**14.** $\frac{j}{-1.9} + 2.7 = -8.6$

_____

**15.** $14.9 = 8.6 + 0.9m$

_____

**16.** $84 = 19 + \frac{z}{12}$

_____

**17.** $15w - 21 = -111$

_____

**18.** $-12.4 = -19.1 + \frac{n}{-7.9}$

_____

**19.** Hugo received $100 for his birthday. He then saved $20 per week until he had a total of $460 to buy a printer. Use an equation to show how many weeks it took him to save the money.

_____

**20.** A health club charges a $50 initial fee plus $2 for each visit. Moselle has spent a total of $144 at the health club this year. Use an equation to find how many visits she has made.

_____

**Solve each equation to find the value of the variable. Write the answer in the puzzle. Do not include any negative signs or any decimals.**

**ACROSS**

**1.** $6n - 12 = 2.4$

**2.** $\frac{n}{3} + 4.6 = 21.6$

**4.** $x - 3 = 51.29$

**6.** $2z + 2 = 7.6$

**DOWN**

**1.** $\frac{j}{5} - 14 = -9$

**2.** $3x - 2 = 169$

**3.** $\frac{x}{4} + 1 = 19$

**4.** $\frac{x}{3} + 4 = 22$

**5.** $2x - 2 = 182$

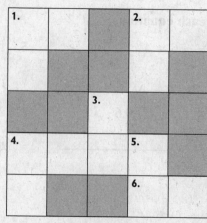

# Reteaching 2-3

A *term* is a number, a variable, or the product of a number and variable(s). The two terms in $-2x + 4y$ are $-2x$ and $4y$.

Terms with exactly the same variable factor are called *like terms*. In $-3x + 4y + 5x$, $-3x$ and $5x$ are like terms.

One way to *combine like terms* is by addition or subtraction.

• Add to combine like terms in $4y + y$.

$$4y + y = (4 + 1)y = 5y$$

• Subtract to combine like terms in $2m - 5m$.

$$2m - 5m = (2 - 5)m = -3m$$

To *simplify* an expression, combine its like terms. Perform as many of its operations as possible.

Simplify:
$$3a + 5b - a + 2b$$
$$= (3a - a) + (5b + 2b)$$
$$= 2a + 7b$$

Simplify:
$$2(x - 4)$$
$$= 2x - 2(4)$$
$$= 2x - 8$$

**Combine like terms.**

**1.** $6x + 2x = $ _____

**2.** $4c - c = $ _____

**3.** $-h - h = $ _____

**4.** $-3y + 4y = $ _____

**5.** $m - 5m = $ _____

**6.** $6n + n = $ _____

**7.** $2s - 6s = $ _____

**8.** $-t - 2t = $ _____

**9.** $3b - 9b = $ _____

**10.** $-2p - 5p = $ _____

**11.** $v + 9v = $ _____

**12.** $-4j + j = $ _____

**Simplify each expression.**

**13.** $8(c - 5) = $ _____

**14.** $4(d + 6) = $ _____

**15.** $5n + 3 + n = $ _____

**16.** $x + 2y + x + y = $ _____

**17.** $3(m + 4) - 5m = $ _____

**18.** $(v - 4)5 = $ _____

**19.** $4a + 2 - 8a + 1 = $ _____

**20.** $6s + 5 - (s - 6) = $ _____

**21.** $3(u + 4) - 5u = $ _____

**22.** $2x + y - (9 - 4x) = $ _____

**23.** $-5x + 3(x - y) = $ _____

**24.** $v + 6v - 2v = $ _____

**25.** $-2s + 6 - s - 4 = $ _____

**26.** $-x + 4(x - 2) = $ _____

**27.** $3(k + j) - 4k - k = $ _____

**28.** $4a - 6 - a + 1 = $ _____

# Practice 2-3

**Simplifying Algebraic Expressions**

• • • • • • • • • • • • • • • • • • • • • • • • • • • • • • • • • • • • • • • • • • • • • • •

**Simplify each expression.**

**1.** $4a + 7 + 2a$

_____

**2.** $8(k - 9)$

_____

**3.** $5n + 6n - 2n$

_____

**4.** $(w + 3)7$

_____

**5.** $5(b - 6) + 9$

_____

**6.** $-4 + 8(2 + t)$

_____

**7.** $-4 + 3(6 + k)$

_____

**8.** $12j - 9j$

_____

**9.** $6(d - 8)$

_____

**10.** $-9 + 8(x + 6)$

_____

**11.** $4(m + 6) - 3$

_____

**12.** $27 + 2(f - 19)$

_____

**13.** $4v - 7 + 8v + 4 - 5$

_____

**14.** $5(g + 8) + 7 + 4g$

_____

**15.** $12h - 17 - h + 16 - 2h$

_____

**16.** $7(e - 8) + 12 - 2e$

_____

**17.** $-3y + 7 + y + 6y$

_____

**18.** $(3.2m + 1.8) - 1.07m$

_____

**Simplify each expression.**

**19.** $28k + 36(7 + k)$

_____

**20.** $3.09(j + 4.6)$

_____

**21.** $12b + 24(b - 42)$

_____

**22.** $7.9y + 8.4 - 2.04y$

_____

**23.** $4.3(5.6 + c)$

_____

**24.** $83x + 15(x - 17)$

_____

**25.** $9.8c + 8d - 4.6c + 2.9d$

_____

**26.** $18 + 27m - 29 + 36m$

_____

**27.** $8(j + 12) + 4(k - 19)$

_____

**28.** $4.2r + 8.1s + 1.09r + 6.32s$

_____

**29.** $43 + 16c - 18d + 56c + 16d$

_____

**30.** $9(a + 14) + 8(b - 16)$

_____

**31.** Tyrone bought 15.3 gal of gasoline priced at $g$ dollars per gal, 2 qt of oil priced at $q$ dollars per qt, and a wiper blade priced at $3.79. Write an expression that represents the total cost of these items.

_____

**32.** Choose a number. Multiply by 2. Add 6 to the product. Divide by 2. Then subtract 3. What is the answer? Repeat this process using two different numbers. Explain.

_____

_____

_____

# Reteaching 2-4

Combining terms can help solve equations.

Solve: $5n + 6 + 3n = 22$
$5n + 3n + 6 = 22$ ← Commutative Property
$8n + 6 = 22$
$8n + 6 - 6 = 22 - 6$
$8n = 16$
$\frac{8n}{8} = \frac{16}{8}$
$n = 2$

Check: $5n + 6 + 3n = 22$
$5(2) + 6 + 3(2) \stackrel{?}{=} 22$
$22 = 22$ ✔

When an equation has a variable on both sides, add or subtract to get the variable on one side.

Solve: $-6m + 45 = 3m$
$-6m + 6m + 45 = 3m + 6m$ ← Add 6m to each side.
$45 = 9m$
$\frac{45}{9} = \frac{9m}{9}$
$5 = m$

Check: $-6m + 45 = 3m$
$-6(5) + 45 \stackrel{?}{=} 3(5)$
$15 = 15$ ✔

---

**Solve each equation. Check the solution.**

**1.** $a - 4a = 36$

$a =$ _____

**2.** $3b - 5 - 2b = 5$

$b =$ _____

**3.** $5n + 4 - 8n = -5$

$n =$ _____

**4.** $12k + 6 = 10$

$k =$ _____

**5.** $3(x - 4) = 15$

$x =$ _____

**6.** $y - 8 + 2y = 10$

$y =$ _____

**7.** $3(s - 10) = 36$

$s =$ _____

**8.** $-15 = p + 4p$

$p =$ _____

**9.** $2g + 3g + 5 = 0$

$g =$ _____

**10.** $6c + 4 - c = 24$

$c =$ _____

**11.** $3(x - 2) = 15$

$x =$ _____

**12.** $4y + 9 - 7y = -6$

$y =$ _____

**13.** $4(z - 2) + z = -13$

$z =$ _____

**14.** $24 = -2(b - 3) + 8$

$b =$ _____

**15.** $17 = 3(g + 3) - g$

$g =$ _____

**16.** $5(k - 4) = 4 - 3k$

$k =$ _____

**17.** $8 - m - 3m = 16$

$m =$ _____

**18.** $6n + n + 14 = 0$

$n =$ _____

**19.** $7(p + 1) = 9 - p$

$p =$ _____

**20.** $36 = 4(q - 5)$

$q =$ _____

**21.** $25 + 2t = 5(t + 2)$

$t =$ _____

# Practice 2-4

**Solving Multi-Step Equations**

**Solve each equation. Check the solution.**

**1.** $2(2.5b - 9) + 6b = -7$

**2.** $12y = 2y + 40$

**3.** $6(c + 4) = 4c - 18$

**4.** $0.7w + 16 + 4w = 27.28$

**5.** $24 = -6(m + 1) + 18$

**6.** $0.5m + 6.4 = 4.9 - 0.1m$

**7.** $7k - 8 + 2(k + 12) = 52$

**8.** $14b = 16(b + 12)$

**9.** $4(1.5c + 6) - 2c = -9$

**10.** $7y = y - 42$

**11.** $9(d - 4) = 5d + 8$

**12.** $0.5n + 17 + n = 20$

**13.** $20 = -4(f + 6) + 14$

**14.** $12j = 16(j - 8)$

**15.** $0.7p + 4.6 = 7.3 - 0.2p$

**16.** $9a - 4 + 3(a - 11) = 23$

**17.** $6(f + 5) = 2f - 8$

**18.** $15p = 6(p - 9)$

**19.** $0.5t + 4.1 = 5.7 - 0.3t$

**20.** $9q - 14 + 3(q - 8) = 7$

**21.** A banquet is planned for 50 people. The caterer charges $1,500 for the food. How much is that per person? Write an equation and solve.

**22.** Stephanie is six years old. She is one year older than one-sixth the age of her mother. How old is Stephanie's mother? Write an equation and solve.

# Reteaching 2-5

**Problem Solving: Draw a Diagram and Write an Equation**

If a problem has many steps, try to write an equation by first defining a variable. Drawing a diagram can help you visualize a problem.

**Read and Understand**    Mrs. Harris is fencing a rectangular dog kennel and has 180 feet of fencing. If she wants the length to be 15 feet longer than the width, what will be the dimensions of the kennel?

What are you asked to do?    *Find the dimensions of the dog kennel.*

**Plan and Solve**    Let $x$ represent the width of the fence. The length of the kennel is 15 feet longer than the width. So, let $x + 15$ equal the length of the dog kennel.

Words    | kennel width | + | kennel width | + | kennel length | + | kennel length | = 180 ft

Equation    $\boxed{x}$ + $\boxed{x}$ + $\boxed{x + 15}$ + $\boxed{x + 15}$ = 180 ft

$$x + x + (x + 15) + (x + 15) = 180$$
$$4x + 30 = 180 \leftarrow \text{Combine like terms.}$$
$$4x = 150 \leftarrow \text{Subtract 30 from each side.}$$
$$\frac{4x}{4} = \frac{150}{4}$$
$$x = 37.5 \text{ ft} \quad \text{the width}$$
$$x + 15 = 52.5 \text{ ft} \quad \text{the length}$$

**Look Back**    How could you check your answer? *Substitute the dimensions back in the problem. Two times the width plus 2 times the length does give you 180 feet. The answer checks.*

---

**Solve each problem by either drawing a diagram or writing an equation.**

1. Tickets for an adult and three children to attend a soccer game cost $20. An adult's ticket costs $2 more than a child's ticket. Find the cost of each ticket.

_____

2. A rectangular deck has a perimeter of 42 feet. The length is 3 feet longer than the width. What is the length and width of the deck?

_____

3. On a family vacation, the Martins drove 842 miles in 2 days. On the second day they drove 24 more miles than the first day. How many miles did they drive each day?

_____

4. On the third day of a school fundraiser, Nichole sold 14 bags of flower bulbs. This was twice as many as the second day. On the second day, she sold two more bags than on the first day. How many bags of flower bulbs did she sell on the first day?

_____

# Practice 2-5

**Problem Solving: Draw a Diagram and Write an Equation**

**Solve each problem by either drawing a diagram or writing an equation. Explain why you chose the method you did.**

1. The cost of a long-distance phone call is $.56 for the first minute and $.32 for each additional minute. What was the total length of a call that cost $9.20?

_____

_____

2. An elevator started on the 7th floor. It went up 6 floors, down 4 floors, up 9 floors, and down 5 floors. On what floor did the elevator finally stop?

_____

_____

_____

3. Two cars start at the same point, at the same time, and travel in opposite directions. In how many hours will the cars be 232 miles apart if the slower car travels at 26 mi/h, and the faster car travels at 32 mi/h?

_____

_____

**Use any strategy to solve each problem. Show your work.**

4. Mary and Jim have tickets to a concert. Mary's ticket number is one less than Jim's ticket number. The product of their numbers is 812. What are the two numbers?

_____

5. The Beards' budget is shown at the right. Their house payment is raised $120. Their income will be no more than it is now, so they plan on subtracting an equal amount from each of the other categories. How much will be available to spend on bills?

| Beards' Budget | |
|---|---|
| **Item** | **Amount** |
| House | $650 |
| Food | $300 |
| Bills | $250 |
| Other | $140 |

6. Antonio watches $\frac{2}{3}$ of a movie at home and then decides to finish watching it later. If he already has watched 2 hours of the movie, how long is it?

_____

Name _____ Class _____ Date _____

# Reteaching 2-6

**Solving Inequalities by Adding and Subtracting**

You can graph inequality solutions on a number line.

| Inequality | Graph | How to Read the Graph |
|---|---|---|
| $x > 2$<br>$x$ is *greater than* 2 | −3 −2 −1 0 1 2 3 | An open dot at 2 shows that 2 is not included.<br>All numbers greater than 2 are included. |
| $x < 2$<br>$x$ is *less than* 2 | −3 −2 −1 0 1 2 3 | An open dot at 2 shows that 2 is not included.<br>All numbers less than 2 are included. |
| $x \geq 2$<br>$x$ is *equal to or greater than* 2 | −3 −2 −1 0 1 2 3 | A solid dot at 2 shows that 2 is included.<br>All numbers greater than 2 are also included. |
| $x \leq 2$<br>$x$ is *equal to or less than* 2 | −3 −2 −1 0 1 2 3 | A solid dot at 2 shows that 2 is included.<br>All numbers less than 2 are also included. |

To help solve an inequality, you can subtract the same number from or add the same number to each side.

Solve: $x + 5 > 8$.

$$x + 5 > 8$$
$$x + 5 - 5 > 8 - 5 \quad \leftarrow \text{Subtract 5 from each side.}$$
$$x > 3 \quad \leftarrow \text{Simplify.}$$

Graph the solution:

−2 −1 0 1 2 3 4

Solve: $y - 4 \leq 1$.

$$y - 4 \leq 1$$
$$y - 4 + 4 \leq 1 + 4 \quad \leftarrow \text{Add 4 to each side.}$$
$$y \leq 5 \quad \leftarrow \text{Simplify.}$$

Graph the solution:

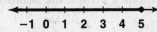

−1 0 1 2 3 4 5

**Graph each inequality on a number line.**

**1.** $x > -2$

−5 −4 −3 −2 −1 0 1 2 3 4 5

**2.** $4 \geq a$

−5 −4 −3 −2 −1 0 1 2 3 4 5

**3.** $y \leq -1$

−5 −4 −3 −2 −1 0 1 2 3 4 5

**4.** $t \geq 0$

−5 −4 −3 −2 −1 0 1 2 3 4 5

**Solve each inequality. Graph the solution.**

**5.** $9 + a > 11$ _____

−5 −4 −3 −2 −1 0 1 2 3 4 5

**6.** $-4 + r < 0$ _____

−5 −4 −3 −2 −1 0 1 2 3 4 5

**7.** $2 > n - 1$ _____

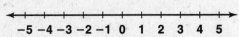

−5 −4 −3 −2 −1 0 1 2 3 4 5

**8.** $1 + s \leq 5$ _____

−5 −4 −3 −2 −1 0 1 2 3 4 5

# Practice 2-6

**Write an inequality for each graph.**

1.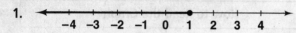

_____

2.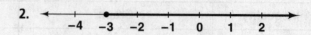

_____

3.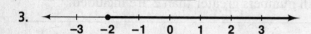

_____

4.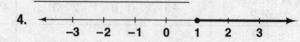

_____

5.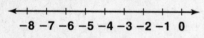

_____

**Graph each inequality on a number line.**

6. $x \geq -6$

7. $x < -5$

8. $x \leq 0$

9. $x \leq 7$

10. $x < 5$

**Solve each inequality. Graph the solutions.**

11. $m + 6 > 2$

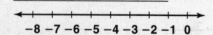

12. $q + 4 \leq 9$

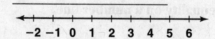

13. $w - 6 > -9$

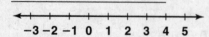

14. $y - 3 < -4$

15. $k + 9 \leq 12$

16. $u + 6 \geq 8$

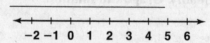

**Write and solve an inequality to answer each question.**

17. The amount of snow on the ground increased by 8 in. between 7 P.M. and 10 P.M. By 10 P.M., there was less than 2 ft of snow. How much snow was there by 7 P.M.?

_____

18. The school record for points scored in a basketball season by one player is 462. Maria has 235 points so far this season. How many more points does she need to break the record?

_____

# Reteaching 2-7

To help solve an inequality, you can divide or multiply each side by the same number. However, if the number is a negative number, you must also *reverse* the direction of the inequality.

Solve: $-3y \geq 6$.     Graph the solution.
$$-3y \geq 6$$

$$\frac{-3y}{-3} \leq \frac{6}{-3} \quad \leftarrow \text{Divide each side by } -3.$$
$$\leftarrow \text{Reverse the direction of the inequality.}$$
$$y \leq -2 \quad \leftarrow \text{Simplify.}$$

Graph:

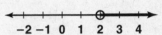

Solve: $\frac{a}{2} > 1$.     Graph the solution.
$$\frac{a}{2} > 1$$

$$2\left(\frac{a}{2}\right) > 1(2) \quad \leftarrow \text{Multiply each side by 2.}$$
$$a > 2 \quad \leftarrow \text{Simplify.}$$

Graph:

---

**Solve each inequality and graph the solutions.**

1. $2a > 8$     _____

2. $12 < -3r$     _____

3. $\frac{1}{3}n > 1$     _____

4. $12 \geq 6s$     _____

5. $\frac{m}{4} < 1$     _____

6. $5q \geq 5$     _____

7. $-4x \leq 8$     _____

8. What is the least whole number solution of $-9x < -27$?

_____

9. Donna sings on average $2\frac{1}{2}$ minutes per song. If a cassette holds 20 minutes of songs, what is the greatest number of songs she can record on a cassette?

_____

# Practice 2-7

**Solving Inequalities by Multiplying and Dividing**

**Solve each inequality and graph the solutions.**

1. $-5m < 20$

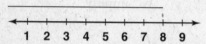

2. $\frac{j}{6} \le 0$

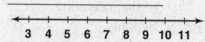

3. $4v > 16$

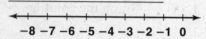

4. $\frac{b}{2} < 4$

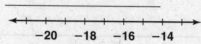

5. $5a > -10$

6. $\frac{c}{-3} \ge 6$

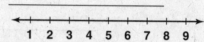

7. $\frac{c}{-6} > 1$

8. $-4i \le -16$

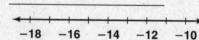

9. $5d < -75$

10. $\frac{d}{12} < -1$

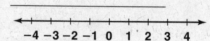

11. $0.5n \ge -2.5$

12. $\frac{p}{0.2} \le 10$

**Write an inequality for each problem. Solve the inequality. Then give the solution to the problem.**

13. Dom wants to buy 5 baseballs. He has $20. What is the most each baseball can cost?

14. A typing service charges $5.00 per page. Mrs. Garza does not want to spend more than $50 for the typing. What is the maximum number of pages she can have typed?

15. The tables at a restaurant can each seat 8 people. A dinner at the restaurant will be attended by 125 people. How many tables does the restaurant need in order for every person at the dinner to have a seat?

# Reteaching 2-8 ....................................

You can solve a two-step inequality by isolating the variable on one side of the inequality symbol.

① First add or subtract the same number on each side to undo the addition or subtraction.

② Then multiply or divide both sides by the same nonzero number to undo the multiplication or division.

Solve: $4x + 5 < -27$.

| | | Check: |
|---|---|---|
| $4x + 5 < -27$ | ← Undo addition first. | |
| $4x + 5 - 5 < -27 - 5$ | ← Subtract 5 from each side. | $4(-10) + 5 < -27$ |
| $4x < -32$ | ← Then undo multiplication. | $-40 + 5 < -27$ |
| $\frac{4x}{4} < \frac{-32}{4}$ | ← Divide each side by 4. | $-35 < -27$ ✔ |
| $x < -8$ | | |

The solution is $x < -8$.

Solve: $\frac{x}{5} - 20 \geq 35$

| | | Check: |
|---|---|---|
| $\frac{x}{5} - 20 \geq 35$ | ← Undo subtraction first. | |
| $\frac{x}{5} - 20 + 20 \geq 35 + 20$ | ← Add 20 from each side. | $\frac{300}{5} - 20 \geq 35$ |
| $\frac{x}{5} \geq 55$ | ← Then undo division. | $60 - 20 \geq 35$ |
| $\frac{x}{5}(5) \geq 55(5)$ | ← Multiply each side by 5. | $40 \geq 35$ ✔ |
| $x \geq 275$ | | |

The solution is $x \geq 275$.

---

**Solve each inequality. Check your work.**

**1.** $3x - 10 < 20$ _____

**2.** $\frac{x}{5} + 3 < 63$ _____

**3.** $16 > 2x + 6$ _____

**4.** $2x - 7 \leq 35$ _____

**5.** $28 \leq 3x + 1$ _____

**6.** $9 \geq \frac{x}{8} - 2$ _____

**7.** $3x - 17 \geq 43$ _____

**8.** $\frac{x}{6} + 3 < -15$ _____

**9.** $\frac{1}{5}x - 9 < 16$ _____

**10.** $8 > \frac{x}{4} + 1$ _____

**11.** $2x - 0.75 \geq 3.25$ _____

**12.** $7.8 \leq 2x + 3.2$ _____

# Practice 2-8

**Solving Two-Step Inequalities**

**Solve each inequality.**

**1.** $6x + 5 \le -19$

**2.** $2x + 12 < 24$

**3.** $15x - 9 > 21$

**4.** $5x - 11 \ge -36$

**5.** $18x - 6 \ge 84$

**6.** $9x + 2.3 > -10.3$

**7.** $11x + 4 \le -29$

**8.** $8x + 15 < 71$

**9.** $\frac{1}{2}x + 3 < 5$

**10.** $\frac{x}{6} - 7 \le 3$

**11.** $\frac{1}{4}x + 10 > -7$

**12.** $\frac{x}{9} - 15 \ge 5$

**13.** $12x + 7 \ge 139$

**14.** $3x - 8 \le 55$

**15.** $7x - 5.8 > 13.1$

**16.** $4x + 13 < 61$

**17.** $\frac{x}{8} - 7 > -12$

**18.** $\frac{1}{5}x + 8 < -2$

**19.** $\frac{n}{11} + 2 \le 6$

**20.** $\frac{x}{7} - 9 \ge -4$

**21.** $20n - 2 \le 138$

**22.** $10x - 3 \ge -83$

**23.** $8x - 3.2 > 37.6$

**24.** $12x - 10 > -130$

**25.** $\frac{w}{10} - 11 > 6$

**26.** $\frac{1}{3}x + 3 < -9$

**27.** $\frac{u}{12} + 4 \le 8$

**Write and solve an inequality to answer each question.**

**28.** A drama club's production of "Oklahoma!" is going to cost $1,250 to produce. How many tickets will they need to sell for $8 each in order to make a profit of at least $830?

**29.** A pet store is selling hamsters for $3.50 each if you purchase a cage for $18.25. You have at most $30 you can spend. How many hamsters can you buy?

# Reteaching 3-1

You can graph a point on a *coordinate plane*. Use an *ordered pair* $(x, y)$ to record the coordinates. The first number in the pair is the *x-coordinate*. The second number is the *y-coordinate*.

To graph a point, start at the origin, $O$. Move horizontally according to the value of $x$. Move vertically according to the value of $y$.

*Example 1:* $(4, -2)$
Start at $O$, move right 4, then down 2.

*Example 2:* $(-3, 2)$
Start at $O$, move left 3, then up 2.

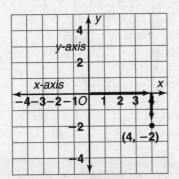 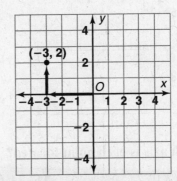

---

**Graph each ordered pair on the coordinate plane. Label each point with its letter. Then connect the points in order from A to S. Connect point S with point A to complete a picture.**

| | |
|---|---|
| $A(7, 7)$ | $J(-4, -6)$ |
| $B(6, 3)$ | $K(-7, -7)$ |
| $C(6, 2)$ | $L(-5, 1)$ |
| $D(5, 1)$ | $M(-6, 2)$ |
| $E(7, -7)$ | $N(-6, 3)$ |
| $F(4, -6)$ | $P(-7, 7)$ |
| $G(1, -2)$ | $Q(-1, 3)$ |
| $H(0, -4)$ | $R(0, 4)$ |
| $I(-1, -2)$ | $S(1, 3)$ |

# Practice 3-1

**Name the coordinates of each point in the graph.**

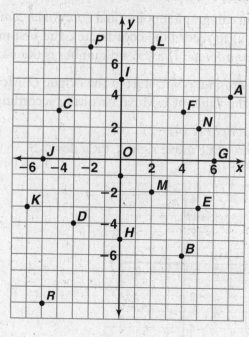

1. *J*

   _____

2. *R*

   _____

3. *K*

   _____

4. *M*

   _____

5. *I*

   _____

6. *P*

   _____

7. *N*

   _____

8. *L*

   _____

**In which quadrant or on which axis is each point located?**

9. $(-3, -2)$

   _____

10. $(7, 0)$

    _____

11. $(4, 0)$

    _____

12. $(-3, -9)$

    _____

13. $(4, -7)$

    _____

14. $(7, -5)$

    _____

15. $(2, 9)$

    _____

16. $(0, 9)$

    _____

17. $(0, -6)$

    _____

18. $(4, 2)$

    _____

19. $(-3, 2)$

    _____

20. $(0, 0)$

    _____

21. Arnie plotted points on the graph below. He placed his pencil point at *A*. He can move either right or down any number of units until he reaches point *B*. In how many ways can he do this?

    _____

22. Marika had to draw $\triangle ABC$ that fit several requirements.

    a. It must fit in the box shown.

    b. The side $\overline{AB}$ has coordinates $A(-2, 0)$ and $B(2, 0)$.

    c. Point C must be on the y-axis.

    Name all the points that could be point C.

    _____

    _____

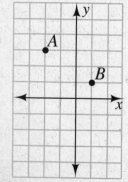

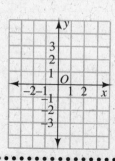

# Reteaching 3-2

**Graphing Equations with Two Variables**

You can use a table to help graph a *linear equation* on a coordinate plane.

① Choose a value for *x*. Solve for *y*.

② Find at least 3 such solutions.

③ Graph the solutions.

④ Draw a line through the points.

Graph $y = 2x - 1$.

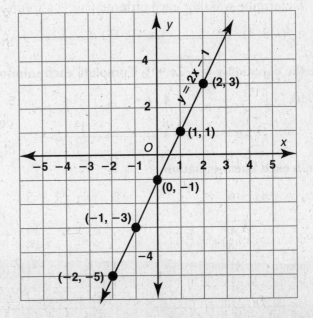

| Choose *x*. | Solve for *y*. $(y = 2x - 1)$ | *y* | *(x, y)* |
|---|---|---|---|
| −2 | 2(−2) − 1 | −5 | (−2, −5) |
| −1 | 2(−1) − 1 | −3 | (−1, −3) |
| 0 | 2(0) − 1 | −1 | (0, −1) |
| 1 | 2(1) − 1 | 1 | (1, 1) |
| 2 | 2(2) − 1 | 3 | (2, 3) |

**Complete the table. Graph each (*x, y*) solution. Draw a line through the points.**

**1.** $y = \frac{1}{2}x + 3$

| *x* | *y* |
|---|---|
| −2 | 2 |
| 0 | |
| 2 | |
| 4 | |

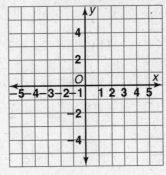

**2.** $y = -2x + 1$

| *x* | *y* |
|---|---|
| −1 | 3 |
| 0 | |
| 1 | |
| 2 | |

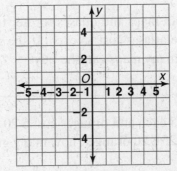

# Practice 3-2

**Graphing Equations with Two Variables**

1. Determine whether each ordered pair is a solution of $y = 3x - 8$.

   **a.** $(0, -8)$ _____   **b.** $(6, -10)$ _____   **c.** $(-2, -2)$ _____   **d.** $(4, 4)$ _____

2. Determine whether each ordered pair is a solution of $y = -5x + 19$.

   **a.** $(-3, 4)$ _____   **b.** $(0, 19)$ _____   **c.** $(2, 9)$ _____   **d.** $(-4, 39)$ _____

**Use the equation $y = -2x + 1$. Complete each solution.**

3. $(0, \underline{\ ?\ })$       4. $(-5, \underline{\ ?\ })$       5. $(20, \underline{\ ?\ })$       6. $(-68, \underline{\ ?\ })$

   _____       _____       _____       _____

**Graph each linear equation.**

7. $y = -4x + 6$

8. $y = \frac{5}{2}x - 5$

9. $y = -\frac{1}{2}x + 3$

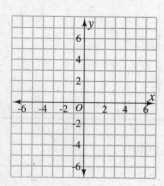   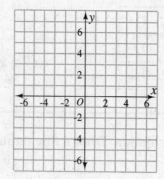   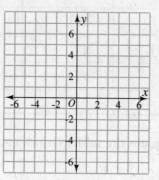

10. $y = \frac{1}{2}x - \frac{1}{2}$

11. $y = -2x + 7$

12. $y = -3x - 1$

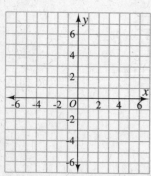   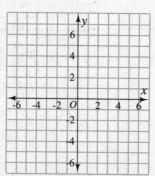   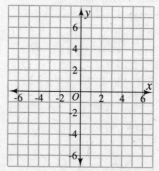

13. Jan wants to buy both maps and atlases for her trip. The maps cost $2 each, and the atlases cost $5 each. If she spends $25 and buys 3 atlases, how many maps can she buy?

   _____

14. Grapefruits cost $.65 each and oranges cost $.20 each. If Keiko spends $5 and buys 25 $.20 oranges, how many grapefruits can she buy?

   _____

# Reteaching 3-3

The *slope of a line* is $\frac{\text{change in } y}{\text{change in } x}$, found by using two points on the line.

Find the slope of the line that passes through these two points: $(4, 3)$ and $(2, -1)$.

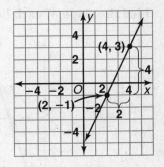

- To find the change in $y$, subtract one $y$-coordinate from the other: $(3 - (-1)) = 4$.

- To find the change in $x$, subtract one $x$-coordinate from the other: $(4 - 2) = 2$.

When you find the slope of a line, the $y$-coordinate you use first for the rise must belong to the same point as the $x$-coordinate you use for the run.

The slope of the line is: $\frac{\text{change in } y}{\text{change in } x} = \frac{3 - (-1)}{4 - 2} = \frac{4}{2} = 2$

A table of values from the graph also shows the slope.

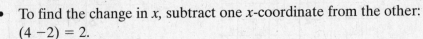

| $x$ | 5 | 4 | 3 | 2 | 1 |
|-----|---|---|---|----|----|
| $y$ | 5 | 3 | 1 | -1 | -3 |

Compare the change in each coordinate.

$\frac{\text{change in } y}{\text{change in } x} = \frac{-2}{-1} = 2$

$-2$ *change in y*

---

**Find the slope of each line.**

1.

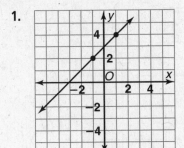

slope = _____

2.

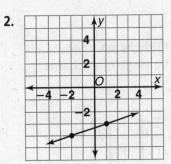

slope = _____

3.

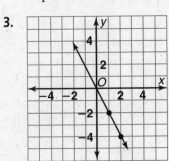

slope = _____

4.

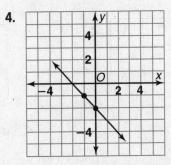

slope = _____

# Practice 3-3

**Understanding Slope**

**Find the slope of each line.**

1.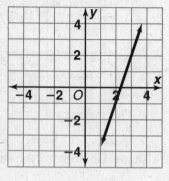

2.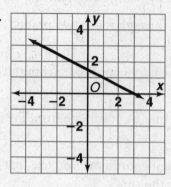

3.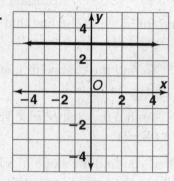

_____   _____   _____

4.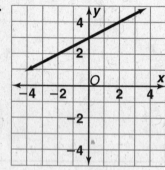

5.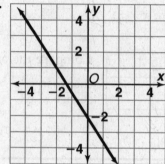

_____   _____

**The points from each table lie on a line.**
**Use the table to find the slope of each line.**
**Then graph the line**

6.

| x | 0 | 1 | 2 | 3 | 4 |
|---|---|---|---|---|---|
| y | −3 | −1 | 1 | 3 | 5 |

slope = _____

7.

| x | 0 | 1 | 2 | 3 | 4 |
|---|---|---|---|---|---|
| y | 5 | 3 | 1 | −1 | −3 |

slope = _____

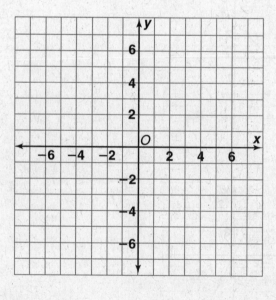

# Reteaching 3-4
**Using the y-Intercept**

An equation of a line can be written in the *slope-intercept form:* $y = mx + b$. The slope of the line is $m$ and the y-intercept is $b$.

The *y-intercept* is the y-coordinate of the point where the line crosses the y-axis.

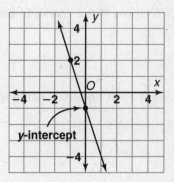

*Example:* For $y = -3x - 1$, the slope is $-3$. The y-intercept is $-1$.

Use the graph to write an equation for the line through $(-1, 2)$ and $(0, -1)$.

① Find $m$: slope $\frac{\text{change in } y}{\text{change in } x} = \frac{2 - (-1)}{-1 - 0} = \frac{3}{-1} = -3$

② Find $b$: y-intercept $= -1$

③ In the equation $y = mx + b$, substitute $m = -3$ and $b = -1$.

The equation for the line is $y = -3x - 1$.

---

**Find the slope and y-intercept of each equation.**

1. $y = 2x + 3$

   $m = $ _____

   $b = $ _____

2. $y = -5x - 2$

   $m = $ _____

   $b = $ _____

3. $y = -3x + 2$

   $m = $ _____

   $b = $ _____

4. $y = x - 3$

   $m = $ _____

   $b = $ _____

5. $y = \frac{1}{2}x - 4$

   $m = $ _____

   $b = $ _____

6. $y = 5x$

   $m = $ _____

   $b = $ _____

**Write an equation for each line.**

7.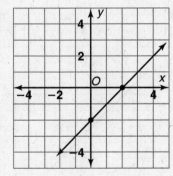

   _____

8.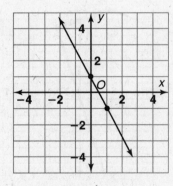

   _____

# Practice 3-4

**Determine if the equation has the same slope as the equation**
$y = 2x - 4$.

**1.** $y = 2x + 4$ _____   **2.** $y = -2x + 3$ _____   **3.** $y = 4x - 2$ _____   **4.** $y = 3x - 4$ _____

**Graph each equation using the slope and the *y*-intercept.**

**5.** $y = \frac{3}{4}x - 3$

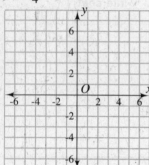

**6.** $y = -\frac{2}{5}x + 2$

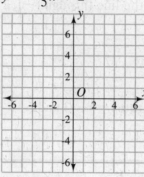

**7.** $y = -\frac{4}{3}x + 4$

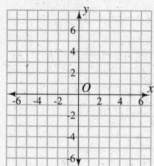

**8.** $y = \frac{4}{5}x + 4$

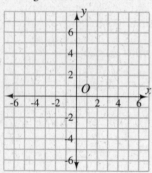

**9.** $y = x + 4$

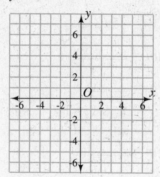

**10.** $y = \frac{5}{3}x - 5$

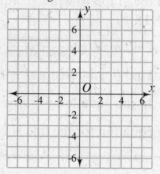

**Write an equation for each line.**

**11.**

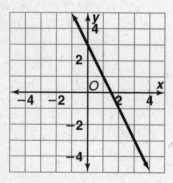

_____

**12.**

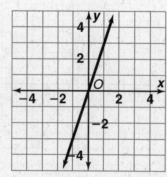

_____

**13.**

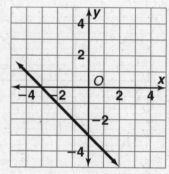

_____

# Reteaching 3-5

**Problem Solving: Write an Equation and Make a Graph**

**You can write an equation with two variables and make a graph to describe a real-world situation.**

Suppose you are planning your sister's bridal shower at a restaurant. A buffet dinner costs $12 per person. You are going to buy a cake and bring it to the shower. The cake costs $38.

Write an equation and make a graph to describe the total cost of the bridal shower. Use the graph to estimate the number of people you can invite for $200.

**Read and Understand** Your goal is to estimate the number of people you can invite for $200, including your sister, you, and your family. The cake costs $38 and the buffet costs $12 per person. Assume there is no tax or tip.

**Plan and Solve** First, write an equation to represent the total cost of the shower. The cost of the cake is a fixed cost, but the cost per person depends on the total number of people you invite.

| Words | total cost | = | cost of cake | + | cost per person | × | number of people |
|-------|-----------|---|--------------|---|-----------------|---|------------------|

↓  Let $t$ = the total cost    Let $p$ = the number of people

| Equation | $t$ | = | 38 | + | 12 | × | $p$ |
|----------|-----|---|----|---|----|----|-----|

Write the equation, $t = 38 + 12p$, in slope intercept form.

$$y = mx + b$$

$$t = 12p + 38$$
$$\quad\uparrow\qquad\uparrow$$
slope = 12    $y$-intercept = 38

Graph $t = 12p + 38$.

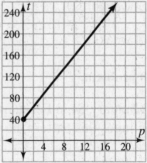

You can invite no more than 13 people to spend less than $200.

**Look Back and Check**

$t = 12p + 38; t = 12(13) + 38; t = \$194$

This is less than $200.

---

You are planning a party where it costs $200 to rent the hall and $10 per person. Write and graph an equation with two variables to model the situation. Use your equation to find the maximum number of people you can invite if you only want to spend $1,500.

_____

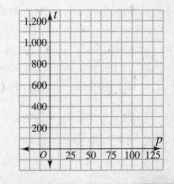

# Practice 3-5

**Problem Solving: Write an Equation and Make a Graph**

**Write and graph an equation with two variables to model each situation.**

1. You order books through a catalog. Each book costs $12 and the shipping and handling cost is $5. Write an equation and make a graph that represents your total cost.

   _____

   a. What is the total cost if you buy 6 books? _____

   b. What is the total cost if you buy 4 books? _____

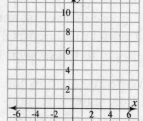

2. A ride in a taxicab costs $2.50 for the first mile and $1.50 for each additional mile, or part of a mile. Write an equation and make a graph that represents the total cost.

   _____

   a. What is the total cost of a 10-mile ride? _____

   b. What is the total cost of a 25-mile ride? _____

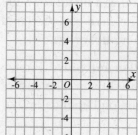

3. A tree is 3 ft tall and grows 3 in. each day. Write an equation and make a graph that represents how much the tree grows over time.

   _____

   a. How tall is the tree in a week? _____

   b. How tall is the tree in 4 weeks? _____

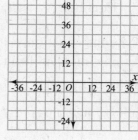

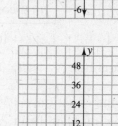

**Use any strategy to solve each problem.**

4. Marcy plans to save $3 in January, $4 in February, $6 in March, and $9 in April. If she continues this pattern, how much money will she save in December? _____

5. Inez is building a fence around her square garden. She plans to put 8 posts along each side. The diameter of each post is 6 inches. How many posts will there be? _____

6. Alain, Betina, Coley, and Dimitri are artists. One is a potter, one a painter, one a pianist, and one a songwriter. Alain, and Coley saw the pianist perform. Betina and Coley have modeled for the painter. The writer wrote a song about Alain and Dimitri. Betina is the potter. Who is the songwriter? _____

7. Luis is reading a book with 520 pages. When he has read 4 times as many pages as he already has, he will be 184 pages from the end. How many pages has Luis read? _____

# Reteaching 3-6

**Using Graphs of Equations**

The accounting department is having its annual luncheon. They have budgeted $120 for the luncheon. Each table costs $10, and lunch will cost $5 per person.

You can write an equation to represent the number of tables and people who attend. Use a graph to show how the number of tables will vary with the number who attend.

- *Words*      $120 = $10 × number of tables + $5 × number who attend

   Let $x$ = number of tables and $y$ = number who attend.

- *Equation*      $120 = 10x + 5y$

(1) Find the coordinates of the $x$-intercept ($\underline{?}$, 0).
   Let $y = 0$ and solve for $x$.

   $120 = 10x + 5(0)$
   $120 = 10x$
   $\frac{120}{10} = 10x$
   $12 = x$

   The coordinates of the $x$-intercept are (12, 0).

(2) Find the coordinates of the $y$-intercept, ($\underline{?}$, 0).
   Let $y = 0$ and solve for $x$.

   $120 = 10(0) + 5y$
   $120 = 5y$
   $\frac{120}{5} = 5y$
   $24 = y$

   The coordinates of the $y$-intercept are (0, 20).

(3) Plot the $x$- and $y$-intercepts and draw the line to graph the equation.

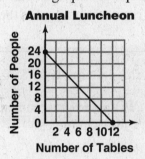

**Annual Luncheon**

---

**Write an equation with two variables for each situation. Then graph the equation.**

1. The Nature Club is renting vans. The vans costs $6 per student. The van company also charges a $24 service fee per van. The club can spend $168.

   Equation: _____

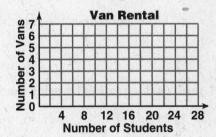

**Van Rental**

2. Kim has $30 to spend at a garden shop. Plants are $2 each and bags of potting soil are $5 each.

   Equation: _____

**Write the coordinates of the $x$-intercept and $y$-intercept for each equation.**

3. $y = 3x + 6$

4. $2x + 4y = 16$

_____         _____

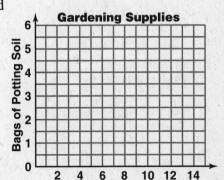

**Gardening Supplies**

# Practice 3-6

**Using Graphs of Equations**

**Use the graph at the right for Exercises 1–5.**

1. What earnings will produce $225 in savings?

   _____

2. How much is saved from earnings of $400?

   _____

3. What is the slope of the line in the graph?

   _____

4. For each increase of $200 in earnings, what is the increase in savings?

   _____

5. Write an equation for the line.

   _____

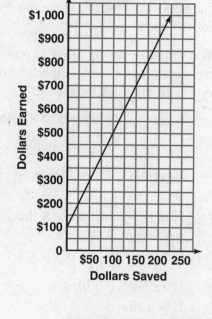

**Earned vs. Saved**

6. A ride in a cab costs $.40 plus $.15 per mile.

   a. Write and graph an equation for traveling *x* miles in the cab.

   _____

   b. The cab charges $.70 for a ride of how many miles?

   _____

   c. How much does the cab charge for a trip of 8 miles?

   _____

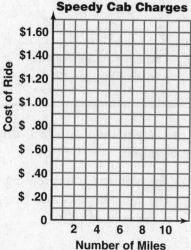

**Speedy Cab Charges**

**Graph each equation by using the *x*- and *y*-intercepts.**

7. $2x + 3y = 6$

8. $x - 2y = 4$

9. $2x - y = -4$

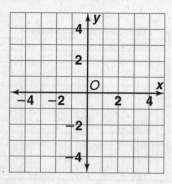

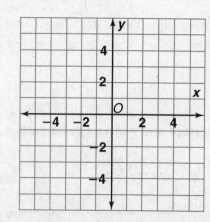

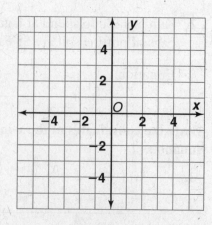

# Reteaching 3-7

When two linear equations are considered together, they form a *system of linear equations*. An ordered pair that is a solution to both equations is called a *solution* of the system.

*Example:* Solve the system of equations by graphing $y = x - 1$ and $y = -x + 3$.

Find three solutions for each equation and graph each line. Find the point where the lines intersect.

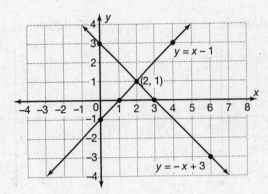

| $x$ | 0 | 1 | 4 |
|---|---|---|---|
| $y$ | −1 | 0 | 3 |

$y = x - 1$

| $x$ | 0 | 3 | 6 |
|---|---|---|---|
| $y$ | 3 | 0 | −3 |

$y = -x + 3$

The solution for this system of linear equations is the ordered pair $(2, 1)$. Check the coordinates for $x$ and $y$ in both equations.

| $y = x - 1$ | $y = -x + 3$ |
|---|---|
| $1 \overset{?}{=} 2 - 1$ | $1 \overset{?}{=} -2 + 3$ |
| $1 = 1$ ✔ | $1 = 1$ ✔ |

---

**Find three solutions for each equation. Then solve the system of equations by graphing both equations on the grid at the right.**

**1.** $y = -x + 1$

**2.** $y = -\frac{1}{2}x + 2$

| $x$ | | | |
|---|---|---|---|
| $y$ | | | |

| $x$ | | | |
|---|---|---|---|
| $y$ | | | |

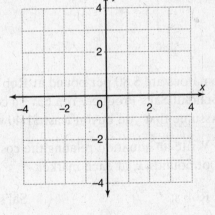

**3.** Solution for system of equations: _____

**4.** Check your solution.

_____

_____

_____

# Practice 3-7

**Solving Linear Systems by Graphing**

**Solve each system of equations by graphing.**

**1.** $y = x + 2$
$y = 2x + 1$

Solution: _____

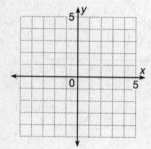

**2.** $y = -2x + 2$
$y = 3x + 2$

Solution: _____

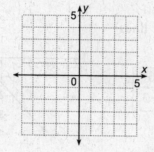

**3.** $y = -\frac{1}{2}x - 1$
$y = x - 4$

Solution: _____

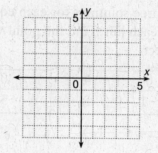

**4.** $y = 2x + 3$
$y = \frac{1}{2}x$

Solution: _____

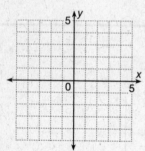

**5.** $y = -\frac{3}{2}x + 2$
$y = \frac{1}{2}x - 2$

Solution: _____

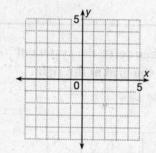

**6.** $y = 2x - 5$
$y = \frac{1}{4}x + 2$

Solution: _____

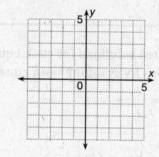

**7.** Tomatoes are $.80 per pound at Rob's Market, and $1.20 per pound at Sal's Produce. You have a coupon for $1.40 off at Sal's. (Assume that you buy at least $1.40 worth of tomatoes.)

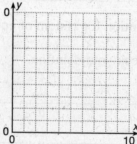

**a.** Write an equation relating the cost, $y$, to the number of pounds, $x$, at each market.

Rob's: _____   Sal's: _____

**b.** Use a graph to estimate the number of pounds for which the cost is the same at either store.

_____

# Reteaching 3-8

**Translations**

A *translation* moves every point of a figure the same distance in the same direction.

Triangle *ABC* is translated 5 units to the right and 4 units up. The *image* of △*ABC* is △*A'B'C'*.

You can write a rule to describe a translation in the coordinate plane.

For the translation of △*DEF*, the rule is:

Add 5 to each *x*-coordinate.
Add 1 to each *y*-coordinate.

$D(-4, -1) \rightarrow D'(1, 0)$

$E(-6, -2) \rightarrow E'(-1, -1)$

$F(-6, -5) \rightarrow F'(-1, -4)$

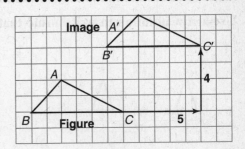

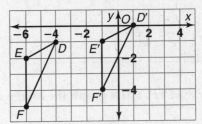

---

**Copy each figure. Then graph the image after the given translation. Name the coordinates of the image.**

**1.** right 5 units, up 1 unit

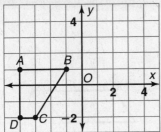

_____

_____

**2.** left 3 units, down 2 units

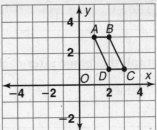

_____

_____

**Use arrow notation to write a rule that describes the translation shown on each graph.**

**3.**

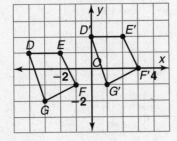

_____

_____

**4.**

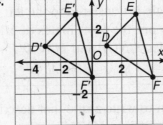

_____

_____

# Practice 3-8

**Use arrow notation to write a rule that describes the translation shown on each graph.**

**1.**

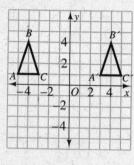

_____

**2.**

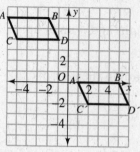

_____

**3.**

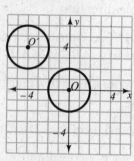

_____

**Copy △MNP. Then graph the image after each translation.**

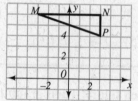

**4.** left 2 units, down 2 units

_____

**5.** right 2 units, down 1 unit

_____

**6.** left 2 units, up 3 units

_____

**Copy ▱RSTU. Then graph the image after each translation.**

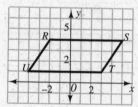

**7.** right 1 unit, down 2 units

_____

**8.** left 3 units, up 0 units

_____

**9.** right 2 units, up 4 units

_____

**10.** A rectangle has its vertices at $M(1, 1)$, $N(6, 1)$, $O(6, 5)$, and $P(1, 5)$. The rectangle is translated to the left 4 units and down 3 units. What are the coordinates of $M'$, $N'$, $O'$, and $P'$? Graph the rectangles $MNOP$ and $M'N'O'P'$.

_____

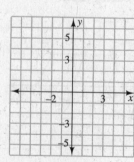

**11.** Use arrow notation to write a rule that describes the translation of $M'N'O'P'$ to $MNOP$.

_____

# Reteaching 3-9

**Reflections and Symmetry**

A *reflection* flips a figure over a line (the *line of reflection*). Figure $A'B'C'$ is the image of figure $ABC$ after a reflection over the *y*-axis.

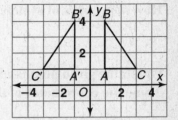

Each point of the image is the same distance from the line of reflection as the corresponding point of the original figure.

Since $A$ is 1 unit to the right of the *y*-axis, locate $A'$ 1 unit to the left of the *y*-axis.

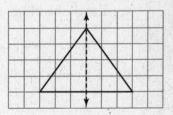

If the image is identical to the original figure, then the figure has *reflectional symmetry* and has a *line of symmetry*.

---

**Copy each figure.**

**1.** Reflect the figure over the *x*-axis.

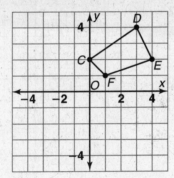

**2.** Reflect the figure over the *y*-axis.

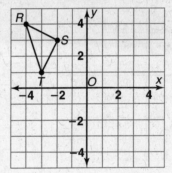

**Copy each figure. Does the figure have reflectional symmetry? If it does, draw all the lines of symmetry.**

**3.**

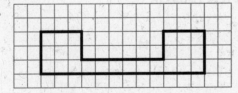

_____

**4.**

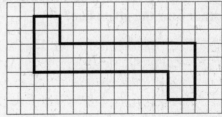

_____

Name _____ Class _____ Date _____

# Practice 3-9

**Reflections and Symmetry**

How many lines of symmetry can you find for each letter?

1. W _____ 2. X _____ 3. H _____ 4. T _____

**Graph the given point and its image after each reflection. Name the coordinates of the reflected point.**

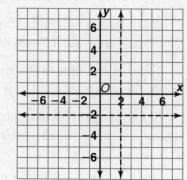

5. $A(5, -4)$ over the vertical dashed line

6. $B(-3, 2)$ over the horizontal dashed line

_____

_____

7. $C(-5, 0)$ over the $y$-axis

8. $D(3, 4)$ over the $x$-axis

_____

_____

$\triangle ABC$ has vertices $A(2, 1)$, $B(3, -5)$, and $C(-2, 4)$. Graph $\triangle ABC$ and its image, $\triangle A'B'C'$, after a reflection over each line. Name the coordinates of $A'$, $B'$, and $C'$.

9. the $x$-axis

10. the line through $(-1, 2)$ and $(1, 2)$

11. the $y$-axis

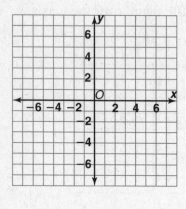

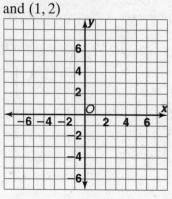

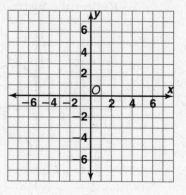

_____

_____

_____

**Fold your paper over each dashed line. Are the figures reflections of each other over the given line?**

12.

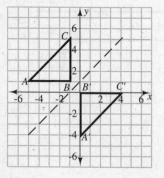

13.

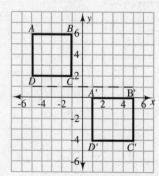

14.

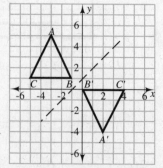

_____

_____

_____

# Reteaching 3-10

A *rotation* is a turn of a figure about a center point, the *center of rotation*.

A figure can be rotated up to 360° counterclockwise.

A figure has *rotational symmetry* if an image matches the original figure after a rotation of 180° or less.

The angle measure the figure rotates is the *angle of rotation*.

The shaded triangle is rotated about its lower vertex.

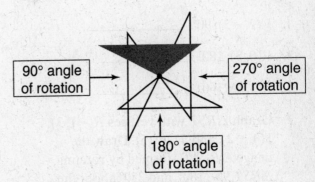

90° angle of rotation

270° angle of rotation

180° angle of rotation

The triangle does not have rotational symmetry.

---

**The shaded figure is rotated 90°, 180°, or 270° about point _X_.
The unshaded figure is its image. What is the angle of rotation?**

1.

_____

2.

_____

3.

_____

**Judging by appearance, determine whether each figure has rotational symmetry. If it does, find the angle of rotation.**

4.

_____

5.

_____

6.

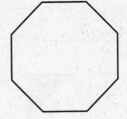

_____

# Practice 3-10

**Graph each point. Then rotate it the given number of degrees about the origin. Give the coordinates of the image.**

1. $V(2, -3)$; 90° _____

2. $M(-4, 5)$; 270° _____

3. $V(0, 5)$; 180° _____

4. $M(6, 0)$; 90° _____

5. $V(3, 4)$; 360° _____

6. $M(0, -1)$; 90° _____

7. Graph $\triangle RST$ with vertices $R(-1, 3)$, $S(4, -2)$, and $T(2, -5)$. Draw the image $\triangle R'S'T'$, formed by rotating $\triangle RST$ 90°, 180°, and 270° about the origin. Give the coordinates of $R'$, $S'$, and $T'$.

90° _____

180° _____

270° _____

**Determine if each figure could be a rotation of the figure at the right. For each figure that could be a rotation, tell what the angle of rotation appears to be.**

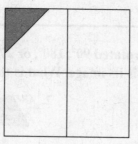

8.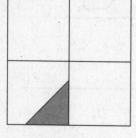

_____

9.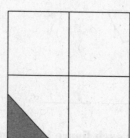

_____

10.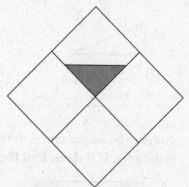

_____

11.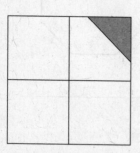

_____

12.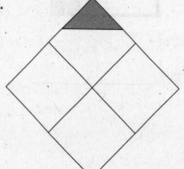

_____

13.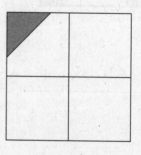

_____

# Reteaching 4-1

A *prime number* is a number with only two factors, 1 and itself.

The number 17 is prime.
Its only factors are 1 and 17.

Use a factor tree to find prime factors. The product of prime factors is called the *prime factorization*.

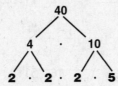

The prime factorization of 40 is
$2 \cdot 2 \cdot 2 \cdot 5$ or $2^3 \cdot 5$.

The *greatest common factor (GCF)* of a set of numbers is the greatest factor common to the numbers.

Find the GCF of 20 and 30.

① Use factor trees to find prime factors.

② Circle the common factors. The product of the common factors is the GCF.

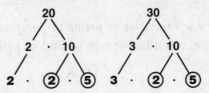

$2 \cdot 5 = 10$
The GCF of 20 and 30 is 10.

**Complete these factor trees. Write the prime factorization for each number.**

**1.**

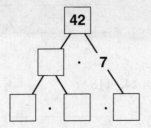

42 = _____

**2.** 52

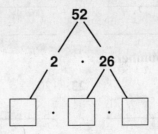

52 = _____

**3.** 91

91 = _____

**4.** 54

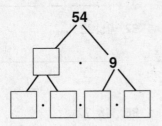

54 = _____

**5.** 90

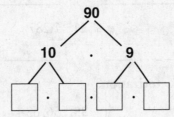

90 = _____

**6.** 94

94 = _____

**Find the GCF by finding the prime factorization.**

**7.** 10, 12

_____

**8.** 15, 8

_____

**9.** 24, 30

_____

**10.** 12, 18

_____

**11.** 27, 18

_____

**12.** 20, 15

_____

Name _____ Class _____ Date _____

# Practice 4-1

**List all the factors of each number.**

**1.** 36 _____     **2.** 42 _____     **3.** 50 _____     **4.** 41 _____

_____        _____        _____        _____

**Tell whether the first number is a factor of the second.**

**5.** 2; 71 _____        **6.** 1; 18 _____        **7.** 3; 81 _____        **8.** 4; 74 _____

**9.** 9; 522 _____       **10.** 8; 508 _____       **11.** 13; 179 _____       **12.** 17; 3,587 _____

**Identify each number as *prime* or *composite*. If the number is *composite*, use a factor tree to find its prime factorization.**

**13.** 74            **14.** 83            **15.** 23            **16.** 51

_____        _____        _____        _____

_____        _____        _____        _____

**17.** 73            **18.** 91            **19.** 109           **20.** 211

_____        _____        _____        _____

_____        _____        _____        _____

**Write the prime factorization of each number.**

**21.** 70            **22.** 92            **23.** 120           **24.** 118

_____        _____        _____        _____

**25.** 200           **26.** 180           **27.** 360           **28.** 500

_____        _____        _____        _____

**29.** 187           **30.** 364           **31.** 1,287         **32.** 1,122

_____        _____        _____        _____

**Find the GCF by finding the prime factorization.**

**33.** 24, 40         **34.** 20, 42         **35.** 56, 63         **36.** 48, 72

_____        _____        _____        _____

**37.** 18, 24, 36      **38.** 20, 45, 75      **39.** 120, 150, 180      **40.** 200, 250, 400

_____        _____        _____        _____

**41.** Mr. Turner distributed some supplies in his office. He distributed 120 pencils, 300 paper clips, and 16 pens. What is the greatest number of people there can be in the office if each person received the same number of items? _____

**42.** The baseball league bought new equipment for the teams. The managers bought 288 baseballs, 40 bats, and 24 equipment bags. How many teams are there if all the new equipment is distributed equally among the teams? _____

# Reteaching 4-2

**Equivalent Forms of Rational Numbers**

A fraction is in simplest form when the *greatest common factor* (GCF) of the numerator and denominator is 1.

*Example 1:* Write $\frac{24}{36}$ in simplest form.

Use prime factorization and circle the common factors.

$$24 = (2) \cdot (2) \cdot 2 \cdot (3)$$
$$36 = (2) \cdot (2) \cdot 3 \cdot (3)$$

So, $\frac{24}{36} = \frac{2}{3}$.

To write a fraction as a decimal:

① Divide numerator by denominator.

② Divide until the remainder is 0 or until the remainder repeats.

③ Use a bar to show digits repeating.

*Example 2:* Write $\frac{5}{6}$ as a decimal.

$$
\begin{array}{r}
0.833 \\
6\overline{)5.000} \\
-48 \\
\hline
20 \\
-18 \\
\hline
20 \\
-18 \\
\hline
2 \leftarrow \text{Remainder repeats.}
\end{array}
$$

So, $\frac{5}{6} = 0.833\ldots$, or $0.8\overline{3}$.

Use algebra to write a repeating decimal as a fraction.

*Example 3:* Write $0.\overline{7}$ as a fraction.

① Let *n* be the decimal.   $n = 0.\overline{7}$

② Multiply each side by 10 because *one* digit repeats.   $10n = 7.\overline{7}$

③ Subtract the equations.
$$
\begin{array}{r}
10n = 7.777\ldots \\
- \quad n = 0.777\ldots \\
\hline
9n = 7
\end{array}
$$

④ Solve for *n*.
$$9n = 7$$
$$\frac{9n}{9} = \frac{7}{9}$$
$$n = \frac{7}{9}$$

So, $0.\overline{7} = \frac{7}{9}$.

**Write each fraction in simplest form.**

**1.** $\frac{16}{64}$ _____

**2.** $\frac{-30}{48}$ _____

**3.** $\frac{42}{63}$ _____

**4.** $\frac{-32}{40}$ _____

**5.** $\frac{12}{-28}$ _____

**6.** $\frac{18}{27}$ _____

**Write each fraction or mixed number as a decimal rounded to three decimal places.**

**7.** $\frac{7}{9}$ _____

**8.** $-3\frac{2}{7}$ _____

**9.** $\frac{5}{9}$ _____

**10.** $5\frac{3}{7}$ _____

**11.** $\frac{4}{3}$ _____

**12.** $\frac{1}{11}$ _____

**Write each decimal as a mixed number or fraction in simplest form.**

**13.** $0.\overline{1}$ _____

**14.** $0.1\overline{6}$ _____

**15.** $0.\overline{3}$ _____

**16.** $0.\overline{8}$ _____

**17.** $0.\overline{6}$ _____

**18.** $0.\overline{36}$ _____

# Practice 4-2

**Write each fraction in simplest form.**

1. $-5$ _____  2. $0.63$ _____  3. $-3.9$ _____  4. $4\frac{5}{6}$ _____

5. $\frac{77}{99}$ _____  6. $\frac{21}{-56}$ _____  7. $-\frac{28}{52}$ _____  8. $\frac{195}{105}$ _____

9. A baseball player averaged 0.375 last season. Express the batting average as a fraction. _____

**Write each fraction or mixed number as a decimal rounded to three places.**

10. $\frac{7}{21}$ _____  11. $-\frac{9}{21}$ _____  12. $-\frac{2}{3}$ _____  13. $1\frac{6}{7}$ _____

14. $3\frac{1}{6}$ _____  15. $-4\frac{7}{8}$ _____  16. $3\frac{11}{12}$ _____  17. $5\frac{7}{11}$ _____

18. $-4\frac{7}{11}$ _____  19. $3\frac{1}{18}$ _____  20. $-1\frac{7}{18}$ _____  21. $2\frac{5}{12}$ _____

22. $-2\frac{7}{9}$ _____  23. $5\frac{7}{15}$ _____  24. $-4\frac{14}{15}$ _____  25. $3\frac{8}{11}$ _____

**Write each decimal as a mixed number or fraction in simplest form.**

26. $0.006$ _____  27. $-4.\overline{8}$ _____  28. $0.97$ _____  29. $0.\overline{53}$ _____

30. $0.\overline{4}$ _____  31. $9.05$ _____  32. $-0.28$ _____  33. $5.\overline{618}$ _____

34. $3.082$ _____  35. $-1.\overline{41}$ _____  36. $4.\overline{23}$ _____  37. $17.\overline{3}$ _____

38. $8.\overline{05}$ _____  39. $-3.0\overline{2}$ _____  40. $7.1\overline{3}$ _____  41. $0.\overline{2}$ _____

**Solve.**

42. The eighth grade held a magazine sale to raise money for their spring trip. They wanted each student to sell subscriptions. After the first day of the sale, 25 out of 125 students turned in subscription orders. Write a rational number in simplest form to express the student response on the first day.

_____

43. Pete wanted to win the prize for selling the most subscriptions. Of 240 subscriptions sold, Pete sold 30. Write a rational number in simplest form to express Pete's part of the total sales.

_____

# Reteaching 4-3

The *least common multiple* (LCM) of two or more numbers is the least multiple common to all of the numbers. The LCM of the denominators is called the *least common denominator* (LCD).

| To compare fractions that have the *same* denominator, compare their numerators.<br><br>Compare $\frac{3}{4}$ and $\frac{1}{4}$.<br><br>$\quad 3 > 1$<br>$\quad$ So, $\frac{3}{4} > \frac{1}{4}$. | To compare fractions with *different* denominators, rewrite the fractions using the LCD.<br><br>Compare $\frac{2}{3}$ and $\frac{7}{9}$.<br><br>Rewrite: $\quad \frac{6}{9} \qquad \frac{7}{9}$<br><br>$\qquad \frac{6}{9} < \frac{7}{9}$<br><br>So, $\frac{2}{3} < \frac{7}{9}$. | Another way to compare numbers involving fractions is to *write them as decimals*.<br><br>Compare $-1.7$ and $-1\frac{3}{4}$.<br><br>Rewrite: $-1.7$ and $-1.75$<br><br>$\qquad -1.7 > -1.75$<br><br>So, $-1.7 > -1\frac{3}{4}$. |
|---|---|---|

**Determine which rational number is greater by rewriting each pair of fractions with the *same* common denominator.**

**1.** $\frac{6}{7}, \frac{4}{5}$

**2.** $\frac{5}{11}, \frac{8}{12}$

**3.** $\frac{2}{5}, \frac{2}{4}$

_____

_____

_____

**4.** $\frac{4}{8}, \frac{10}{12}$

**5.** $\frac{3}{4}, \frac{8}{10}$

**6.** $\frac{4}{6}, \frac{1}{3}$

_____

_____

_____

**7.** $\frac{2}{3}, \frac{3}{6}$

**8.** $\frac{2}{4}, \frac{4}{5}$

**9.** $\frac{1}{7}, \frac{1}{3}$

_____

_____

_____

**10.** $\frac{2}{8}, \frac{1}{5}$

**11.** $\frac{5}{7}, \frac{9}{10}$

**12.** $\frac{7}{8}, \frac{3}{4}$

_____

_____

_____

**Compare. Write >, <, or =.**

**13.** $\frac{8}{9} \,\square\, -2$

**14.** $-10.2 \,\square\, \frac{-51}{5}$

**15.** $-\frac{12}{24} \,\square\, -\frac{9}{24}$

**16.** $1.2 \,\square\, 1\frac{1}{2}$

**17.** $\frac{1}{9} \,\square\, \frac{1}{3}$

**18.** $\frac{1}{5} \,\square\, 0.15$

**19.** $0.375 \,\square\, \frac{3}{8}$

**20.** $\frac{-5}{9} \,\square\, \frac{-7}{12}$

**21.** $\frac{-1}{2} \,\square\, \frac{-3}{4}$

**22.** $-\frac{3}{5} \,\square\, -\frac{3}{7}$

**23.** $\frac{3}{10} \,\square\, \frac{1}{5}$

**24.** $\frac{5}{6} \,\square\, 0.72$

# Practice 4-3

**Determine which rational number is greater by rewriting each pair of fractions with the same common denominator.**

**1.** $\frac{2}{9}, \frac{3}{6}$

**2.** $\frac{2}{4}, \frac{4}{5}$

**3.** $\frac{1}{9}, \frac{1}{3}$

_____

_____

_____

**4.** $\frac{2}{12}, \frac{1}{4}$

**5.** $\frac{5}{12}, \frac{9}{15}$

**6.** $\frac{7}{10}, \frac{3}{5}$

_____

_____

_____

**7.** $\frac{6}{16}, \frac{4}{9}$

**8.** $\frac{5}{10}, \frac{8}{12}$

**9.** $\frac{2}{5}, \frac{1}{3}$

_____

_____

_____

**10.** $\frac{4}{6}, \frac{1}{3}$

**11.** $\frac{3}{8}, \frac{8}{9}$

**12.** $\frac{3}{6}, \frac{1}{3}$

_____

_____

_____

**13.** $\frac{2}{6}, \frac{4}{5}$

**14.** $\frac{5}{20}, \frac{1}{2}$

**15.** $\frac{1}{7}, \frac{1}{10}$

_____

_____

_____

**16.** During the 1992 Summer Olympic Games, the top three women's long jumpers were Inessa Kravets ($23\frac{3}{8}$ ft), Jackie Joyner-Kersee ($23\frac{5}{24}$ ft), and Heike Drechsler ($23\frac{7}{16}$ ft). Write these women's names in order from the shortest jump to the longest.

_____

**Compare. Write >, <, or =.**

**17.** $-\frac{4}{9}$ ☐ $-\frac{5}{8}$

**18.** $\frac{1}{3}$ ☐ $\frac{6}{18}$

**19.** $\frac{5}{7}$ ☐ 0.63

**20.** $-0.76$ ☐ $-\frac{3}{4}$

**21.** $-1\frac{9}{12}$ ☐ $-1\frac{15}{20}$

**22.** $\frac{6}{11}$ ☐ $\frac{5}{9}$

**23.** $\frac{7}{12}$ ☐ 0.59

**24.** $\frac{6}{13}$ ☐ 0.45

**Order each set of numbers from greatest to least.**

**25.** $0.74, \frac{3}{4}, \frac{6}{7}, 0.64$ _____

**26.** $\frac{16}{32}, 0.45, \frac{2}{5}, \frac{9}{25}$ _____

**27.** $\frac{7}{8}, -\frac{5}{8}, \frac{15}{30}, -\frac{8}{11}$ _____

**28.** $\frac{14}{15}, 0.743, -0.65, \frac{14}{31}$ _____

**29.** $\frac{17}{28}, 0.95, \frac{11}{15}, \frac{17}{30}$ _____

**30.** $0.8, 0.5, \frac{5}{8}, \frac{3}{8}$ _____

**31.** $\frac{7}{10}, \frac{1}{2}, -0.3, -\frac{3}{4}$ _____

**32.** $-\frac{9}{10}, -\frac{4}{5}, -\frac{1}{2}, -\frac{17}{18}$ _____

# Reteaching 4-4

**Adding and Subtracting Rational Numbers**

To add or subtract fractions and mixed numbers with unlike denominators, first rewrite the fractions using the least common denominator (LCD).

Subtract: $2\frac{3}{4} - 5\frac{1}{3}$

$$2\frac{3}{4} - 5\frac{1}{3} = \frac{11}{4} - \frac{16}{3}$$

$$= \frac{33}{12} - \frac{64}{12} \qquad \leftarrow \text{The LCD is 12.}$$

$$= \frac{-31}{12} \qquad \leftarrow \text{Subtract numerators.}$$

$$= -2\frac{7}{12} \qquad \leftarrow \text{Simplify.}$$

$$2\frac{3}{4} - 5\frac{1}{3} = -2\frac{7}{12}$$

You can use addition or subtraction to solve equations with rational numbers.

Solve: $h - \frac{3}{8} = \frac{1}{6}$

$$h - \frac{3}{8} + \frac{3}{8} = \frac{1}{6} + \frac{3}{8} \qquad \leftarrow \text{Add } \frac{3}{8}.$$

$$h = \frac{4}{24} + \frac{9}{24} \qquad \leftarrow \text{The LCD is 24.}$$

$$h = \frac{13}{24}$$

**Find each sum or difference as a fraction or mixed number in simplest form.**

**1.** $6\frac{1}{4} - 2\frac{3}{8}$

**2.** $\frac{5}{6} + \left(-\frac{1}{2}\right)$

**3.** $-4\frac{1}{3} - \left(-\frac{3}{5}\right)$

_____

**4.** $\frac{1}{8} - \left(-\frac{1}{6}\right)$

**5.** $-1\frac{3}{8} - 4\frac{1}{12}$

**6.** $\frac{7}{10} + \left(-1\frac{2}{5}\right)$

_____

**7.** $1\frac{5}{8} - \left(-2\frac{1}{2}\right)$

**8.** $-2\frac{1}{3} - \left(-1\frac{5}{12}\right)$

**9.** $-10 - \left(3\frac{11}{12}\right)$

_____

**10.** $1\frac{1}{3} - 4\frac{3}{4}$

**11.** $9 + \left(-6\frac{5}{9}\right)$

**12.** $-2\frac{5}{6} - 5\frac{5}{12}$

_____

**Solve each equation. Write each answer as a mixed number or as a fraction in simplest form.**

**13.** $y + \frac{7}{8} = -\frac{1}{4}$

**14.** $c + -\frac{3}{5} = \frac{1}{2}$

**15.** $m - 3\frac{2}{3} = 1\frac{1}{6}$

_____

**16.** $x - 2\frac{1}{4} = -3$

**17.** $n + \frac{1}{2} = -2\frac{5}{6}$

**18.** $\frac{1}{2} + d = -3\frac{1}{5}$

_____

**19.** $7.3 + g = 1\frac{4}{5}$

**20.** $y - 4.1 = 2\frac{3}{4}$

**21.** $z + 2.6 = 0.37$

_____

# Practice 4-4

**Find each sum or difference as a mixed number or fraction in simplest form.**

1. $\frac{3}{4} + \frac{7}{8}$ _____

2. $-1\frac{1}{6} + 2\frac{2}{3}$ _____

3. $4\frac{1}{2} - 7\frac{7}{8}$ _____

4. $-3\frac{5}{6} - \left(-4\frac{1}{12}\right)$ _____

5. $\frac{5}{18} + \frac{7}{12}$ _____

6. $-4\frac{7}{20} + 3\frac{9}{10}$ _____

7. $5\frac{8}{21} - \left(-3\frac{1}{7}\right)$ _____

8. $1\frac{19}{24} + 2\frac{23}{20}$ _____

9. $3\frac{16}{25} - 4\frac{7}{20}$ _____

10. $5\frac{1}{14} + 2\frac{3}{7} + 1\frac{4}{21}$ _____

11. $\frac{11}{12} - \frac{5}{16} + \frac{11}{18}$ _____

12. $\frac{5}{6} + \frac{7}{8} - \frac{11}{12}$ _____

13. $-19\frac{5}{6} + 10\frac{9}{10}$ _____

14. $4\frac{7}{18} - 3\frac{7}{12}$ _____

15. $-1\frac{4}{5} - \left(-4\frac{1}{12}\right)$ _____

**Write each answer as a fraction or mixed number in simplest form.**

16. $14.6 + \left(-3\frac{1}{5}\right)$

17. $-7\frac{3}{4} - 4.125$

18. $5.75 + \left(-2\frac{1}{8}\right)$

_____   _____   _____

19. $1\frac{3}{4} - 2.75 - 4\frac{5}{8}$

20. $3\frac{1}{2} - 6\frac{7}{10} + 4\frac{1}{5}$

21. $\frac{3}{16} + \frac{1}{8} - \frac{1}{4}$

_____   _____   _____

**Solve each equation. Write each answer as a mixed number or as a fraction in simplest form.**

22. $x + \frac{3}{8} = -\frac{1}{4}$

23. $y - \frac{1}{5} = -\frac{4}{5}$

24. $z + \left(-\frac{2}{3}\right) = -\frac{1}{6}$

_____   _____   _____

25. $m - \frac{9}{10} = \frac{1}{5}$

26. $n - 1\frac{1}{3} = -3$

27. $p + \frac{7}{12} = -\frac{1}{4}$

_____   _____   _____

28. $c - 7.2 = -3.7$

29. $d - 0.16 = 2.3$

30. $\frac{1}{8} + a = -2\frac{1}{4}$

_____   _____   _____

31. Stanley is helping in the library by mending torn pages. He has cut strips of tape with lengths of $5\frac{1}{2}$ in., $6\frac{7}{8}$ in., $3\frac{3}{4}$ in., and $4\frac{3}{16}$ in. What is the total length of tape he has used?

_____

Name _____  Class _____  Date _____

# Reteaching 4-5

To multiply rational numbers in fraction form, multiply numerators, then multiply denominators.

Multiply: $\frac{7}{12} \cdot 1\frac{4}{5}$

$\frac{7}{12} \cdot \frac{9}{5}$ ← fraction form

$\frac{7 \cdot 9}{12 \cdot 5}$ ← Multiply numerators.
← Multiply denominators.

$\frac{63}{60} = 1\frac{3}{60} = 1\frac{1}{20}$ ← Simplify.

To divide, multiply by the reciprocal of the divisor.

Divide: $-3\frac{1}{8} \div \frac{2}{3}$

$\frac{-25}{8} \div \frac{2}{3}$ ← fraction form

$\frac{-25}{8} \cdot \frac{3}{2}$ ← reciprocal of divisor

$\frac{-25 \cdot 3}{8 \cdot 2} = \frac{-75}{16}$ ← Multiply.

$= -4\frac{11}{16}$ ← Simplify.

---

**Find each product. Write each answer as a fraction or mixed number in simplest form.**

1. $\frac{8}{9} \cdot \left(-\frac{3}{4}\right)$

2. $-\frac{1}{2} \cdot \frac{4}{5}$

3. $-\frac{2}{3} \cdot \left(-\frac{1}{8}\right)$

4. $\frac{5}{6} \cdot \frac{3}{7}$

5. $\frac{3}{4} \cdot \left(-\frac{2}{3}\right)$

6. $3 \cdot 2\frac{1}{4}$

7. $-5\frac{1}{2} \cdot 1\frac{3}{4}$

8. $-2\frac{1}{8} \cdot (-3)$

9. $4\frac{1}{5} \cdot 2\frac{1}{2}$

10. $\frac{13}{15} \cdot \frac{5}{6}$

11. $-3\frac{2}{5} \cdot 2\frac{1}{2}$

12. $-5 \cdot \left(-2\frac{1}{4}\right)$

13. $-\frac{5}{8} \cdot 4\frac{2}{3}$

14. $-5 \cdot 3\frac{3}{10}$

15. $-2\frac{3}{5} \cdot \left(-3\frac{1}{3}\right)$

**Find each quotient.**

16. $\frac{5}{6} \div \frac{3}{5}$

17. $-\frac{3}{8} \div \left(-\frac{1}{2}\right)$

18. $-6 \div \frac{3}{4}$

19. $4 \div \left(-\frac{2}{3}\right)$

20. $5\frac{1}{4} \div 1\frac{1}{2}$

21. $1\frac{1}{4} \div \left(-\frac{2}{5}\right)$

22. $-\frac{3}{4} \div \left(-1\frac{1}{2}\right)$

23. $-1\frac{3}{5} \div \frac{1}{4}$

24. $2\frac{1}{2} \div \frac{3}{10}$

25. $-\frac{5}{9} \div \left(-\frac{2}{3}\right)$

26. $-6 \div 3\frac{5}{8}$

27. $\frac{3}{4} \div (-9)$

# Practice 4-5

Multiplying and Dividing Rational Numbers

• • • • • • • • • • • • • • • • • • • • • • • • • • • • • • • • • • • • • • • • • • • • • • • • • • • •

**Find each product or quotient. Write each answer as a fraction or mixed number in simplest form.**

1. $-\frac{1}{6} \cdot 2\frac{3}{4}$ _____

2. $\frac{3}{16} \div \left(-\frac{1}{8}\right)$ _____

3. $-\frac{31}{56} \cdot (-8)$ _____

4. $-5\frac{7}{12} \div 12$ _____

5. $-8 \div \frac{1}{4}$ _____

6. $-3\frac{1}{6} \div \left(-2\frac{1}{12}\right)$ _____

7. $8\frac{3}{4} \cdot 3\frac{7}{8}$ _____

8. $-\frac{11}{12} \div \frac{5}{6}$ _____

9. $4\frac{9}{28} \cdot (-7)$ _____

10. $-1\frac{1}{15} \div 15$ _____

11. $-3 \div \frac{3}{4}$ _____

12. $-2\frac{7}{8} \div 3\frac{3}{4}$ _____

13. $-\frac{23}{24} \cdot (-8)$ _____

14. $\frac{7}{8} \cdot \left(-\frac{2}{7}\right)$ _____

15. $-7 \div \frac{1}{9}$ _____

16. $-6\frac{5}{6} \div \frac{1}{6}$ _____

17. $-8 \cdot 3\frac{3}{4}$ _____

18. $\frac{7}{10} \cdot \left(-3\frac{1}{4}\right)$ _____

19. $5 \cdot \left(-3\frac{5}{6}\right)$ _____

20. $-\frac{8}{9} \div \left(-3\frac{2}{3}\right)$ _____

21. $2\frac{1}{3} \div \frac{2}{3}$ _____

**Solve each equation.**

22. $\frac{1}{3}a = \frac{3}{10}$

_____

23. $-\frac{3}{4}b = 9$

_____

24. $-\frac{7}{8}c = 4\frac{2}{3}$

_____

25. $\frac{5}{6}n = -3\frac{3}{4}$

_____

26. $-\frac{3}{5}x = 12$

_____

27. $-2\frac{2}{3}y = 3\frac{1}{3}$

_____

28. $\frac{7}{12}y = -2\frac{4}{5}$

_____

29. $2\frac{1}{4}z = -\frac{1}{9}$

_____

30. $2\frac{1}{5}d = -\frac{1}{2}$

_____

31. One pound of flour contains about four cups. A recipe calls for $2\frac{1}{4}$ c of flour. How many full recipes can you make from a two-pound bag of flour?

_____

32. Kim needs $2\frac{1}{2}$ ft of wrapping paper to wrap each package. She has five packages to wrap. How many packages can she wrap with a 12-ft roll of wrapping paper?

_____

33. Gina and Paul are making pizza for the cast and crew of the school play. They estimate that the boys in the cast and crew will eat $\frac{1}{2}$ pizza each. They estimate that the girls will each eat $\frac{1}{3}$ of a pizza. There are 7 boys and 10 girls working on the play. How many pizzas do they need to make?

_____

# Reteaching 4-6

You can use a *formula* to find the area of a figure.

*Example:* Find the area of a square with side length 1.2 m.

$A = s \cdot s$     ← Write the formula.
$A = (1.2)(1.2)$     ← Substitute known values.
$A = 1.44$     ← Simplify.

The area of the square is 1.44 m$^2$.

Knowing how to *transform a formula* by solving for one of its variables can be useful.

Write a formula to find the width of a rectangle.

Use $A = \ell w$. Solve for $w$.

$$\frac{A}{\ell} = \frac{\ell w}{\ell}$$

$$\frac{A}{\ell} = w; \text{ or } w = \frac{A}{\ell}$$

| **Area Formulas** |
| --- |
| Rectangle: $A = $ length $\cdot$ width<br>$\qquad\qquad A = \ell w$ |
| Square:     $A = $ side length $\cdot$ side length<br>$\qquad\qquad A = s \cdot s$ |
| Trapezoid: $A = \frac{1}{2}$ height (sum of bases)<br>$\qquad\qquad A = \frac{1}{2} h(b_1 + b_2)$ |

---

**Find the area of each figure.**

1. Square: side 3.4 ft

2. Rectangle: 6 m $\times$ 2.3 m

3. Trapezoid: $b_1 = 6$ m, $b_2 = 12$ m, $h = 4.2$ m

**Solve each formula for the variable indicated.**

4. Solve for $r$.
   $d = rt$

5. Solve for $\ell$.
   $A = \ell w$

6. Solve for $b$.
   $y = rx + b$

7. Solve for $t$.
   $I = prt$

8. Solve for $h$.
   $A = bh$

9. Solve for $h$.
   $V = \ell wh$

**Use the formula $d = rt$ to find each of the following.**

10. time for $d = 500$ miles and $r = 50$ mi/h _____

11. rate for $d = 52.5$ miles and $t = 1.5$ hour _____

12. time for $d = 75$ km and $r = 25$ km/h _____

# Practice 4-6

**Find the area and the perimeter of each figure.**

**1.**

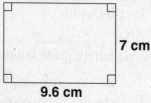

7 cm

9.6 cm

_____

**2.**

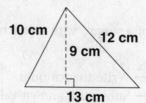

10 cm   12 cm

9 cm

13 cm

_____

**3.**

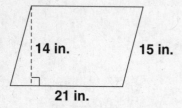

14 in.   15 in.

21 in.

_____

_____

**4.**

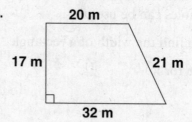

20 m

17 m   21 m

32 m

_____

_____

**Write an equation to find the solution for each problem. Solve the equation. Then give the solution for the problem.**

**5.** The Kents left home at 7:00 A.M. and drove to their parents' house 400 mi away. They arrived at 3:00 P.M. What was their average speed?

_____

**6.** An airplane flew for 4 h 30 min at an average speed of 515 mi/h. How far did it fly?

_____

**7.** Marcia rowed her boat 18 mi downstream at a rate of 12 mi/h. How long did the trip take?

_____

**In Exercises 8–11, use the formula $F = \frac{9}{5}C + 32$ or $C = \frac{5}{9}(F - 32)$ to find a temperature in either degrees Fahrenheit, °F, or degrees Celsius, °C.**

**8.** What is the temperature in degrees Fahrenheit when it is 0°C?

_____

**9.** What is the temperature in degrees Fahrenheit when it is 100°C?

_____

**10.** What is the temperature in degrees Celsius when it is −4°F?

_____

**11.** What is the temperature in degrees Celsius when it is 77°F?

_____

# Reteaching 4-7

**Problem Solving: Try, Check, and Revise and Work Backward**

You have $25 left from your paycheck. You spent $200 on rent, $50 on gas, $150 on food, and $40 on clothing. How much was your paycheck?

**Read and Understand**   What do you know? *You have $25 left from your paycheck and spent $200, $50, $150, and $40.*

**Plan and Solve**   Use the *Work Backward* strategy to solve.
Add the expenses and the remaining amount.

$$
\begin{array}{rl}
\$ \ 25 & \text{remaining} \\
200 & \text{rent} \\
50 & \text{gas} \\
150 & \text{food} \\
+ \ \ 40 & \text{clothing} \\
\hline
\$ \ 465 & \text{paycheck}
\end{array}
$$

**Look Back and Check**   How can you check your answer? *Subtract the total expenses from $465 and see if you get the $25 you have left from your paycheck.*

---

**Solve each problem by either testing and revising or working backward.**

1. The next month you get a roommate who pays half the rent. You split a $50 phone bill. How much did you pay for clothing if gas and food expenses and your paycheck remained the same and you were left with $55?

   _____

2. You and your roommate go grocery shopping. At the bakery, you spend $6.50. At the fish market, you spend $4.75. Then you return home with $5.00. How much did you start with?

3. Your car breaks down. The new battery costs $125 and other necessary parts cost $217. The total cost to fix the car is $650. What is the cost for labor?

   _____

4. In February you deposited $75 in savings. In March you deposited $50, in April you deposited $120, and in May you deposited $20. By June you had $300 in savings. How much money did you start with in January?

   _____

5. If you multiply your roommate's age by 4, add 7, divide by 3, and subtract 9, the result is 20. How old is your roommate?

   _____

6. You spend $20 on gas. You spend half of your remaining cash for lunch. Then you buy a newspaper for $1.75. You have $6.25 left. How much cash did you start with?

   _____

# Practice 4-7

**Problem Solving: Try, Check, and Revise and Work Backward**

**Solve each problem by either testing and revising or working backward.**

1. Alli withdrew some money from the bank for shopping. She spent two thirds of what she withdrew on groceries. She spent $25 on a sweater. She spent half of what remained on a necklace. She went home with $15. How much did Alli withdraw from the bank?

   _____

2. Jill met her friends at the movies at 2 P.M. on Saturday after washing windows. It took her $\frac{3}{4}$ h to wash the windows at the first house. It took twice as long to wash the windows at the next house. The last house took $1\frac{1}{2}$ h. After that, it took her $\frac{1}{2}$ h to walk to the movie theater. At what time did Jill start washing windows?

   _____

3. If you start with a number, add 4, multiply by 3, subtract 10, then divide by 4, the result is 5. What is the number?

   _____

4. Phil had a busy day with his tow truck. He did not return to the garage until 4:00 P.M. It took $1\frac{3}{4}$ h to get the car back to the garage from the last call. The call before that took Phil twice as long. He took a half hour for lunch. One call in the morning took Phil only a half hour, but the one before that took five times as long. What time did Phil's work day begin?

   _____

5. A ball is bouncing on the floor. After each bounce, the height of the ball is one-half its previous height. After the fifth bounce, the height of the ball is 6 in. What was the height of the ball before the first bounce?

   _____

6. If you start with a number, subtract 4, multiply by $\frac{1}{4}$, add 6, then divide by 2, the result is 10. What is the number?

   _____

7. Matt spent $\frac{1}{5}$ of his money on a concert ticket. He spent $60 on a new jacket and $2.50 for bus fare. He reached home with $17.50. How much did he have to begin with?

   _____

8. Bob sells planters at craft shows. At the first craft show, he sold a fourth of his planters. At the next craft show, he sold 14 more. At the third he sold half of what remained. At the fourth show he sold the remaining 20. How many planters did Bob sell?

   _____

*Course 3* Chapter 4

Name _____ Class _____ Date _____

# Reteaching 4-8

**Exploring Square Roots and Irrational Numbers**

- The *square* of 5 is 25.
 $5 \cdot 5 = 5^2 = 25$
- The *square root* of 25 is 5
 because $5^2 = 25$.

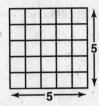

$$\left.\begin{array}{l} 1^2 = 1 \\ 2^2 = 4 \\ 3^2 = 9 \\ 4^2 = 16 \\ 5^2 = 25 \end{array}\right\} \textit{perfect squares}$$

$$\sqrt{25} = 5$$

*Example:* You can use a calculator to find square roots.
Find $\sqrt{36}$ and $\sqrt{21}$ to the nearest tenth.

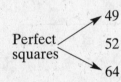

$36 \;\boxed{\sqrt{}}\; = 6 \qquad 21 \;\boxed{\sqrt{}}\; \approx 4.5825757 \approx 4.6$

You can estimate square roots like $\sqrt{52}$ and $\sqrt{61}$.

Perfect squares
49
52    Estimate
64

$\sqrt{49} = 7$
$\sqrt{52} \approx 7$
$\sqrt{64} = 8$

Estimate

$\sqrt{49} = 7$
$\sqrt{61} \approx 8$
$\sqrt{64} = 8$

---

**Find each square root. Round to the nearest integer if necessary.**
**Use ≈ to show that a value is rounded.**

1. $\sqrt{16}$  2. $\sqrt{85}$  3. $\sqrt{26}$  4. $\sqrt{36}$

5. $\sqrt{98}$  6. $\sqrt{40}$  7. $\sqrt{100}$  8. $\sqrt{18}$

9. $\sqrt{5}$  10. $\sqrt{121}$  11. $\sqrt{68}$  12. $\sqrt{144}$

13. $\sqrt{29}$  14. $\sqrt{64}$  15. $\sqrt{37}$  16. $\sqrt{75}$

17. $\sqrt{225}$  18. $\sqrt{54}$  19. $\sqrt{169}$  20. $\sqrt{103}$

21. $\sqrt{61}$  22. $\sqrt{400}$  23. $\sqrt{119}$  24. $\sqrt{84}$

25. If a whole number is not a perfect square, its square root is an
 *irrational number.* List the numbers from Exercises 1–24
 that are irrational.

_____

_____

# Practice 4-8

**Exploring Square Roots and Irrational Numbers**

**Find each square root. Round to the nearest tenth if necessary.**

1. $\sqrt{81}$ _____

2. $\sqrt{76}$ _____

3. $\sqrt{121}$ _____

4. $\sqrt{289}$ _____

5. $\sqrt{130}$ _____

6. $\sqrt{8}$ _____

7. $\sqrt{144}$ _____

8. $\sqrt{160}$ _____

9. $\sqrt{182}$ _____

10. $\sqrt{256}$ _____

11. $\sqrt{301}$ _____

12. $\sqrt{350}$ _____

13. $\sqrt{361}$ _____

14. $\sqrt{410}$ _____

15. $\sqrt{441}$ _____

16. $\sqrt{500}$ _____

**Identify each number as rational or irrational.**

17. $\sqrt{16}$ _____

18. $\sqrt{11}$ _____

19. $\sqrt{196}$ _____

20. $\sqrt{200}$ _____

21. $\sqrt{1,521}$ _____

22. $\sqrt{785}$ _____

23. $\sqrt{529}$ _____

24. $\sqrt{1,680}$ _____

25. $\sqrt{2,000}$ _____

26. $\sqrt{3,969}$ _____

27. $\sqrt{3,192}$ _____

28. $\sqrt{15,376}$ _____

29. $\frac{4}{5}$ _____

30. $0.\overline{712}$ _____

31. $-8$ _____

32. $\sqrt{3}$ _____

33. $5.2$ _____

34. $52$ _____

35. $-\sqrt{25}$ _____

36. $\sqrt{306}$ _____

37. $2.7064$ _____

**Find each square root. Where necessary, round to the nearest tenth.**

38. $\sqrt{5}$ _____

39. $\sqrt{4}$ _____

40. $\sqrt{3}$ _____

41. $\sqrt{245}$ _____

42. $\sqrt{21}$ _____

43. $\sqrt{50}$ _____

# Reteaching 4-9

| The Pythagorean Theorem | |
|---|---|
| The sum of the squares of the lengths of the *legs* of a right triangle is equal to the square of the length of the *hypotenuse*.<br><br>Also, if $a^2 + b^2 = c^2$, then the triangle is a right triangle. | 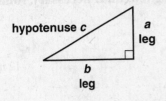<br><br>$a^2 + b^2 = c^2$ |

*Example 1:* Find the length of a leg of a right triangle if the length of the other leg is 12 cm and the length of the hypotenuse is 13 cm.

$$a^2 + b^2 = c^2$$
$$12^2 + b^2 = 13^2$$
$$144 + b^2 = 169$$
$$144 - 144 + b^2 = 169 - 144$$
$$b^2 = 25$$
$$b = \sqrt{25}$$
$$b = 5$$

The length of the leg is 5 cm.

*Example 2:* Is a triangle with sides 6 m, 7 m, and 10 m a right triangle?

$$a^2 + b^2 = c^2$$
$$6^2 + 7^2 \stackrel{?}{=} 10^2 \quad \leftarrow \text{Substitute.}$$
$$36 + 49 \stackrel{?}{=} 100 \quad \leftarrow \text{Simplify.}$$
$$85 \neq 100$$

The triangle is *not* a right triangle.

---

**The lengths of two sides of a right triangle are given. Find the length of the third side.**

**1.** legs: 6 ft and 8 ft
hypotenuse:

_____

**2.** leg: 15 m
hypotenuse: 17 m
leg:

_____

**3.** leg: 12 in.
hypotenuse: 15 in.
leg:

_____

**4.** leg: 1.5 km
hypotenuse: 2.5 km
leg:

_____

**5.** legs: 15 in. and 20 in.
hypotenuse:

_____

**6.** leg: 16 m
hypotenuse: 34 m
leg:

_____

**Is a triangle with the given side lengths a right triangle?**

**7.** 10 cm, 24 cm, 26 cm

_____

**8.** 5 ft, 7 ft, 9 ft

_____

**9.** 6 m, 12 m, 15 m

_____

**10.** 5 in., 12 in., 13 in.

_____

**11.** 30 mm, 40 mm, 50 mm

_____

**12.** 2 yd, 5 yd, 8 yd

_____

# Practice 4-9

**The Pythagorean Theorem**

Find the missing length. If necessary, round the answer to the nearest tenth.

**1.**

17 cm

15 cm

_____

**2.**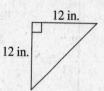

12 in.

12 in.

_____

**3.**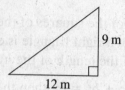

9 m

12 m

_____

**4.**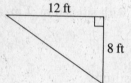

12 ft

8 ft

_____

**5.**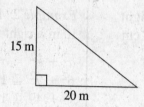

15 m

20 m

_____

**6.**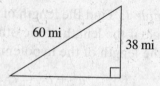

60 mi

38 mi

_____

**Is a triangle with the given side lengths a right triangle?**

**7.** 8 cm, 12 cm, 15 cm

_____

**8.** 9 in., 12 in., 15 in.

_____

**9.** 5 m, 12 m, 25 m

_____

**10.** 15 in., 36 in., 39 in.

_____

**11.** 10 m, 20 m, 25 m

_____

**12.** 7 mm, 24 mm, 25 mm

_____

**13.** 9 yd, 40 yd, 41 yd

_____

**14.** 10 cm, 25 cm, 26 cm

_____

**15.** 27 yd, 120 yd, 130 yd

_____

**16.** 11 mi, 60 mi, 61 mi

_____

You are given three circles, as shown. Points *A, B, C, D, E, F,* and *G*
lie on the same line. Find each length to the nearest tenth.

**17.** *HD* _____

**18.** *IE* _____

**19.** *JD* _____

# Reteaching 5-1

A *ratio* is a comparison between two quantities. Suppose that an apple pie is cut into 12 pieces. 8 are to be served hot and 4 are to be served cold. Two possible ratios are:

$$\frac{\text{hot}}{\text{cold}} = \frac{8}{4} \ \frac{(part)}{(part)} \qquad \frac{\text{hot}}{\text{total}} = \frac{8}{12} \ \frac{(part)}{(whole)}$$

*Example 1:* Write the ratios in simplest form.

$$\frac{8}{4} = \frac{8 \div 4}{4 \div 4} = \frac{2}{1} \qquad \frac{8}{12} = \frac{8 \div 4}{12 \div 4} = \frac{2}{3}$$

A *rate* compares two different types of quantities. To find a unit rate, divide both the numerator and the denominator by the denominator.

*Example 2:* Find the unit rate for 150 miles in 6 hours.

① Compare.  $\dfrac{\text{miles}}{\text{hours}} = \dfrac{150}{6}$

② Divide.  $= \dfrac{150 \div 6}{6 \div 6}$

③ Simplify.  $= \dfrac{25}{1}$

The unit rate is 25 miles per hour, or 25 mi/h.

---

**Write each ratio in simplest form.**

**1.** 8 in. to 10 in.

**2.** $\dfrac{16 \text{ cm}}{12 \text{ cm}}$

**3.** 15 m : 18 m

**4.** $\dfrac{16 \text{ yd}}{24 \text{ yd}}$

**5.** 30 ft : 10 ft

**6.** $\dfrac{9 \text{ mi}}{15 \text{ mi}}$

**7.** $\dfrac{12 \text{ ft}}{28 \text{ ft}}$

**8.** 12 cm to 9 cm

**9.** 6 m : 16 m

**10.** 18 km to 10 km

**11.** $\dfrac{8 \text{ cm}}{15 \text{ cm}}$

**12.** 30 in. : 35 in.

**Use a calculator, paper and pencil, or mental math to find each unit rate.**

**13.** $3.75 for 3 pounds of bird seed

**14.** 270 miles for 12 gallons of gas

**15.** 45 minutes for 15 songs

**16.** $10.50 for 3 pairs of socks

**17.** 72 plants in 9 planters

**18.** 192 jars in 8 cases

**19.** 3 pounds of cheese for 4 pizzas

**20.** 270 miles in 6 hours

Name _____ Class _____ Date _____

# Practice 5-1

Write three ratios that each diagram can represent.

1.

_____

_____

_____

2.

_____

_____

_____

3.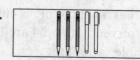

_____

_____

_____

Write each ratio in simplest form.

4. 9 cm : 12 cm

_____

5. 20 in. out of 25 in.

_____

6. 16 ft to 24 ft

_____

7. $\frac{6 \text{ m}}{21 \text{ m}}$

_____

8. 100 yd to 85 yd

_____

9. $\frac{18 \text{ km}}{30 \text{ km}}$

_____

10. 6 in. to 2 ft

_____

11. 10 min to 3 h

_____

12. 20 s to 5 min

_____

Use a calculator, paper and pencil, or mental math to find each unit rate.

13. $67.92 for 4 gal

_____

14. $21.00 for 6 h

_____

15. 250 mi in 4 h

_____

16. 141 words in 3 min

_____

17. $5.94 for 6 carnations

_____

18. 36 min for 12 songs

_____

The table at the right shows the results of a survey. Write each of the ratios in simplest form and as a decimal to the nearest hundredth.

**Which Meal Do You Want for the Party?**

| Tacos | Pizza |
|-------|-------|
| ℍℍ //// | ℍℍ ℍℍ |
| ℍℍ | ℍℍ / |

19. *Tacos* to *Pizza* _____

20. *Pizza* to *Tacos* _____

21. *Tacos* to the total _____

22. *Pizza* to the total _____

23. Which is the better buy: a 16-oz box of cereal for $3.89 or a 6-oz box of cereal for $1.55?

_____

24. A bag contains 8 yellow marbles and 6 blue marbles. What number of yellow marbles can you add to the bag so that the ratio of yellow to blue marbles is 2 : 1?

_____

Name _____ Class _____ Date _____

# Reteaching 5-2

Sometimes you must select the appropriate unit for a measurement.

What customary unit would you use for the weight of a car? *ton, because a ton is a very large unit of weight*

What metric unit would you use for the capacity of a glass of milk? *milliliter, because a milliliter is a small unit of capacity*

| **Equivalent Units of Measurement** | |
| --- | --- |
| **Customary** | **Metric** |
| 1 ft = 12 in. | 1 m = 100 cm |
| 1 yd = 3 ft | 1 km = 1,000 m |
| 1 mi = 5,280 ft | |
| 1 c = 8 fl oz | 1 L = 1,000 mL |
| 1 pt = 2 c | |
| 1 qt = 2 pt | |
| 1 gal = 4 qt | |
| 1 lb = 16 oz | 1 kg = 1,000 g |
| 1 t = 2,000 lb | |

To convert units of measure, multiply by a conversion factor, or a ratio equal to 1. This process is called *dimensional analysis*.

*Example:* Convert 4.5 c to fluid ounces.

From the table you know that 1 c = 8 fl oz.

To convert cups to ounces, multiply by $\frac{8 \text{ fl oz}}{1 \text{ c}}$.

$4.5 \text{ c} = \frac{4.5 \text{ c}}{1} \cdot \frac{8 \text{ fl oz}}{1 \text{ c}} = \frac{(4.5)(8) \text{ fl oz}}{1} = 36 \text{ fl oz}$

So, 4.5 cups equals 36 fluid ounces.

---

**Choose an appropriate customary unit.**

**1.** weight of a peach

_____

**2.** capacity of a pitcher of lemonade

_____

**3.** length of a crayon

_____

**Choose an appropriate metric unit.**

**4.** distance to Mexico City

_____

**5.** mass of a hummingbird

_____

**6.** capacity of a jug of milk

_____

**Use dimensional analysis to convert each measure.**

**7.** 48 in. = _?_ ft

_____

**8.** 8,400 cm = _?_ m

_____

**9.** 6 km = _?_ m

_____

**Use compatible numbers to find a reasonable estimate.**

**10.** 15 qt is about _?_ c.

_____

**11.** 32,688 g is about _?_ kg.

_____

**12.** 88 oz is about _?_ lb.

_____

# Practice 5-2

**Choose an appropriate customary unit.**

1. length of a stapler

    _____

2. weight of a cookie

    _____

3. capacity of a teakettle

    _____

4. height of a door

    _____

5. distance to the moon

    _____

6. weight of a jet aircraft

    _____

**Choose an appropriate metric unit.**

7. mass of a cat

    _____

8. length of a playground

    _____

9. capacity of a test tube

    _____

10. length of an insect

    _____

11. capacity of a bathtub

    _____

12. mass of a coin

    _____

**Use dimensional analysis to convert each measure. Round answers to the nearest hundredth where necessary.**

13. 56 in. = __?__ ft

    _____

14. 240 d = __?__ h

    _____

15. 4 gal = __?__ pt

    _____

16. 0.75 d = __?__ h

    _____

17. 2.25 t = __?__ lb

    _____

18. 84 ft = __?__ yd

    _____

19. 0.25 d = __?__ min

    _____

20. 18 d = __?__ h

    _____

21. 0.01 t = __?__ oz

    _____

**Use dimensional analysis to solve each problem.**

22. At one time, trains were not permitted to go faster than 12 mi/h. How many yards per minute is this?

    _____

23. A mosquito can fly at 0.6 mi/h. How many inches per second is this?

    _____

24. An Arctic tern flew 11,000 miles in 115 days. How many feet per minute did the bird average?

    _____

25. A sneeze can travel up to 100 mi/h. How many feet per second is this?

    _____

**Use compatible numbers to find a reasonable estimate.**

26. 118 in. is about __?__ ft.

    _____

27. 3,540 seconds is about __?__ hours.

    _____

# Reteaching 5-3

You can write an equation as a strategy when solving some problems that have ratios or rates.

A home decorating store offers to mix any paint for free. You need a certain shade of orange that the store person tells you needs 5 parts of red and 3 parts of yellow. If you need 5 gallons of paint, how many ounces of red and orange paint do you need?

| | |
|---|---|
| **Read and Understand** | There are 640 oz in 5 gallons. The ratio of paint colors in 5 to 3. Find how many ounces of each color are needed. |
| **Plan and Solve** | Setting up an equation will help you solve the problem. Using the ratio given, you know the amount of red paint is a multiple of 5 and the amount of yellow paint is a multiple of 3. |

The ratio of red to yellow is 5 : 3. So $5p$ represents the amount of red paint and $3p$ represents the amount of yellow paint.

| Words | amount of red | + | amount of yellow | = | total amount of paint |
|---|---|---|---|---|---|
| Equation | $5p$ | + | $3p$ | = | 640 |

$5p + 3p = 640$
$\quad 8p = 640 \quad$ ← Combine like terms.
$\quad \dfrac{8p}{8} = \dfrac{640}{8} \quad$ ← Divide each side by 8.
$\quad\quad p = 80 \quad$ ← Simplify.

Substitute 80 for $p$ in the expression for each color

red: $5(80) = 400$ oz

yellow: $3(80) = 240$ oz

**Look Back and Check**  Since $400 + 240 = 640$, the answer is correct.

---

**Solve each problem by writing an equation.**

1. A cleaning solution contains a mixture of ammonia and water in a ratio of 5 : 2. If you need 7 gallons of cleaning solution, how many ounces of ammonia and water do you need?

   _____

2. Concrete is made of cement and sand in a ratio of 1 : 2. How many pounds of cement and sand are needed to make 27 pounds of concrete?

   _____

3. Juice concentrate is mixed with water in a ratio of 1 : 3. How many quarts of concentrate and water do you need to make 12 quarts of juice?

   _____

# Practice 5-3

**Solve each problem by writing an equation.**

1. The P.E. department has a set of 40 jump ropes. There are 4 times more red jump ropes than blue jump ropes. How many of each color are there?

   _____

2. A snack is made from granola and nuts. In a 28-oz container, there is 1 more ounce of granola than twice the ounces of nuts. How many ounces of each are in the snack?

   _____

3. The local fair sells tickets for both children and adults. The price of a child's ticket is $5 and the price of an adult ticket is $8. The fair had its greatest turn out so far on Friday; 1,050 people attended. The fair took in $7,350. How many of each type of ticket were sold?

   _____

4. A bathroom cleaner contains 1 part of bleach with 4 parts of water. If you need 10 parts of bathroom cleaner, how much water and bleach do you need?

   _____

5. Your teacher has a container of yellow and green marbles on her desk. Your teacher says there are 3 times more green marbles than yellow marbles and there are 164 marbles in all. How many of each is in the container?

   _____

**Use any strategy to solve each problem. Show your work.**

6. Of 24 students questioned, 6 belong to the Music Club, 8 belong to the Math Club, 5 belong to both. How many students belong to neither club?

   _____

7. You want to carpet a room that is 9 ft long and 4 yd wide. Carpet costs $8.95 per square yard. How much carpet do you need?

   _____

8. Suppose you bought some 32¢ stamps and some 20¢ stamps. You spent $3.92 for sixteen stamps. How many of each stamp did you buy?

   _____

# Reteaching 5-4

A *proportion* states that two ratios are equal. To solve a proportion that contains a variable, find a value of the variable that makes the statement true. Use *cross products*.

*Example 1:* Solve the proportion $\frac{3}{4} = \frac{n}{20}$.

① Write the proportion.    $\frac{3}{4} = \frac{n}{20}$

② Use cross products.    $3 \cdot 20 = 4 \cdot n$

③ Solve.    $60 = 4n$
              $15 = n$

When you write a proportion, remember that matching terms in the ratios should represent the same thing.

*Example 2:* Minh makes bouquets having 4 roses out of 7 flowers. How many roses are there out of 14 flowers?

① Write the proportion.    $\frac{4}{7} = \frac{n}{14} \frac{(roses)}{(flowers)}$

② Use cross products.    $4 \cdot 14 = 7n$

③ Solve.    $56 = 7n$
              $8 = n$

There are 8 roses out of 14 flowers.

---

**Solve each proportion.**

1. $\frac{5}{3} = \frac{n}{6}$

   $30 =$ _____

   $n =$ _____

2. $\frac{s}{4} = \frac{7}{2}$

   $2s =$ _____

   $s =$ _____

3. $\frac{15}{12} = \frac{5}{y}$

   $15y =$ _____

   $y =$ _____

4. $\frac{5}{7} = \frac{w}{21}$

   $105 =$ _____

   $w =$ _____

5. $\frac{b}{10} = \frac{6}{15}$

   $15b =$ _____

   $b =$ _____

6. $\frac{9}{12} = \frac{3}{n}$

   $9n =$ _____

   $n =$ _____

**Write a proportion for each situation. Then solve.**

7. Eight out of 10 fish are trout. How many trout are there out of 40 fish?

   _____

   $w =$ _____

8. There is 1 robin for every 5 birds. How many robins are there for 15 birds?

   _____

   $b =$ _____

9. Two flowers cost $.66. How much does 1 flower cost?

   _____

   $n =$ _____

# Practice 5-4

**Solve each proportion.**

1. $\frac{3}{8} = \frac{m}{16}$ _____

2. $\frac{9}{4} = \frac{27}{x}$ _____

3. $\frac{18}{6} = \frac{j}{1}$ _____

4. $\frac{b}{18} = \frac{7}{6}$ _____

5. $\frac{12}{q} = \frac{3}{4}$ _____

6. $\frac{3}{2} = \frac{15}{r}$ _____

7. $\frac{5}{x} = \frac{25}{15}$ _____

8. $\frac{80}{20} = \frac{4}{n}$ _____

**Estimate the solution of each proportion.**

9. $\frac{m}{25} = \frac{16}{98}$ _____

10. $\frac{7}{3} = \frac{52}{n}$ _____

11. $\frac{30}{5.9} = \frac{k}{10}$ _____

12. $\frac{2.8}{j} = \frac{1.3}{2.71}$ _____

13. $\frac{y}{12} = \frac{2.89}{4.23}$ _____

14. $\frac{5}{8} = \frac{b}{63}$ _____

15. $\frac{9}{4} = \frac{35}{d}$ _____

16. $\frac{c}{7} = \frac{28}{50}$ _____

**Solve each proportion.**

17. $\frac{4}{5} = \frac{b}{40}$

18. $\frac{11}{7} = \frac{88}{c}$

19. $\frac{x}{1.4} = \frac{28}{5.6}$

20. $\frac{0.99}{a} = \frac{9}{11}$

21. $\frac{42.5}{20} = \frac{x}{8}$

22. $\frac{15}{25} = \frac{7.5}{y}$

23. $\frac{16}{b} = \frac{56}{38.5}$

24. $\frac{z}{54} = \frac{5}{12}$

25. $\frac{8}{12} = \frac{e}{3}$

26. $\frac{v}{35} = \frac{15}{14}$

27. $\frac{60}{n} = \frac{12}{5}$

28. $\frac{6}{16} = \frac{9}{w}$

29. $\frac{4}{7} = \frac{r}{35}$

30. $\frac{18}{16} = \frac{27}{t}$

31. $\frac{n}{12} = \frac{12.5}{15}$

32. $\frac{27}{f} = \frac{40.5}{31.5}$

33. 5 is to 8 as 15 is to $w$

34. $y$ is to 8 as 22.5 is to 10

35. 14 is to $b$ as 28 is to 18

36. 10 is to 7 as $m$ is to 10.5

37. 30 is to 16 as $j$ is to 8

38. $r$ is to 17 as 81 is to 51

**Write a proportion for each situation. Then solve.**

39. Jaime paid $1.29 for three ponytail holders. At that rate, what would eight ponytail holders cost her?

40. According to a label, there are 25 calories per serving of turkey lunch meat. How many calories are there in 2.5 servings?

41. Arturo paid $8 in tax on a purchase of $200. At that rate, what would the tax be on a purchase of $150?

42. Chris drove 200 mi in 4 h. At that rate, how long would it take Chris to drive 340 mi?

# Reteaching 5-5

Similar polygons have congruent corresponding angles and corresponding sides that are in proportion.
The symbol ~ means *is similar to*.

*Example:* Is parallelogram
*ABCD* ~ parallelogram *KLMN*?

① Check corresponding angles.　　$\angle A \cong \angle K$, $\angle B \cong \angle L$, $\angle C \cong \angle M$, and $\angle D \cong \angle N$

② Compare corresponding sides.　　$\dfrac{AB}{KL} = \dfrac{8}{4} = \dfrac{2}{1}$　$\dfrac{BC}{LM} = \dfrac{12}{6} = \dfrac{2}{1}$

$\dfrac{CD}{MN} = \dfrac{8}{4} = \dfrac{2}{1}$　$\dfrac{DA}{NK} = \dfrac{12}{6} = \dfrac{2}{1}$

Corresponding angles are congruent. Corresponding sides are in proportion. The parallelograms are similar.

You can use proportions to find unknown lengths in similar figures.

① To find *EF*, use a proportion.　　$\dfrac{AB}{DE} = \dfrac{BC}{EF}$　　$\triangle ABC \sim \triangle DEF$

② Substitute.　　　　　　　　　　$\dfrac{12}{6} = \dfrac{10}{n}$

③ Use cross products.　　　　　　$12n = 60$

④ Solve.　　　　　　　　　　　　$n = 5$

　　$EF = 5$

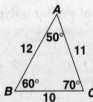

---

**Tell whether each pair of polygons is similar. Explain why or why not.**

1.
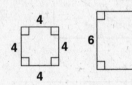

2.
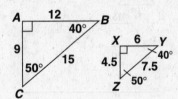

3.

_____　　_____　　_____

**Exercises 4–6 show pairs of similar polygons. Find the unknown length.**

4.
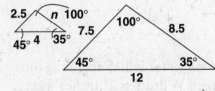

5.
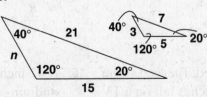

6.
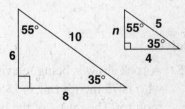

_____　　_____　　_____

# Practice 5-5

**Similar Figures and Proportions**

**Tell whether each pair of polygons is similar. Explain why or why not.**

1.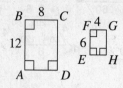

2.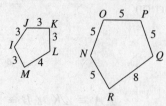

3.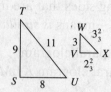

_____

_____

_____

4.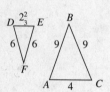

5.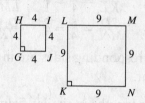

6.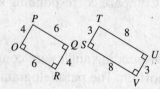

_____

_____

_____

**Exercises 7–14 show pairs of similar polygons. Find the unknown lengths.**

7.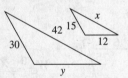

8.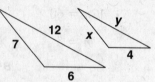

9.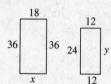

_____

_____

_____

10.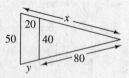

11.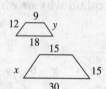

12.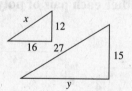

_____

_____

_____

13.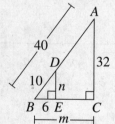

_____

14.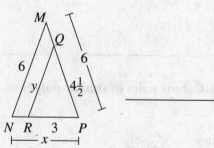

_____

## Solve.

15. A rock show is being televised. The lead singer, who is 75 inches tall, is 15 inches tall on a TV monitor. The image of the bass player is 13 inches tall on the monitor. How tall is the bass player?

16. A 42-inch-long guitar is 10.5-feet-long on a stadium screen. A drum is 21 inches wide. How wide is the image on the stadium screen?

_____

_____

Name _____  Class _____  Date _____

# Reteaching 5-6

**Similarity Transformations**

Draw the image of quadrilateral *ABCD*
for the *dilation* with *scale factor* 2.
Then graph the image.

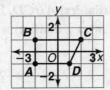

*Example:*

① Write the coordinates of
each point.

② Multiply the *x*- and *y*-
coordinates of each point
by the scale factor, 2.

③ Graph the image
*A′B′C′D′*.

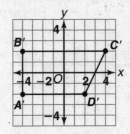

$$A(-2, -1) \longrightarrow A'(-4, -2)$$
$$B(-2, 1) \longrightarrow B'(-4, 2)$$
$$C(2, 1) \longrightarrow C'(4, 2)$$
$$D(1, -1) \longrightarrow D'(2, -2)$$

Image *A′B′C′D′* is an *enlargement* of *ABCD* because the scale
factor is greater than 1. If the scale factor had been less than 1,
then the dilation of *ABCD* would be a *reduction*.

---

**Graph quadrilateral *ABCD* and its image *A′B′C′D′* after a
dilation with the given scale factor. Classify each dilation as
an enlargement or a reduction.**

1. $A(-1, 1), B(1, 1), C(0, -1), D(-1, -1)$;
   scale factor 2

2. $A(-2, -2), B(-2, 2), C(2, 2), D(2, 0)$;
   scale factor $\frac{1}{2}$

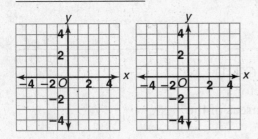

3. $A(-2, -2), B(-2, 2), C(2, 2), D(2, -2)$;
   scale factor $\frac{1}{2}$

4. $A(-2, 2), B(2, 0), C(2, -2), D(-2, -2)$;
   scale factor 2

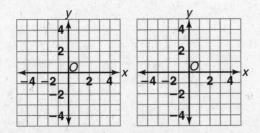

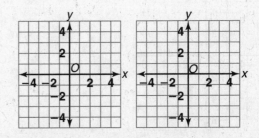

# Practice 5-6

**Similarity Transformations**

**Graph the coordinates of the quadrilateral *ABCD*. Find the coordinates of its image *A'B'C'D'* after a dilation with the given scale factor.**

**1.** $A(2, -2), B(3, 2), C(-3, 2), D(-2, -2)$;
scale factor 2

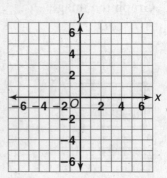

**2.** $A(6, 3), B(0, 6), C(-6, 2), D(-6, -5)$;
scale factor $\frac{1}{2}$

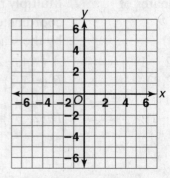

**Quadrilateral *A'B'C'D'* is a dilation of quadrilateral *ABCD*. Find the scale factor. Classify each dilation as an enlargement or a reduction.**

**3.**

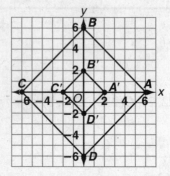

**4.**

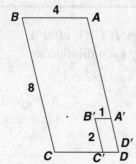

**5.**

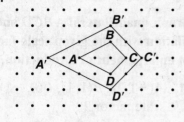

_____  _____  _____

**6.** A triangle has coordinates $A(-2, -2), B(4, -2)$, and $C(1, 1)$.
Graph its image $A'B'C'$ after a dilation with scale factor $\frac{3}{2}$.
Give the coordinates of $A'B'C'$, and the ratio of the areas of the
figures $A'B'C'$ and $ABC$.

_____

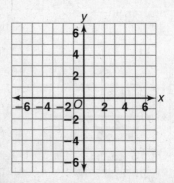

# Reteaching 5-7

A carpenter is making some furniture based on tiny furniture from an old dollhouse. The *scale* of the models is $\frac{5}{2}$ in. : 1 ft. The height of a footstool in the dollhouse is 3 in. What is the height of the carpenter's footstool?

① Write a proportion. Let $h$ = height of the carpenter's footstool. Be sure the terms of the ratios match.

$$\frac{\frac{5}{2}}{1} = \frac{3}{h} \quad \frac{\text{model height (in.)}}{\text{actual height (ft)}}$$

② Use cross products.

$$\frac{5}{2}h = 3$$

③ Solve.

$$h = \frac{6}{5}$$

$$h = 1\frac{1}{5}$$

The height of the carpenter's footstool is $1\frac{1}{5}$ ft.

---

**Write a proportion. Then solve.**

1. The carpenter wants to make a dresser based on the dollhouse furniture. The scale is $\frac{5}{2}$ in. : 1 ft. The height of the dresser in the dollhouse is 10 in. What is the height of the carpenter's dresser?

_____

2. The carpenter uses colonial doll furniture with a scale of $\frac{9}{2}$ in. : 1 ft as a model. The length of a doll's bed is 27 in. What is the length of the carpenter's bed?

_____

3. The scale of some Victorian doll furniture is $\frac{15}{4}$ in. : 1 ft. The height of the doll's table is 12 in. What is the height of the carpenter's table?

_____

4. The scale of some modern doll furniture is $\frac{7}{2}$ in. : 1 ft. The length of a doll's sofa is 28 in. What is the length of the carpenter's sofa?

_____

5. The carpenter wants to make a desk like a doll's desk that is $10\frac{1}{2}$ in. high. The scale is $\frac{7}{2}$ in. : 1 ft. What is the height of the carpenter's desk?

_____

6. Ruth makes a scale drawing of her room. She uses the scale $\frac{3}{2}$ in. : 1 ft. In the drawing, the dimensions of her room are 18 in. by 24 in. What are the actual dimensions of her room?

_____

# Practice 5-7

**Solve each problem.**

1.  A scale model of a whale is being built. The actual length of the whale is 65 ft. The scale of the model is 2 in. : 3 ft. What will be the length of the model?

    _____

2.  The smallest frog known is only $\frac{1}{2}$ in. long. A local science museum is planning to build a model of the frog. The scale used will be 3 in. : $\frac{1}{4}$ in. How long will the model be?

    _____

3.  Two cities on a map were $2\frac{1}{4}$ in. apart. The cities are actually 56.25 mi apart. What scale was used to draw the map?

    _____

4.  Four ounces of a certain perfume cost $20.96. How much would six ounces of perfume cost?

    _____

5.  The human brain weighs about 1 lb for each 100 lb of body weight. What is the approximate weight of the brain of a person weighing 85 lb to the nearest ounce?

    _____

6.  Two towns are 540 km apart. If the scale on the map is 2 cm to 50 km, how far apart are the towns on the map?

    _____

7.  Cans of tuna cost $1.59 for $6\frac{1}{2}$ oz. At that rate, how much would 25 oz of tuna cost?

    _____

8.  Students are building a model of a volcano. The volcano is about 8,000 ft tall. The students want the model to be 18 in. tall. What scale should they use?

    _____

9.  A certain shade of paint requires 3 parts of blue to 2 parts of yellow to 1 part of red. If 18 gal of that shade of paint are needed, how many gal of blue are needed?

    _____

# Reteaching 5-8

**Similarity and Indirect Measurement**

You can use similar triangles to solve problems.

*Example:* Sam is 5 ft tall and casts a shadow 8 ft long. The nearby flagpole casts a shadow 24 feet long. How tall is the flagpole?

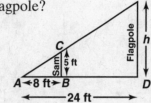

① Draw a diagram. Show similar triangles formed by the flagpole, Sam, and the shadows. Let $h$ = height of the flagpole.

② Write a proportion. Use the similar triangles.

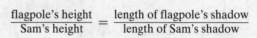

$$\frac{\text{flagpole's height}}{\text{Sam's height}} = \frac{\text{length of flagpole's shadow}}{\text{length of Sam's shadow}}$$

③ Substitute.

$$\frac{h}{5} = \frac{24}{8}$$

④ Use cross products.

$$8h = 5 \cdot 24$$

⑤ Solve.

$$h = \frac{120}{8} = 15$$

The height of the flagpole is 15 ft.

---

**In each figure, find $h$.**

**1.**

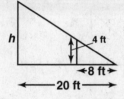

_____

**2.**

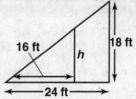

_____

**Use similar triangles to answer each question.**

**3.** A child 4 ft tall casts a shadow 12 ft long. She stands next to a sculpture that has a 36 ft long shadow. How tall is the sculpture?

_____

**4.** A building 35 ft tall casts a shadow 105 ft long. Patty casts a shadow 16.5 ft long. How tall is Patty?

_____

**5.** A man 6 ft tall casts a shadow 3 ft long. He stands next to a tree that has a 47.5 ft shadow. How tall is the tree?

_____

**6.** A fence post 3 ft tall casts a shadow 16 ft long. At the same time the barn casts a shadow 96 ft long. How tall is the barn?

_____

# Practice 5-8

**Similarity and Indirect Measurement**

**In each figure, find *x*.**

**1.**

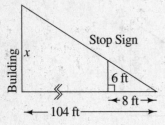

**2.**

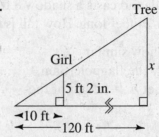

_____

_____

**3.**

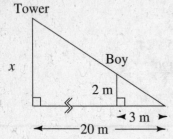

**4.**

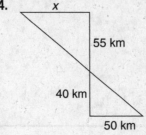

_____

_____

**5.**

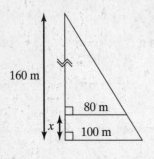

**6.**

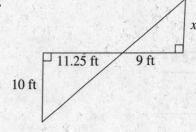

_____

_____

## Solve.

**7.** An office building 55 ft tall casts a shadow 30 ft long. How tall is a person standing nearby who casts a shadow 3 ft long?

**8.** A 20-ft pole casts a shadow 12 ft long. How tall is a nearby building that casts a shadow 20 ft long?

_____

_____

**9.** A fire tower casts a shadow 30 ft long. A nearby tree casts a shadow 8 ft long. How tall is the fire tower if the tree is 20 ft tall?

**10.** A house casts a shadow 12 m long. A tree in the yard casts a shadow 8 m long. How tall is the tree if the house is 20 m tall?

_____

_____

# Reteaching 5-9

**The Sine and Cosine Ratios**

Find the sine and cosine ratios for $\angle A$.

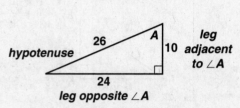

$$sine \text{ of } \angle A = \sin A \qquad cosine \text{ of } \angle A = \cos A$$

$$= \frac{opposite}{hypotenuse} \qquad = \frac{adjacent}{hypotenuse}$$

$$= \frac{24}{26} \qquad = \frac{10}{26}$$

$$= \frac{12}{13} \qquad = \frac{5}{13}$$

You can use a calculator to find the sine and cosine of any acute angle.

*Example 1:* Find sin 47°.

① Enter the angle measure.

② Press the SIN key.

47 SIN 0.7313537

So, sin 47° ≈ 0.7314.

*Example 2:* Find cos 47°.

① Enter the angle measure.

② Press the COS key.

47 COS 0.6819984

So, cos 47° ≈ 0.6820.

You can use the sine and cosine ratios to find measures indirectly.

*Example 3:* Find the length $x$ to the nearest tenth.

① Use the cosine ratio. $\qquad \cos 54° = \frac{x}{35}$

② Solve for $x$. $\qquad x = 35(\cos 54°)$

③ Use a calculator. $\qquad$ 35 ✖ 54 COS ▤ 20.5725

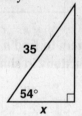

The length $x$ is about 20.6 ft.

---

**Find each trigonometric ratio as a fraction in simplest form.**

**1.** sin $D$

**2.** cos $D$

_____ _____

**3.** sin $E$

**4.** cos $E$

_____ _____

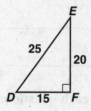

**Find each sine or cosine ratio to the nearest ten-thousandth.**

**5.** sin 32° $\qquad$ **6.** cos 56° $\qquad$ **7.** cos 18° $\qquad$ **8.** sin 65°

_____ _____ _____ _____

**9.** Find $n$ to the nearest tenth. $n = $ _____

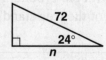

# Practice 5-9

**Find each trigonometric ratio as a fraction in simplest form.**

1. sin *J*

_____

2. cos *J*

_____

3. sin *L*

_____

4. cos *L*

_____

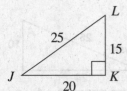

**Find each sine or cosine ratio to the nearest ten-thousandth.**

5. sin 48°

_____

6. cos 57°

_____

7. sin 18°

_____

8. cos 18°

_____

9. sin 89°

_____

10. cos 89°

_____

11. sin 37°

_____

12. cos 8°

_____

13. sin 54°

_____

14. cos 62°

_____

15. sin 75°

_____

16. cos 15°

_____

**Use the Pythagorean theorem to find *n* in Exercises 17–19. Then write sin *X* and cos *X* as fractions in simplest form.**

17.

_____

_____

18.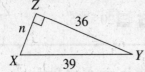

_____

_____

19.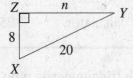

_____

_____

**Answer each question.**

20. A man on a 135-ft vertical cliff looks down at an angle of 16° and sees his friend. How far away is the man from his friend? How far is the friend from the base of the cliff?

_____

21. A 12-ft tree fell against a house during a thunderstorm. The tree formed a 56° angle with the ground. How far away from the house does the base of the tree stand?

_____

# Reteaching 6-1

A *percent* is a ratio that compares a number to 100.

- To *write a fraction as a percent*, find the equivalent fraction with denominator 100. Write the numerator to show the percent.

$$\frac{3}{10} = \frac{3 \cdot 10}{10 \cdot 10} = \frac{30}{100}$$

- To *write a decimal as a percent*, move the decimal point two places to the right and write the % sign.

$$0.78 = 78\%$$
$$0.054 = 5.4\%$$
$$3.9 = 390\%$$

- To *write a percent as a fraction*, compare the number to 100, then simplify.

$$40\% = \frac{40}{100} = \frac{2}{5}$$

- To *write a percent as a decimal*, remove the % sign and move the decimal point two places to the left.

$$34\% = 0.34$$
$$0.9\% = 0.009$$
$$460\% = 4.6$$

Another way to change between a fraction and a percent is to use a decimal as an intermediate step.

| Fraction | → | Decimal | → | Percent | | Percent | → | Decimal | → | Fraction |
|---|---|---|---|---|---|---|---|---|---|---|
| $\frac{3}{8} = 3 \div 8$ | = | 0.375 | = | 37.5% | | 250% | = | 2.50 | = | $2\frac{50}{100} = 2\frac{1}{2}$ |

**Write each decimal as a percent.**

**1.** 0.39 _____

**2.** 0.08 _____

**3.** 4.2 _____

**4.** 0.5 _____

**5.** 9 _____

**6.** 0.056 _____

**Write each fraction as a percent.**

**7.** $\frac{3}{4}$ _____

**8.** $\frac{1}{5}$ _____

**9.** $\frac{7}{10}$ _____

**10.** $\frac{5}{8}$ _____

**11.** $\frac{1}{4}$ _____

**12.** $\frac{3}{5}$ _____

**Write each percent as a decimal.**

**13.** 45% _____

**14.** 90% _____

**15.** 0.2% _____

**16.** 150% _____

**17.** 4% _____

**18.** 32% _____

**Write each percent as a fraction in simplest form.**

**19.** 25% _____

**20.** 10% _____

**21.** 68% _____

**22.** 450% _____

**23.** 12% _____

**24.** 375% _____

Name _____ Class _____ Date _____

# Practice 6-1

**Fractions, Decimals, and Percents**

**Use mental math to write each decimal as a percent.**

1. 0.95 _____
2. 0.06 _____
3. 0.004 _____
4. 0.27 _____

5. 0.63 _____
6. 0.005 _____
7. 1.4 _____
8. 2.57 _____

**Choose a calculator or a paper and pencil to write each fraction as a percent. Round to the nearest tenth of a percent.**

9. $\frac{4}{5}$ _____
10. $\frac{7}{10}$ _____
11. $\frac{5}{6}$ _____
12. $4\frac{1}{2}$ _____

13. $\frac{5}{8}$ _____
14. $\frac{1}{15}$ _____
15. $\frac{9}{25}$ _____
16. $1\frac{7}{8}$ _____

17. $\frac{1}{6}$ _____
18. $\frac{11}{12}$ _____
19. $\frac{1}{20}$ _____
20. $3\frac{9}{20}$ _____

**Use mental math to write each percent as a decimal.**

21. 70% _____
22. 10% _____
23. 800% _____
24. 37% _____

25. 2.6% _____
26. 234% _____
27. 9% _____
28. $3\frac{1}{2}$% _____

**Write each percent as a fraction in simplest form.**

29. 10% _____
30. 47% _____
31. $5\frac{1}{2}$% _____
32. 473% _____

33. 15% _____
34. 92% _____
35. $3\frac{1}{4}$% _____
36. 548% _____

37. 85% _____
38. 42% _____
39. 70% _____
40. 150% _____

**Solve.**

41. There are twelve pairs of cranial nerves connected to the brain. Ten of these pairs are related to sight, smell, taste, and sound. What percent of the pairs are related to sight, smell, taste, and sound?

_____

42. If a person weighs 150 lb, then calcium makes up 3 lb of that person's weight. What percent of a person's weight does calcium make up?

_____

43. A quality control inspector found that 7 out of every 200 flashlights produced were defective. What percent of the flashlights were *not* defective?

_____

44. In 1992, 80 varieties of reptiles were on the endangered species list. Eight of these were found only in the United States. What percent of the reptiles on the endangered species list were found only in the United States?

_____

# Reteaching 6-2

You can use common percents and their multiples to estimate a percent of a number. Some common percents are listed below.

| | | | |
|---|---|---|---|
| $25\% = \frac{1}{4}$ | $20\% = \frac{1}{5}$ | $12\frac{1}{2}\% = \frac{1}{8}$ | $10\% = \frac{1}{10}$ |
| $50\% = \frac{1}{2}$ | $40\% = \frac{2}{5}$ | $37\frac{1}{2}\% = \frac{3}{8}$ | $30\% = \frac{3}{10}$ |
| $75\% = \frac{3}{4}$ | $60\% = \frac{3}{5}$ | $62\frac{1}{2}\% = \frac{5}{8}$ | $70\% = \frac{7}{10}$ |
| | $80\% = \frac{4}{5}$ | $87\frac{1}{2}\% = \frac{7}{8}$ | $90\% = \frac{9}{10}$ |

Here are two ways to estimate percent.

*Use fractions.*

*Example 1:* Estimate 74% of $79.

① Use a fraction that is close to 74%.

$$75\% \approx \frac{3}{4}$$
$$79 \approx 80$$

② Multiply.

$$\frac{3}{4} \times 80 = 60$$

74% of $79 is about $60.

*Use decimals.*

*Example 2:* Estimate 18% of 165.

① Use a decimal that is close to 18%.

$$18\% \approx 0.2$$
$$165 \approx 170$$

② Multiply.

$$0.2 \cdot 170 = 34$$

34 is about 18% of 165.

---

**Estimate the percent of each number. Use fractions or decimals.**

1. 20% of 36 _____

2. 75% of 41 _____

3. 60% of 49 _____

4. 30% of 42 _____

5. $12\frac{1}{2}$% of 66 _____

6. 25% of 17 _____

7. 9.7% of 68 _____

8. 40% of 19.9 _____

9. 5% of 60 _____

10. 69% of 150 _____

11. 0.8% of 153 _____

12. 55% of 400 _____

**Estimate a 15% tip for each restaurant bill.**

13. $9.25

14. $39.50

15. $28.85

_____

_____

_____

16. $48.45

17. $21.20

18. $12.34

_____

_____

_____

# Practice 6-2

**Estimate.**

**1.** 6% of 140

**2.** 18.9% of 44

**3.** 61% of 180

_____

_____

_____

**4.** 5.1% of 81

**5.** $16\frac{1}{2}$% of 36

**6.** 81% of 241

_____

_____

_____

**7.** 67% of 300

**8.** 51% of 281

**9.** 62.9% of 400

_____

_____

_____

**10.** 76% of 600

**11.** 88% of 680

**12.** 37% of 481

_____

_____

_____

**13.** 19.1% of 380

**14.** 41% of 321

**15.** 33% of 331

_____

_____

_____

**16.** 83% of 453

**17.** 76.3% of 841

**18.** 67.1% of 486

_____

_____

_____

**19.** 84% of 93

**20.** 0.3% of 849

**21.** 81.2% of 974

_____

_____

_____

**22.** 0.87% of 250

**23.** 57.9% of 500

**24.** 62% of 400

_____

_____

_____

**Estimate.**

**25.** Of the 307 species of mammals on the endangered list in 1992, 12.1% of them were found only in the United States. Estimate the number of mammal species in the United States that were on the endangered list.

_____

**26.** In 1990, 19% of the people of Mali lived in urban settings. If the population that year was 9,200,000, estimate the number of people who lived in urban settings.

_____

**27.** Of the 1,267 students at the school, 9.8% live within walking distance of school. Estimate the number of students within walking distance.

_____

**28.** Of the 1,267 students at the school, 54.6% have to ride the bus. About how many students have to ride the bus?

_____

# Reteaching 6-3

**Percents and Proportions**

You can use proportions to solve percent problems.

Find the part.

*Example 1:* Find 10% of 92.

① Think of the percent
   as a ratio. $\qquad 10\% = \frac{10}{100}$

② Write a proportion. $\qquad \frac{10}{100} = \frac{n}{92}$

③ Solve. $\qquad 100n = 920$
   $$\frac{100n}{100} = \frac{920}{100}$$
   $$n = 9.2$$

10% of 92 is 9.2.

Find the whole.

*Example 3:* 50 is 20% of what number?

① Write a proportion. $\qquad \frac{50}{n} = \frac{20}{100}$

② Solve. $\qquad 20n = 5,000$
   $$\frac{20n}{20} = \frac{5,000}{20}$$
   $$n = 250$$

Find the percent.

*Example 2:* What percent of 80 is 20?

① Write a proportion. $\qquad \frac{20}{80} = \frac{n}{100}$

② Solve. $\qquad 80n = 2,000$
   $$\frac{80n}{80} = \frac{2,000}{80}$$
   $$n = 25$$

20 is 25% of 80.

50 is 20% of 250.

---

**Complete the proportion. Then solve each problem.**

**1.** 6 is $n$% of 30.

$$\frac{n}{100} = $$

$n =$ _____

**2.** 2 is 25% of $n$.

$$\frac{2}{n} = $$

$n =$ _____

**3.** 75% of 80 is $n$.

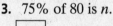 $= \frac{n}{80}$

$n =$ _____

**4.** $n$% of 50 is 20.

$$\frac{n}{100} = $$

$n =$ _____

**5.** 49 is $n$% of 140.

$$\frac{n}{100} = $$

$n =$ _____

**6.** 45 is 15% of $n$.

$$\frac{45}{n} = $$

$n =$ _____

**Use a proportion to solve each problem.**

**7.** Find 50% of 90.

_____

**8.** Find 75% of 980.

_____

**9.** 60 is 30% of what number?

_____

# Practice 6-3

**Percents and Proportions**

**Write a proportion that will help you answer the problem. Then solve each problem.**

1. What percent is 21 of 50?

   _____

2. What is 45% of 72?

   _____

3. 83 is 70% of what number?

   _____

4. 45 is what percent of 65?

   _____

**Use a proportion to solve each problem.**

5. 78% of 58 is _____.

6. 86 is 12% of _____.

7. 90 is _____ of 65.

8. 40 is 17% of _____.

9. 57 is 31% of _____.

10. 280% of _____ is 418.

11. 53% of 92 is _____.

12. 56 is 25% of _____.

13. 51 is _____ of 14.

14. What percent of 42 is 18?

    _____

15. 58 is 40% of what number?

    _____

16. What is 70% of 93?

    _____

17. 240 is what percent of 150?

    _____

18. What percent of 16 is 40?

    _____

19. 65 is 60% of what number?

    _____

20. What is 175% of 48?

    _____

21. 210 is what percent of 70?

    _____

22. What percent of 56 is 7?

    _____

23. 68 is 50% of what number?

    _____

24. What is 63% of 148?

    _____

25. 215 is what percent of 400?

    _____

**Solve.**

26. In 1990, the population of El Paso, Texas, was 515,342. Of this population, 69% were of Hispanic origin. How many people were of Hispanic origin?

    _____

27. Bangladesh covers 55,598 mi². Of this land, 2,224 mi² are meadows and pastures. What percent of the land is meadow and pasture?

    _____

# Reteaching 6-4

You can use an equation to solve percent problems.

| Find the whole. | Find the part. |
|---|---|

*Example 1:* 25% of what number is 20?

① Think of the percent
   as a decimal.        25% = 0.25

② Write an equation.    $0.25n = 20$

③ Solve.               $n = \frac{20}{0.25}$
                       $= 80$

25% of 80 is 20.

*Example 2:* Find 12% of 48.

① Think of the percent
   as a decimal.        12% = 0.12

② Write an equation.   $0.12 \times 48 = n$

③ Solve.               $5.76 = n$

12% of 48 is 5.76.

Find the percent.

*Example 3:* What percent of 48 is 30?

① Write an equation.    $n \times 48 = 30$

② Solve.               $n = \frac{30}{48}$
                       $= 0.625$
                       $= 62.5\%$    30 is 62.5% of 48.

**Use an equation to solve each problem.**

**1.** 30% of what number is 6?

_____

**2.** 32 is 25% of what number?

_____

**3.** What percent of 80 is 20?

_____

**4.** What is 10% of 35?

_____

**5.** Find 40% of 90.

_____

**6.** What percent of 60 is 27?

_____

**7.** What is 11% of 99?

_____

**8.** 22 is 55% of what number?

_____

**9.** What is 13% of 56?

_____

**10.** What percent of 96 is 84?

_____

# Practice 6-4

**Use an equation to solve each problem. Round to the nearest tenth.**

1. What percent of 80 is 25? _____

2. 8.6 is 5% of what number? _____

3. What is 140% of 85? _____

4. 70 is what percent of 120? _____

5. What percent of 90 is 42? _____

6. 18.4 is what percent of 10? _____

7. 56% of what number is 82? _____

8. Find 93% of 150. _____

9. 30% of what number is 120? _____

10. What percent of 420 is 7? _____

11. 79 is what percent of 250? _____

12. 9.1 is 3% of what number? _____

13. What is 94% of 260? _____

14. 45 is what percent of 18? _____

15. What percent of 280 is 157? _____

16. 20.7 is what percent of 8? _____

17. 114% of what number is 75? _____

18. Find 72% of 18,495. _____

19. 75% of what number is 200? _____

20. What percent of 940 is 15? _____

21. 80 is what percent of 450? _____

22. Find 65% of 2,190. _____

23. 90 is what percent of 40? _____

24. 45 is what percent of 900? _____

25. 82 is 90% of what number? _____

26. 50 is 120% of what number? _____

**Solve.**

27. In a recent survey, 216 people, or 54% of the sample, said they usually went to a family restaurant when they went out to eat. How many people were surveyed?

_____

28. In a school survey, 248 students, or 32% of the sample, said they worked part time during the summer. How many students were surveyed?

_____

29. Juliet sold a house for $112,000. What percent commission did she receive if she earned $6,720?

_____

30. Jason earns $200 per week plus 8% commission on his sales. How much were his sales last week if Jason earned $328?

_____

31. Stella makes 2% royalties on a book she wrote. How much money did her book earn in sales last year if she made $53,000 in royalties?

_____

32. Linda earns $40 base pay per week, plus 10% commission on all sales. What were her sales if she made $112 in one week?

_____

33. Kevin sold a house for $57,000. His fee, or sales commission, for selling the house was $2,679. What percent of the price of the house was Kevin's commission?

_____

34. Marik agreed to pay a realtor 6.5% commission for selling his house. If the house sold for $68,900, how much does Marik have after paying the realtor's commission?

_____

# Reteaching 6-5

Percent of Increase

*Example 1:* Alex collects rare books. In 1997, he bought a book for $10. In 1998, it was worth $12. What is the percent of increase from 1997 to 1998?

$$\text{Percent increase} = \frac{\text{amount of change}}{\text{original amount}}$$

$$= \frac{12 - 10}{10}$$

$$= \frac{2}{10} = 0.2 = 20\%$$

The value of Alex's book increased by 20%.

Percent of Decrease

*Example 2:* Alex sold one of his books in 1998 for $8. The book cost $12 in 1996. What is the percent of decrease from 1996?

$$\text{Percent increase} = \frac{\text{amount of change}}{\text{original amount}}$$

$$= \frac{12 - 8}{12}$$

$$= \frac{4}{12} = \frac{1}{3} \approx 33.3\%$$

The value of Alex's book decreased by $33\frac{1}{3}\%$.

---

**Find each percent of decrease. Round your answer to the nearest tenth of a percent.**

**1.** $40 to $30

**2.** $80 to $40

**3.** 25 to 20

**4.** 11.5 h to 8 h

**5.** 99 lb to 87 lb

**6.** 55 to 30.8

**7.** 15 ft to 13 ft

**8.** 75 s to 46 s

**9.** 25 to 16.4

**Find each percent of increase. Round your answer to the nearest tenth of a percent.**

**10.** $50 to $60

**11.** $90 to $120.50

**12.** 120 min to 180 min

**13.** 60 to 77

**14.** 20 m to 35.7 m

**15.** 60 to 80

# Practice 6-5

**Find each percent of change. Label your answer as increase or decrease. Round to the nearest tenth of a percent.**

**1.** 15 to 20

_____

**2.** 18 to 10

_____

**3.** 10 to 7.5

_____

**4.** 86 to 120

_____

**5.** 17 to 34

_____

**6.** 32 to 24

_____

**7.** 27 to 38

_____

**8.** 40 to 10

_____

**9.** 8 to 10

_____

**10.** 43 to 86

_____

**11.** 100 to 23

_____

**12.** 846 to 240

_____

**13.** 130 to 275

_____

**14.** 193 to 270

_____

**15.** 436 to 118

_____

**16.** 457 to 318

_____

**17.** 607 to 812

_____

**18.** 500 to 118

_____

**19.** 346 to 843

_____

**20.** 526 to 1,000

_____

**21.** 1,000 to 526

_____

**22.** 489 to 751

_____

**23.** 286 to 781

_____

**24.** 846 to 957

_____

**Solve.**

**25.** In 1995, the price of a laser printer was $1,299. In 2002, the price of the same type of printer had dropped to $499. Find the percent of decrease.

_____

**26.** The amount won in harness racing in 1991 was $1.238 million. In 1992, the amount was $1.38 million. What was the percent of increase?

_____

**27.** In 1980, there were about 3 million people in Chicago. In 1990, the population was about 2.8 million people. Find the percent of decrease in the population of Chicago.

_____

**28.** Caryn was 58 in. tall last year. This year she is 61 in. tall. What is the percent of increase in her height?

_____

**29.** Last month, Dave weighed 175 lb. This month he weighs 164 lb. What is the percent of decrease in Dave's weight?

**30.** Between the ages of 1 and 10 a life insurance policy costs $3.84 per month. At the age of 11, the policy increases to $6.12 per month. Find the percent of increase.

_____

# Reteaching 6-6

*Example 1:* Carissa's Nursery buys plants for $10. She marks them up 20%. What is the selling price?

① Find the *markup.*

$$\text{cost} \times \text{markup rate} = \text{markup}$$
$$\$10 \times \quad 0.20 \quad = \quad \$2$$

② Find the *selling price.*

$$\text{cost} + \text{markup} = \text{selling price}$$
$$\$10 + \quad \$2 \quad = \quad \$12$$

The selling price is $12.

*Example 2:* Carissa's Nursery is having a 25% off sale on trees. The regular price for a maple tree is $200. What is the sale price?

① Find the amount of *discount.*

$$\text{price} \times \text{discount rate} = \text{discount}$$
$$\$200 \times \quad 0.25 \quad = \quad \$50$$

② Find the *sale price.*

$$\text{price} - \text{discount} = \text{sale price}$$
$$\$200 - \quad \$50 \quad = \quad \$150$$

The sale price is $150.

*Example 3:* Carissa's Nursery sells a shrub for $30. This is 20% off the regular price. Find the regular price.

Let $c$ = nursery's cost.

$$c - (0.20 \cdot c) = 30$$
$$0.80c = 30$$
$$\frac{0.80c}{0.80} = \frac{30}{0.8}$$
$$c = 37.50$$

The regular price is $37.50.

---

**Find each selling price. Round to the nearest cent.**

**1.** cost: $20
markup rate: 20%

_____

**2.** cost: $99.99
markup rate: 10%

_____

**3.** cost: $95
markup rate: 50%

_____

**Find each sale price. Round to the nearest cent.**

**4.** regular price: $500
discount: 20%

_____

**5.** regular price: $23.99
discount: 15%

_____

**6.** regular price: $82.75
discount: 10%

_____

**Find each regular price. Round to the nearest cent.**

**7.** sale price: $48
10% off

_____

**8.** sale price: $50
20% off

_____

**9.** sale price: $79.99
30% off

_____

# Practice 6-6

**Find each selling price. Round to the nearest cent.**

1. cost: $10.00
   markup rate: 60%

   _____

2. cost: $12.50
   markup rate: 50%

   _____

3. cost: $15.97
   markup rate: 75%

   _____

4. cost: $21.00
   markup rate: 100%

   _____

5. cost: $25.86
   markup rate: 70%

   _____

6. cost: $32.48
   markup rate: 110%

   _____

7. cost: $47.99
   markup rate: 160%

   _____

8. cost: $87.90
   markup rate: 80%

   _____

9. cost: $95.90
   markup rate: 112%

   _____

10. cost: $120.00
    markup rate: 56%

    _____

11. cost: $150.97
    markup rate: 65%

    _____

12. cost: $2,000.00
    markup rate: 95%

    _____

**Find each sale price. Round to the nearest cent.**

13. regular price: $10.00
    discount rate: 10%

    _____

14. regular price: $12.00
    discount rate: 15%

    _____

15. regular price: $18.95
    discount rate: 20%

    _____

16. regular price: $20.95
    discount rate: 15%

    _____

17. regular price: $32.47
    discount rate: 20%

    _____

18. regular price: $39.99
    discount rate: 25%

    _____

19. regular price: $42.58
    discount rate: 30%

    _____

20. regular price: $53.95
    discount rate: 35%

    _____

21. regular price: $82.99
    discount rate: 50%

    _____

22. regular price: $126.77
    discount rate: 62%

    _____

23. regular price: $250.98
    discount rate: 70%

    _____

24. regular price: $2,000.00
    discount rate: 15%

    _____

**Find each store's cost. Round to the nearest cent.**

25. selling price: $55
    markup rate: 20%

    _____

26. selling price: $25.50
    markup rate: 45%

    _____

27. selling price: $79.99
    markup rate: 30%

    _____

28. selling price: $19.95
    markup rate: 75%

    _____

29. selling price: $95
    markup rate: 25%

    _____

30. selling price: $64.49
    markup rate: 10%

    _____

# Reteaching 6-7

You can write equations to solve many types of problems.

**Read and Understand**    Katrina is looking for a new sports club. She plans to spend between 10% and 15% of her weekly income on a membership. If Katrina earns $450 per week, find the minimum and maximum amounts that she can spend on a membership.

What are you asked to do?    *Find the minimum and maximum she can spend on a membership.*

**Plan and Solve**

| Minimum | Maximum |
|---|---|
| $m = 0.10 \cdot 450$ | $x = 0.15 \cdot 450$ |
| $= 45$ | $= 67.50$ |

Katrina can spend between $45 and $67.50 per week.

**Look Back**    Mentally find 10% of $450, which is $45. Take half of $45 to get $22.50. Add $45 and $22.50 to get $67.50. So, the answers are reasonable.

---

**Solve each problem by writing an equation. Check that your answer is reasonable.**

1. Madeline has sold $500 worth of merchandise this week. She would like to increase her sales 25% to 30% for next week. Find the minimum and maximum amounts she can increase her sales.

   _____

2. Last year, Miquel ran a total of 1,820 miles. This year he plans to run 15% to 20% more miles than last year. Between how many miles must Miquel run this year to reach his goal?

   _____

3. A manufacturing company sold $150,000 of specially produced grommets last year. This year, it plans to decrease sales 20% to 30% less than last year. Between what two dollar amounts should the company try to keep its sales?

   _____

4. Juanita currently has a score of 75 points in Mrs. Johnson's science class. She would like to increase her points by 20% to 25%. Between what two point values does Juanita need to raise her points?

   _____

# Practice 6-7

**Problem Solving: Write an Equation**

**Use any strategy to solve each problem. Show your work.**

1. On a map, the distance between Wauseon and Archbold is 8 cm. What is the actual distance between the cities if 2.5 cm = 1 mi?

   _____

2. The drama club sold adult tickets for $8 and children's tickets for $5. For the final performance a total of 226 tickets were sold for a total of $1,670. How many adult tickets were sold for the performance?

   _____

3. The Caston's budget is shown at the right. They just learned that their house payment will be increased by $120. Their income will be no more than it is now, so they plan on reducing each of the other categories by an equal amount. How much money will they then be able to budget for bills?

   | Caston's Budget | |
   | --- | --- |
   | Item | Amount |
   | House | $750 |
   | Food | $400 |
   | Bills | $350 |
   | Other | $140 |

   _____

4. Rhonda added 140 to one third of a number for a result of 216. What is the number?

   _____

5. The sum of three consecutive integers is 228. What are the integers?

   _____

6. Angie has an equal number of dimes and quarters. The total value of her coins is $3.50. How many dimes does she have?

   _____

7. How many ways can you arrange the letters A, B, C, and D in a row if A and B are never next to each other?

   _____

8. One month, Meredith's parents doubled her monthly allowance. The next month, they increased her allowance by $3. The next month, they cut her allowance in half. Is her allowance more or less now than her original allowance? By how much?

   _____

# Reteaching 6-8

*Simple Interest*

Alicia put $200 in a savings account to earn interest. The interest rate is 5% per year. How much interest will the account earn in $2\frac{1}{2}$ years?

Use this formula to solve:

Interest = *principal* · rate · time in years

$$I = p \cdot r \cdot t$$
$$= 200 \cdot 0.05 \cdot 2.5$$
$$= 25$$

In $2\frac{1}{2}$ years, the account will earn $25 in interest.

*Compound Interest*

Alex put $500 in an account that earns 6% interest, compounded annually. What will be the account balance after $2\frac{1}{2}$ years?

Use this formula to solve:

Balance = principal · (1 + rate)$^{\text{time in years}}$
$$B = p(1 + r)^t$$

Use a calculator to evaluate:
$$B = 500(1 + 0.06)^{2.5}$$

500 ☒ 1.06 $\boxed{y^x}$ 2.5 ▬ 578.41

The balance will be $578.41.

---

**Find the interest earned in each account.**

1. $300 at 5% simple interest for 1 year

   _____

2. $300 at 5% simple interest for 2 years

   _____

3. $500 at 8% simple interest for 2 years

   _____

4. $1,000 at 6% simple interest for 3 years

   _____

5. $1,200 at 4.5% simple interest for 3 years

   _____

6. $950 at $5\frac{1}{2}$% simple interest for 6 years

   _____

**Find the final balance in each account.**

7. $800 at 4% compounded annually for 3 years

   _____

8. $1,200 at 5% compounded annually for 4 years

   _____

9. $2,000 at $3\frac{1}{2}$% compounded annually for 2 years

   _____

10. $4,500 at 8% compounded annually for 3 years

   _____

**Solve.**

11. Ms. Ito is lending her nephew Dan $3,000 for college. She is charging him 2% simple interest each year. He will pay his aunt back in four years. How much interest will he pay?

   _____

# Practice 6-8

**Find the final balance in each account. Round your answers to the nearest cent.**

**1.** $800 at 4.25% simple interest for 6 years

_____

**2.** $800 at 6% compounded annually for 4 years

_____

**3.** $250 at 5% simple interest for 3 years

_____

**4.** $900 at 8% simple interest for 1 year

_____

**5.** $1,250 at 5% simple interest for 2 years

_____

**6.** $1,250 at $4\frac{1}{2}$% compounded annually for 3 years

_____

**7.** $1,500 at 4% compounded annually for 4 years

_____

**8.** $1,750 at 5% simple interest for 2 years

_____

**9.** $2,000 at 6% simple interest for 3 years

_____

**10.** $2,000 at 6% compounded annually for 3 years

_____

**11.** $2,500 at 6% compounded annually for 3 years

_____

**12.** $4,000 at 6% compounded annually for 3 years

_____

**13.** $5,000 at 5% simple interest for 10 years

_____

**14.** $6,000 at 5% simple interest for 6 years

_____

**15.** $5,000 at 5% compounded annually for 10 years

_____

**16.** $6,000 at 5% compounded annually for 8 years

_____

**Solve.**

**17.** Bill invests $500. How much will it grow to in 20 years at 6% compounded annually?

_____

**18.** In Exercise 17, how much less will Bill have in the account if the interest is simple interest?

_____

**19.** Which earns more compound interest, $1,000 at 5% for 10 years or $1,000 at 10% for 5 years? How much more?

_____

**20.** Which earns more simple interest, $1,000 at 5% for 10 years or $1,000 at 10% for 5 years? How much more?

_____

# Reteaching 6-9

Angel has eight baseball hats in his collection. There are 2 blue
baseball hats, 1 red, 2 green, and 3 black. What is the probability of
Angel picking a red baseball hat?

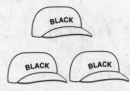

If Angel chose a hat at random, there are 8 possible results, or *outcomes*.
A collection of possible outcomes in an experiment is an *event*.

When each outcome has an equal chance of occurring, you can use
the following formula:

*Probability* of an event = $\frac{\text{number of outcomes in the event}}{\text{total number of possible outcomes}}$

You can list all the possible outcomes. This is called the
*sample space*. Then you can find the probability.

| Sample Space | | | | Probability of red hat |
|---|---|---|---|---|
| green | green | black | black | $P(\text{red hat}) = \frac{1}{8}$ ← favorable outcomes |
| black | red | blue | blue |                  ← all possible outcomes |

There are 8 possible outcomes.

---

**A spinner has 12 spaces with the numbers
1, 2, 3, 4, 5, 5, 5, 6, 6, 7, 8, 8. Find each probability.**

**1.** $P(1)$ _____

**2.** $P(5)$ _____

**3.** $P(8)$ _____

**4.** $P(\text{odd number})$ _____

**5.** $P(\text{even number})$ _____

**6.** $P(\text{number less than 5})$ _____

**7.** $P(\text{number greater than 4})$ _____

**8.** $P(\text{odd or even number})$ _____

**A box has 10 red, 15 yellow, 20 pink, 25 black, and 30 orange jelly
beans. You pick a jelly bean without looking. Find each probability.**

**9.** $P(\text{red})$

**10.** $P(\text{yellow})$

_____

_____

**11.** $P(\text{pink})$

**12.** $P(\text{black})$

_____

_____

# Practice 6-9

**A dart is thrown at the game board shown. Find each probability.**

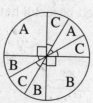

1. $P(A)$ _____
2. $P(B)$ _____
3. $P(C)$ _____
4. $P(A \text{ or } B)$ _____
5. $P(B \text{ or } C)$ _____
6. $P(A, B, \text{ or } C)$ _____

**A bag of uninflated balloons contains 10 red, 12 blue, 15 yellow, and 8 green balloons. A balloon is drawn at random. Find each probability.**

7. $P(\text{red})$ _____
8. $P(\text{blue})$ _____
9. $P(\text{yellow})$ _____
10. $P(\text{green})$ _____

11. What is the probability of picking a balloon that is not yellow?

_____

12. What is the probability of picking a balloon that is not red?

_____

**Solve.**

13. a. You are given a ticket for the weekly drawing each time you enter the grocery store. Last week you were in the store once. There are 1,200 tickets in the box. Find the probability of you winning.

_____

   b. Find the probability of you winning if you were in the store three times last week and there are 1,200 tickets in the box.

_____

14. A cheese tray contains slices of Swiss cheese and cheddar cheese. If you randomly pick a slice of cheese, $P(\text{Swiss}) = 0.45$. Find $P(\text{cheddar})$. If there are 200 slices of cheese, how many slices of Swiss cheese are on the tray?

_____

15. a. Make a table to find the sample space for tossing two coins.

   b. Find the probability that you get one head and one tail when tossing two coins.

_____

# Reteaching 7-1

To write a number such as 67,000 in *scientific notation*, move the decimal point to form a number between 1 and 10. The number of places moved shows which power of 10 to use.

- Write 67,000 in scientific notation.

  6.7 is between 1 and 10. So, move the decimal point in 67,000 to the left 4 places and multiply by $10^4$.

  $67,000 = 6.7 \times 10^4$

To write scientific notation in *standard form,* look at the exponent. The exponent shows the number of places and the direction to move the decimal point.

- Write $8.5 \times 10^5$ in standard form.

  The exponent is positive 5, so move the decimal point 5 places to the right.

  $8.5 \times 10^5 = 850,000$

---

**Write each number in scientific notation.**

1. 6,500 _____

2. 65,000 _____

3. 6,520 _____

4. 345 _____

5. 29,100 _____

6. 93,000,000 _____

7. 200 _____

8. 2,300 _____

9. 23,000 _____

10. 450 _____

11. 90,000 _____

12. 96,000 _____

**Write each number in standard form.**

13. $4 \times 10^4$ _____

14. $4 \times 10^5$ _____

15. $3.6 \times 10^3$ _____

16. $4.85 \times 10^4$ _____

17. $4.05 \times 10^2$ _____

18. $7.1 \times 10^5$ _____

19. $4 \times 10^2$ _____

20. $1.3 \times 10^2$ _____

21. $7 \times 10^1$ _____

22. $2.5 \times 10^3$ _____

23. $1.81 \times 10^3$ _____

24. $1.6 \times 10^4$ _____

25. Jupiter is on the average $7.783 \times 10^8$ kilometers from the sun. _____

**Which number is greater?**

26. $5 \times 10^2$ or $2 \times 10^5$ _____

27. $2.1 \times 10^3$ or $2.1 \times 10^6$ _____

28. $6 \times 10^{10}$ or $3 \times 10^9$ _____

29. $3.6 \times 10^1$ or $3.6 \times 10^3$ _____

# Practice 7-1

**Write each number in scientific notation.**

**1.** 45

**2.** 250

**3.** 90

**4.** 200

_____

_____

_____

_____

**5.** 670

**6.** 4,100

**7.** 500

**8.** 3,000

_____

_____

_____

_____

**9.** 43,200

**10.** 97,100

**11.** 38,050

**12.** 90,200

_____

_____

_____

_____

**13.** 480,000

**14.** 960,000

**15.** 8,750,000

**16.** 407,000

_____

_____

_____

_____

**Write each number in standard form.**

**17.** $3.1 \times 10^1$

**18.** $8.07 \times 10^2$

**19.** $4.96 \times 10^3$

**20.** $8.073 \times 10^2$

_____

_____

_____

_____

**21.** $4.501 \times 10^4$

**22.** $9.7 \times 10^6$

**23.** $8.3 \times 10^7$

**24.** $3.42 \times 10^4$

_____

_____

_____

_____

**25.** $2.86 \times 10^5$

**26.** $3.58 \times 10^6$

**27.** $8.1 \times 10^1$

**28.** $9.071 \times 10^2$

_____

_____

_____

_____

**29.** $4.83 \times 10^9$

**30.** $2.73 \times 10^8$

**31.** $2.57 \times 10^5$

**32.** $8.09 \times 10^4$

_____

_____

_____

_____

**Order each set of numbers from least to greatest.**

**33.** $8.9 \times 10^2, 6.3 \times 10^3, 2.1 \times 10^4, 7.8 \times 10^5$

_____

**34.** $2.1 \times 10^4, 2.12 \times 10^3, 3.46 \times 10^5, 2.112 \times 10^2$

_____

**35.** $8.93 \times 10^3, 7.8 \times 10^2, 7.84 \times 10^3, 8.915 \times 10^4$

_____

**Write each number in scientific notation.**

**36.** The eye's retina contains about 130 million light-sensitive cells.

_____

**37.** A mulberry silkworm can spin a single thread that measures up to 3,900 ft in length.

_____

# Reteaching 7-2

- To multiply numbers or variables with the same base, add the exponents.

Simplify $3^2 \cdot 3^4$.      Simplify $n^3 \cdot n^4$.      Simplify $-4^3 \cdot -4^5$.
$3^2 \cdot 3^4 = 3^{(2+4)}$      $n^3 \cdot n^4 = n^{(3+4)}$      $-4^3 \cdot -4^5 = -4^{(3+5)}$
$\qquad = 3^6$      $\qquad = n^7$      $\qquad = -4^8$

- To multiply numbers in scientific notation.

Find the product $(5 \times 10^4)(7 \times 10^5)$. Write the result in scientific notation.

$(5 \times 10^4)(7 \times 10^5)$

$(5 \cdot 7)(10^4 \cdot 10^5)$       ← Use the Associative and Commutative properties.

$35 \times (10^4 \cdot 10^5)$       ← Multiply 5 and 7.

$35 \times 10^{4+5}$       ← Add the exponents for the powers of 10.

$35 \times 10^9$

$3.5 \times 10^1 \times 10^9$       ← Write 35 in scientific notation.

$3.5 \times 10^{10}$       ← Add the exponents.

---

**Write each expression using a single exponent.**

**1.** $5^3 \cdot 5^4$

**2.** $a^2 \cdot a^5$

**3.** $(-8)^4 \cdot (-8)^5$

**4.** $n^6 \cdot n^2$

**5.** $m^3 \cdot m^6$

**6.** $(-7)^4 \cdot (-7)^2$

**7.** $(-3)^2 \cdot (-3)^2$

**8.** $2^5 \cdot 2^2$

**9.** $c^5 \cdot c^3$

**10.** $7^5 \cdot 7^9$

**11.** $n^3 \cdot n^{11}$

**12.** $3^5 \cdot 3^2$

**Find each product. Write the answer in scientific notation.**

**13.** $(3 \times 10^4)(5 \times 10^3)$

**14.** $(2 \times 10^3)(7 \times 10^6)$

**15.** $(8 \times 10^2)(5 \times 10^2)$

**16.** $(9 \times 10^4)(7 \times 10^4)$

**17.** $(4 \times 10^2)(7 \times 10^5)$

**18.** $(8 \times 10^3)(4 \times 10^5)$

# Practice 7-2

**Write each expression using a single exponent.**

**1.** $3^2 \cdot 3^5$

_____

**2.** $1^3 \cdot 1^4$

_____

**3.** $5^4 \cdot 5^3$

_____

**4.** $a^1 \cdot a^2$

_____

**5.** $(-y)^3 \cdot (-y)^2$

_____

**6.** $-z^3 \cdot z^9$

_____

**7.** $(3x) \cdot (3x)$

_____

**8.** $4.5^8 \cdot 4.5^2$

_____

**9.** $(5x) \cdot (5x)^3$

_____

**10.** $3^3 \cdot 3 \cdot 3^4$

_____

**11.** $x^2y \cdot xy^2$

_____

**12.** $5x^2 \cdot x^6 \cdot x^3$

_____

**Find each product. Write the answers in scientific notation.**

**13.** $(3 \times 10^4)(5 \times 10^6)$

_____

**14.** $(9 \times 10^7)(3 \times 10^2)$

_____

**15.** $(7 \times 10^2)(6 \times 10^4)$

_____

**16.** $(3 \times 10^{10})(4 \times 10^5)$

_____

**17.** $(4 \times 10^5)(7 \times 10^8)$

_____

**18.** $(9.1 \times 10^6)(3 \times 10^9)$

_____

**19.** $(8.4 \times 10^9)(5 \times 10^7)$

_____

**20.** $(5 \times 10^3)(4 \times 10^6)$

_____

**21.** $(7.2 \times 10^8)(2 \times 10^3)$

_____

**22.** $(1.4 \times 10^5)(4 \times 10^{11})$

_____

**Replace each __?__ with =, <, or >.**

**23.** $3^8$ __?__ $3 \cdot 3^7$

_____

**24.** $49$ __?__ $7^2 \cdot 7^2$

_____

**25.** $5^3 \cdot 5^4$ __?__ $25^2$

_____

**26.** Double the number $4.6 \times 10^{15}$. Write the answer in scientific notation.

_____

**27.** Triple the number $2.3 \times 10^3$. Write the answer in scientific notation.

_____

# Reteaching 7-3

To divide powers with the same base, subtract exponents.

$$\frac{8^6}{8^4} = 8^{6-4} \qquad \frac{a^5}{a^3} = a^{5-3}$$

$$= 8^2 \qquad\qquad = a^2$$

$$= 64$$

- For any nonzero number $a$, $a^0 = 1$.

$$3^0 = 1 \qquad\qquad (-6)^0 = 1 \qquad 4t^0 = 4(1) = 4$$

- For any nonzero number $a$ and any integer $n$, $a^{-n} = \frac{1}{a^n}$ .

$$2^{-4} = \frac{1}{2^4} \qquad 3c^{-2} = \frac{3}{c^2} \qquad \frac{5^3}{5^6} = 5^{3-6} \qquad \frac{10z^3}{5z} = 2z^{3-1}$$

$$= \frac{1}{16} \qquad\qquad\qquad\qquad = 5^{-3} \qquad\qquad = 2z^2$$

$$= \frac{1}{5^3}$$

$$= \frac{1}{125}$$

**Simplify each expression.**

1. $\frac{6^5}{6^3} = $ _____

2. $(-4)^5 \div (-4)^3 = $ _____

3. $9^8 \div 9^6 = $ _____

4. $(-3)^{-2} = $ _____

5. $\frac{2^5}{2^7} = $ _____

6. $(-8)^0 = $ _____

7. $\frac{5^0}{5^2} = $ _____

8. $(-4)^{-3} = $ _____

9. $\frac{(-6)^4}{(-6)^6} = $ _____

10. $7^3 \div 7^5 = $ _____

11. $9^8 \div 9^{10} = $ _____

12. $\frac{2^7}{2^3} = $ _____

**Simplify each expression. Use only positive exponents.**

13. $w^8 \div w^3 = $ _____

14. $x^6 \div x^1 = $ _____

15. $\frac{d^7}{d^3} = $ _____

16. $y^6 \div y^9 = $ _____

17. $a^{10} \div a^4 = $ _____

18. $3m^6 \div m^2 = $ _____

19. $\frac{w^2}{w^6} = $ _____

20. $4c^5 \div c^8 = $ _____

21. $\frac{8x^2}{4x^5} = $ _____

22. $8a^4 \div 2a^2 = $ _____

23. $6w^2 \div 2w^5 = $ _____

24. $\frac{6x^6}{3x^9} = $ _____

# Practice 7-3

**Simplify each expression.**

**1.** $8^{-2}$

**2.** $(-3)^0$

**3.** $5^{-1}$

**4.** $18^0$

**5.** $2^{-5}$

**6.** $3^{-3}$

**7.** $2^{-3}$

**8.** $5^{-2}$

**9.** $\frac{4^4}{4}$

**10.** $8^6 \div 8^8$

**11.** $\frac{(-3)^6}{(-3)^8}$

**12.** $\frac{8^4}{8^0}$

**13.** $1^{15} \div 1^{18}$

**14.** $7 \div 7^4$

**15.** $\frac{(-4)^8}{(-4)^4}$

**16.** $\frac{10^9}{10^{12}}$

**17.** $\frac{7^5}{7^3}$

**18.** $8^4 \div 8^2$

**19.** $\frac{(-3)^5}{(-3)^8}$

**20.** $\frac{6^7}{6^8}$

**21.** $\frac{b^{12}}{b^4}$

**22.** $\frac{g^9}{g^{15}}$

**23.** $x^{16} \div x^7$

**24.** $v^{20} \div v^{25}$

**Complete each equation.**

**25.** $\frac{1}{3^5} = 3^{\underline{\,?\,}}$

**26.** $\frac{1}{(-2)^7} = -2^{\underline{\,?\,}}$

**27.** $\frac{1}{x^2} = x^{\underline{\,?\,}}$

**28.** $\frac{1}{-125} = (-5)^{\underline{\,?\,}}$

**29.** $\frac{1}{1,000} = 10^{\underline{\,?\,}}$

**30.** $\frac{5^{10}}{\underline{\,?\,}} = 5^5$

**31.** $\frac{z^{\underline{\,?\,}}}{z^8} = z^{-3}$

**32.** $\frac{q^5}{\underline{\,?\,}} = q^{-7}$

**Write each number in scientific notation.**

**33.** 0.0007

**34.** 0.00000001

**35.** 0.000901

**36.** 0.0000000091

**37.** 0.0000000001

**38.** 0.000032

**39.** Write each term as a power of 4, and write the next three terms
of the sequence 256, 64, 16, 4, . . .

Name _____ Class _____ Date _____

# Reteaching 7-4

The expression $x^n$ is a power. It can also be read as $x$ to the $n$th power.

*Raising a Power to a Power*

To raise a power to a power, multiply exponents.

Arithmetic:
$(2^4)^6$
$= 2^{(4 \cdot 6)}$ ← Multiply the exponents.
$= 2^{24}$ ← Simplify the exponent.

Algebra:
$(a^x)^y$
$= a^{(x \cdot y)}$ ← Multiply the exponents.
$= a^{xy}$ ← Simplify the exponent.

$(x^{-3})^{-5}$
$= x^{(-3 \cdot -5)}$ ← Multiply the exponents.
$= x^{15}$ ← Simplify the exponent.

*Raising a Product to a Power*

To raise a product to a power, raise each factor to the power.

Arithmetic:
$(4 \cdot 7)^2$
$= 4^2 \cdot 7^2$ ← Raise each factor to the power.

Algebra:
$(xy)^a$
$= x^a y^a$ ← Raise each factor to the power.

$(4a^2)^3$

$= 4^3(a^2)^3$ ← Raise each factor to the power.
$= 4^3 a^6$ ← Multiply the exponents.
$= 64a^6$ ← Simplify.

---

**Write each expression using one base and one exponent.**

**1.** $(6^2)^{-4}$

**2.** $(y^6)^{-5}$

**3.** $(7^{-4})^{-5}$

**4.** $(x^b)^c$

**5.** $(5^9)^3$

**6.** $(a^{-3})^{-8}$

**Simplify each expression.**

**7.** $(ht)^n$

**8.** $(5v)^2$

**9.** $(7p^4)^2$

**10.** $(3d^4 f^2)^3$

**11.** $(k^5 j^4)^3$

**12.** $(2s^7 u^6)^4$

**Use <, >, or = to complete each statement.**

**13.** $2^5$ ☐ $(2^3)^2$

**14.** $(5^{-4})^2$ ☐ $5^{-8}$

**15.** $(6 \cdot 4)^2$ ☐ $10^2$

# Practice 7-4

**Power Rules**

**Write each expression using one base and one exponent.**

**1.** $(5^3)^{-6}$

_____

**2.** $(-9^4)^{-2}$

_____

**3.** $(d^5)^6$

_____

**4.** $(8^{-3})^{-9}$

_____

**5.** $(4^{-3}, 4^{-2}, 4^{-1})^{-4}$

_____

**6.** $(y^8)^{-6}$

_____

**7.** $(v^3, v^6, v^9)^2$

_____

**8.** $(k^{-7})^{-5}$

_____

**9.** $((n^3)^2)^5$

_____

**10.** $((a^2)^2)^2$

_____

**Simplify each expression.**

**11.** $(xyz)^6$

_____

**12.** $(10^2 \cdot x^7)^3$

_____

**13.** $(7y^8)^2$

_____

**14.** $(t^2 \cdot t^4)^5$

_____

**15.** $(4g)^3$

_____

**16.** $(x^5 y^4)^8$

_____

**Use >, <, or = to complete each statement.**

**17.** $7^3 \cdot 7^3 \underline{\ ?\ } (7^3)^3$

_____

**18.** $(6^{-2} \cdot 6^5)^3 \underline{\ ?\ } (6^3)^2$

_____

**19.** $(4^6)^0 \underline{\ ?\ } 4^6 \cdot 4^{-6}$

_____

**20.** Find the area of a square whose side is $3 \times 10^4$ millimeters. Write the answer in scientific notation.

_____

**21.** As of October 29, 2002 the Ijen volcano had an active crater with a radius of 1,100 ft. Using the formula for a circle $A = \pi r^2$ and 3.14 for $\pi$, what is the area of the crater?

_____

# Reteaching 7-5

You can write equations to help solve problems involving scientific notation.

The Pacific Ocean is about $6.4 \times 10^7$ square miles. It is about two times bigger than the size of the Atlantic Ocean. About how big is the Atlantic Ocean?

**Read and Understand** The Pacific Ocean has an area two times the size of the Atlantic Ocean. Your goal is to find the area of the Atlantic Ocean.

**Plan and Solve** You know the size of the Pacific Ocean. You can write an equation to solve for the size of the Atlantic Ocean.

Let $x$ = the area of the Atlantic Ocean.

$$2x = 6.4 \times 10^7$$
$$x = \frac{6.4 \times 10^7}{2}$$
$$x = 3.2 \times 10^7$$

The Atlantic Ocean is about $3.2 \times 10^7$ square miles.

**Look Back and Check** Half of 6.4 is 3.2 and the exponent on 10 did not change. So the area of the Atlantic Ocean appears to be correct.

---

**Solve each problem by writing an equation.**

1. The Arctic Ocean is about $5.4 \times 10^6$ square miles. The Indian Ocean is about 5 times the size of the Arctic Ocean. About how big is the Indian Ocean?

   _____

2. The greatest depth of the Arctic Ocean is about $1.8 \times 10^5$ ft. The greatest depth of the Pacific Ocean is about two times this amount. About how deep is the greatest depth of the Pacific Ocean?

   _____

3. Joe is 5 years older than Bijan. If the sum of their ages is 25, how old is each boy?

   Joe _____   Bijan _____

4. A chicken dinner costs $2.50 more than a spaghetti dinner. If the cost of both is $18.40, how much does each meal cost?

   Chicken _____   Spaghetti _____

5. Elaine sold twice as many T-shirts as Kim. How many did each girl sell if the total number of T-shirts sold was 27?

   Elaine _____   Kim _____

6. There are 5 more rows of corn than rows of peas in the garden. How many rows of each are there if there are 19 rows in all?

   Corn _____   Peas _____

# Practice 7-5

**Problem Solving: Write an Equation**

The top 10 United States counties with the greatest population are shown in the table.

| Rank (of 3,141 counties) | County Name | State | Census Population April 1, 1990 | Census Population April 1, 2000 |
|---|---|---|---|---|
| 1 | Los Angeles County | CA | $8.9 \times 10^6$ | $9.6 \times 10^6$ |
| 2 | Cook County | IL | $5.1 \times 10^6$ | $5.4 \times 10^6$ |
| 3 | Harris County | TX | $2.8 \times 10^6$ | $3.4 \times 10^6$ |
| 4 | Maricopa County | AZ | $2.1 \times 10^6$ | $3.1 \times 10^6$ |
| 5 | Orange County | CA | $2.4 \times 10^6$ | $2.8 \times 10^6$ |
| 6 | San Diego County | CA | $2.5 \times 10^6$ | $2.8 \times 10^6$ |
| 7 | Kings County | NY | $2.3 \times 10^6$ | $2.5 \times 10^6$ |
| 8 | Miami-Dade County | FL | $1.9 \times 10^6$ | $2.3 \times 10^6$ |
| 9 | Queens County | NY | $2.0 \times 10^6$ | $2.2 \times 10^6$ |
| 10 | Dallas County | TX | $1.9 \times 10^6$ | $2.2 \times 10^6$ |

**Solve each problem by writing an equation. Check your answer.**

1. In 1990, the population of Pima County in Arizona was about 4 times less than that of the population of Harris County in Texas. What was the population of Pima County in 1990?

   _____

2. In 2000, what was the difference in population between Cook County and Queens County?

   _____

3. About how many times larger was Los Angeles County than Cook County in 1990?

   _____

4. In 2000, the population of Orange County in Florida was 896,344. How many more people lived in Miami-Dade County in 2000 than in Orange County?

   _____

5. The mayor of Kings County in New York expects the population to increase by about 10% from 2000 to 2010. How many people are predicted to populate that county in 2010?

   _____

# Reteaching 7-6

The *binary*, or base-2 number system, uses the digits 0 and 1 with place values using powers of 2. Computers use binary numbers to store information.

- Finding the decimal value of a binary number

Find the decimal value of the binary number $1101_2$.

$1101_2 = (1 \cdot 2^3) + (1 \cdot 2^2) + (0 \cdot 2^1) + (1 \cdot 2^0)$  ← Write the binary number in expanded form.
$= 8 + 4 + 0 + 1$  ← Simplify within the parentheses.
$= 13$  ← Add.

Find the decimal value of the binary number $110101_2$.

$110101_2 = (1 \cdot 2^5) + (1 \cdot 2^4) + (0 \cdot 2^3) +$  ← Write the binary number in expanded form.
$(1 \cdot 2^2) + (0 \cdot 2^1) + (1 \cdot 2^0)$
$= 32 + 16 + 0 + 4 + 0 + 1$  ← Simplify within the parentheses.
$= 53$  ← Add.

- Changing a decimal to a binary number

Write the decimal number 18 as a binary number.

Begin by completing a table of powers of 2.

| $2^7$ | $2^6$ | $2^5$ | $2^4$ | $2^3$ | $2^2$ | $2^1$ | $2^0$ |
|---|---|---|---|---|---|---|---|
| 128 | 64 | 32 | 16 | 8 | 4 | 2 | 1 |
|  |  |  |  |  |  |  |  |

Complete the table by using each power of 2 either once or not at all.
Use a 1 if the power is used and a 0 if the power is not used.

| $2^7$ | $2^6$ | $2^5$ | $2^4$ | $2^3$ | $2^2$ | $2^1$ | $2^0$ |
|---|---|---|---|---|---|---|---|
| 128 | 64 | 32 | 16 | 8 | 4 | 2 | 1 |
|  |  |  | 1 | 0 | 0 | 1 | 0 |

$18 = 16 + 2$  (Use the digits 1 and 0 to write the binary number.)

$18 = 10010_2$

---

**Write the decimal value for each binary number.**

1. $1111_2 =$ _____
2. $11100_2 =$ _____
3. $10111_2 =$ _____
4. $110101_2 =$ _____

**Write each decimal number as a binary number.**

5. 14 _____
6. 7 _____
7. 33 _____
8. 22 _____

# Practice 7-6

**Write the decimal value for each binary number.**

**1.** $11011_2$

_____

**2.** $100110_2$

_____

**3.** $10001_2$

_____

**4.** $11010_2$

_____

**5.** $110010_2$

_____

**6.** $110111_2$

_____

**7.** $110011_2$

_____

**8.** $11110_2$

_____

**9.** $11100_2$

_____

**10.** $1011001_2$

_____

**11.** $1101010_2$

_____

**12.** $10001111_2$

_____

**13.** $10001110_2$

_____

**14.** $1111111_2$

_____

**15.** $1001010_2$

_____

**Write each decimal number as a binary number.**

**16.** 14

_____

**17.** 22

_____

**18.** 58

_____

**19.** 63

_____

**20.** 86

_____

**21.** 102

_____

**22.** 65

_____

**23.** 101

_____

**The base-5 number system uses the digits 0, 1, 2, 3, and 4 with place values using powers of 5. Write the decimal value for each base-5 number.**

**24.** $123_5$

_____

**25.** $222_5$

_____

**26.** $431_5$

_____

**The hexadecimal (base-6) number system uses the digits 0, 1, 2, 3, 4, and 5 with place values using powers of 6. Write the decimal value for each hexadecimal number.**

**27.** $111_6$

_____

**28.** $214_6$

_____

**29.** $152_6$

_____

# Reteaching 8-1

- *Vertical angles* are pairs of opposite angles formed by two intersecting lines. They are congruent.

  *Example 1:* ∠1 and ∠3, ∠4 and ∠2

- *Adjacent angles* have a common vertex and a common side, but no common interior points.

  *Example 2:* ∠1 and ∠2, ∠1 and ∠4

- Two *supplementary angles* form a 180° angle.

  *Example 3:* ∠1 and ∠4 are supplementary angles. ∠3 is also a supplement of ∠4.

If you know the measure of one supplementary angle, you can find the measure of the other.   →   If $m\angle 4$ is 120°, then $m\angle 1$ is $180° - 120°$, or 60°.

- Two *complementary angles* form a 90° angle.

  *Example 4:* ∠5 and ∠6 are complementary angles. ∠6 is a complement of ∠5.

If you know the measure of one complementary angle, you can find the measure of the other.   →   If $m\angle 5$ is 30°, then $m\angle 6$ is $90° - 30°$, or 60°.

---

**Use the diagrams at the right for Exercises 1–6.**

1. Vertical angles ∠7 and _____

2. Adjacent angles ∠10 and _____

3. Supplementary angles ∠8 and _____

4. Complementary angles ∠12 and _____

5. Vertical angles ∠8 and _____

6. Supplementary angles ∠7 and _____

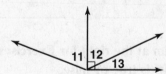

**Find the measure of the supplement of each angle.**

7. 38°          8. 65°          9. 120°          10. 152°

_____   _____   _____   _____

**Find the measure of the complement of each angle.**

11. 25°          12. 18°          13. 40°          14. 64°

_____   _____   _____   _____

# Practice 8-1

**Name a pair of vertical angles and a pair of adjacent angles in each figure. Find** $m\angle 1$**.**

**1.**

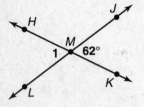

_____

_____

**2.**

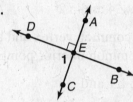

_____

_____

**3.**

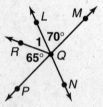

_____

_____

**4.**

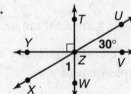

_____

_____

**Find the measure of the supplement and the complement of each angle.**

**5.** $10°$

**6.** $38°$

**7.** $42.5°$

**8.** $n°$

_____  _____  _____  _____

**Use the diagram at the right for Exercises 9–14. Decide whether each statement below is true or false.**

**9.** $\angle GAF$ and $\angle BAC$ are vertical angles. _____

**10.** $\angle EAF$ and $\angle EAD$ are adjacent angles. _____

**11.** $\angle CAD$ is a supplement of $\angle DAF$. _____

**12.** $\angle CAD$ is a complement of $\angle EAF$. _____

**13.** $m\angle GAC = 90°$ _____

**14.** $m\angle DAF = 109°$ _____

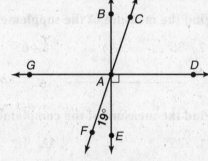

# Reteaching 8-2

Look at the figure at the right.

- Line $\overleftrightarrow{AB}$ is parallel to line $\overleftrightarrow{CD}$ ($\overleftrightarrow{AB} \| \overleftrightarrow{CD}$)

- Line $\overleftrightarrow{EF}$ is a *transversal*.

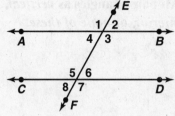

*Alternate interior angles* lie within a pair of lines and on opposite sides of the transversal.

*Example 1:* ∠3 and ∠5, ∠4 and ∠6

Alternate interior angles are congruent. If $m\angle 4$ is 60°, then $m\angle 6$ is also 60°.

*Corresponding angles* lie on the same side of the transversal and in corresponding positions.

*Example 2:* ∠1 and ∠5, ∠3 and ∠7

Corresponding angles are congruent. If $m\angle 1$ is 120°, then $m\angle 5$ is also 120°.

---

**Use the diagram at the right to complete Exercises 1–2.**

1. Name the alternate interior angles.

   a. ∠11 and ∠ _?_          b. ∠12 and ∠ _?_

   _____          _____

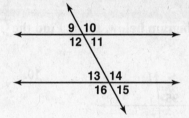

2. Name the corresponding angles.

   a. ∠16 and ∠ _?_          b. ∠14 and ∠ _?_

   _____          _____

   c. ∠9 and ∠ _?_           d. ∠11 and ∠ _?_

   _____          _____

**In the diagram at the right, $\ell \| m$. Find the measure of each angle.**

3. ∠1                    4. ∠3

   _____          _____

5. ∠6                    6. ∠5

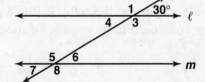

   _____          _____

7. ∠8                    8. ∠7

   _____          _____

# Practice 8-2

**Identify each pair of angles as *vertical, adjacent, corresponding, alternate interior,* or *none of these.***

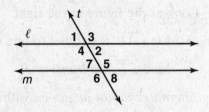

**1.** ∠7, ∠5

**2.** ∠1, ∠2

**3.** ∠1, ∠5

_____

_____

_____

**4.** ∠1, ∠7

**5.** ∠4, ∠7

**6.** ∠4, ∠5

_____

_____

_____

**Use the diagram at the right for Exercises 7 and 8.**

**7.** Name four pairs of corresponding angles.

_____

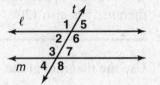

**8.** Name two pairs of alternate interior angles.

_____

**In each diagram below, ℓ ∥ m. Find the measure of each numbered angle.**

**9.**

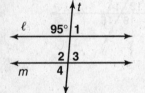

**10.**

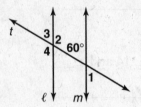

**11.**

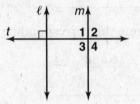

m∠1 = _____

m∠1 = _____

m∠1 = _____

m∠2 = _____

m∠2 = _____

m∠2 = _____

m∠3 = _____

m∠3 = _____

m∠3 = _____

m∠4 = _____

m∠4 = _____

m∠4 = _____

**12.** Use the figure at the right. Is line ℓ parallel to line m? Explain how you could use a protractor to support your conjecture.

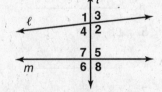

_____

_____

_____

_____

# Reteaching 8-3

**Congruent Polygons**

Congruence statements reveal corresponding parts.

$\triangle ABC \cong \triangle DEF$

*Example 1:* $\overline{AB}$ corresponds to $\overline{DE}$
  $\angle C$ corresponds to $\angle F$.

Corresponding parts are congruent ($\cong$).

*Example 2:* $\overline{AB} \cong \overline{DE}$
  $\angle C \cong \angle F$

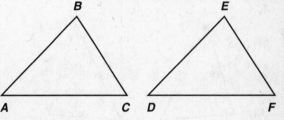

Triangles are congruent if you can show just three parts are congruent.

*side-side-side (SSS)*
(The marks show which
parts are congruent.)

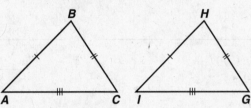

*side-angle-side (SAS)*
(The arcs show which
angles are congruent.)

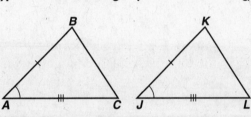

*angle-side-angle (ASA)*

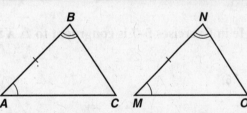

---

**In the diagram at the right, *ABCD* $\cong$ *JKLM*. Complete the following.**

1. $\angle A \cong$ _____

2. $\overline{KL} \cong$ _____

3. $\angle M \cong$ _____

4. $\overline{DC} \cong$ _____

5. $\overline{JM} \cong$ _____

6. $\angle B \cong$ _____

**Is the triangle congruent to $\triangle$ *JKL*? If so, tell why. Use SSS, SAS, or ASA.**

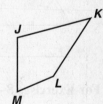

7.

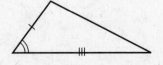

8.

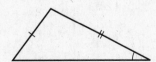

9.

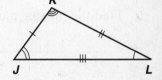

_____  _____  _____

# Practice 8-3

**Congruent Polygons**

**Determine whether each pair of triangles is congruent. Explain.**

**1.**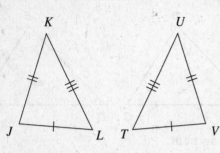

_____

**2.**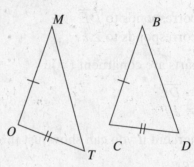

_____

**3.**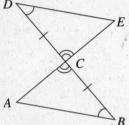

_____

**4.**

_____

**Determine if each triangle in Exercises 5–7 is congruent to △ XYZ at the right.**

**5.**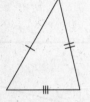

**6.**

**7.**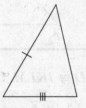

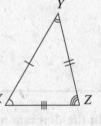

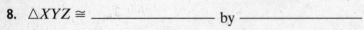

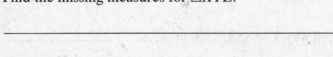

**For Exercises 8–9, use the triangles at the right.**

**8.** △XYZ ≅ _____ by _____

**9.** Find the missing measures for △XYZ.

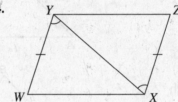

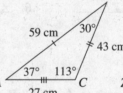

_____

_____

# Reteaching 8-4    Problem Solving: Solve a Simpler Problem and Look for a Pattern

Juan Delgado is creating this mosaic with black and white tiles. If he adds another row, how many tiles in all will be black?

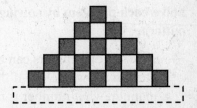

**Read and Understand**    What do you know? *There is 1 black tile in the top row, 2 in row 2, 3 in row 3, 4 in row 4, and 5 in row 5.*

**Plan and Solve**    Look for a pattern. You can make a table that shows the total number of black tiles.

| Rows | 1 | 2 | 3 | 4 | 5 | ⑥ |
|---|---|---|---|---|---|---|
| Black Tiles | 1 | 3 | 6 | 10 | ⑮ | ? |

       ↑       ↑     ↑     ↑     ↑

     **1**   **1 + 2**  **3 + 3**  **6 + 4**  **10 + 5**

How is the total number of black tiles related to the row numbers? *The number of black tiles is equal to the sum of the row numbers.*

Through row 5, there are 15 black tiles.
With row 6, there will be 15 + 6 or 21, black tiles.

**Look Back and Check**    How could you check your solution? *Draw the sixth row and count the black tiles.*

---

**Solve each problem by solving a simpler problem. Then look for a pattern.**

1.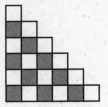

If another row is added at the bottom, how many tiles in all will be white?

_____

2.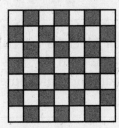

If another row is added at the bottom, how many tiles in all will be black?

_____

3. Find the next number in the pattern: 1, 2, 4, 8, 16, 32, 64, _____

4. Find the next three numbers in the pattern: 1, 1.25, 1.5, 1.75, … _____

5. Draw the fifth figure in the pattern.

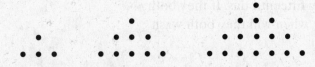

# Practice 8-4

**Problem Solving: Solve a Simpler Problem and Look for a Pattern**

**Solve each problem by solving a simpler problem. Then look for a pattern.**

1. A series of numbers can be represented by dots arranged in the pattern shown below. If the pattern continues in the same manner, what number is represented by the tenth figure?

_____

2. Alma sent out 4 cards on Monday, 8 cards on Tuesday, 16 cards on Wednesday, and 28 cards on Thursday. If this pattern continues, how many cards did Alma send out on Saturday?

_____

3. Find the next number in the pattern. 2, 2, 4, 6, 10, 16, 26, . . .

_____

**Choose a strategy or a combination of strategies to solve each problem.**

4. Jen picked a number, added 9 to it, multiplied the sum by 8, and then subtracted 11. The result was 133. What number did Jen start with?

_____

5. Ajani was offered a job in which he was paid $.01 the first day, $.02 the second day, $.04 the third day, $.08 the fourth day, and so on. On which day was Ajani first paid more than $100?

_____

6. Bruno and Grete work in a flower shop. By noon, Bruno had made twice as many flower baskets as Grete. From noon to 3:00 P.M., Grete made 6 more baskets, while Bruno made only 1 more. At 5:00 P.M., Grete had made 10 more flower baskets, while Bruno had made only 3 more. At 5:00 P.M., Bruno had made a total of 4 fewer flower baskets than Grete made all day. How many flower baskets did each make in all?

_____

7. Doug washes his clothes at the laundromat every sixth day. Janelle washes her clothes there every fifteenth day. If they both wash their clothes on the first of May, when will they both wash their clothes on the same day again?

_____

# Reteaching 8-5

A *quadrilateral* is a 4-sided polygon. A *triangle* is a 3-sided polygon.

| QUADRILATERALS | TRIANGLES |
|---|---|

A *parallelogram* is a quadrilateral with 2 pairs of parallel sides.

An *acute triangle* has 3 angles smaller than 90°.

A *trapezoid* is a quadrilateral with only 1 pair of parallel sides.

A *right triangle* has 1 angle of 90°.

A *rhombus* is a parallelogram with 4 congruent sides.

An *obtuse triangle* has 1 angle larger than 90°.

A *rectangle* is a parallelogram with 4 right angles.

An *equilateral triangle* has 3 congruent sides.

A *square* is a rectangle with 4 congruent sides or a rhombus with 4 right angles.

An *isosceles triangle* has at least 2 congruent sides.

A *scalene triangle* has no congruent sides.

---

**Name all the figures shown that fit each description. If none are shown, write *none*.**

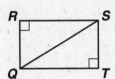   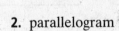

1. obtuse triangle

_____

2. parallelogram

_____

3. right triangle

_____

4. rhombus

_____

5. trapezoid

_____

6. isosceles triangle

_____

7. acute triangle

_____

8. rectangle

_____

Name _____ Class _____ Date _____

# Practice 8-5

Classifying Triangles and Quadrilaterals

• • • • • • • • • • • • • • • • • • • • • • • • • • • • • • • • • • • • • • • • • • • • • • • • • • • •

**Determine the best name for each quadrilateral. Explain your choice.**

1.
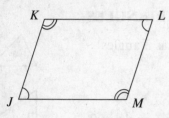

2.
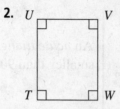

3.
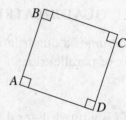

_____

_____

_____

_____

_____

_____

4.
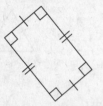

5.

6.
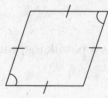

_____

_____

_____

_____

_____

_____

7.

8.

9. $\triangle ABC \cong \triangle CDA$
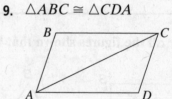

_____

_____

_____

_____

_____

_____

**Classify each triangle by its sides and its angles. Explain your choice.**

10.

11.
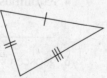

12.
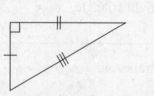

_____

_____

_____

_____

_____

_____

# Reteaching 8-6

**Angles and Polygons**

The sum of the angle measures of a polygon with $n$ sides is $(n - 2) \times 180°$.

*Example 1:* A triangle is a *3*-sided polygon. The sum of the angle measures is:

$$(3 - 2) \times 180° = 1 \times 180°$$
$$= 180°$$

$$m\angle 1 + m\angle 2 + m\angle 3 = 180°$$

*Example 2:* A quadrilateral is a *4*-sided polygon. The sum of the angle measures is:

$$(4 - 2) \times 180° = 2 \times 180°$$
$$= 360°$$

$$m\angle 1 + m\angle 2 + m\angle 3 + m\angle 4 = 360°$$

In a *regular polygon*, all of the sides are congruent and all of the angles are congruent. The measure of each *interior angle* of a regular polygon is:

sum of the angle measures ÷ the number of angles

*Example 3:* Find the measure of each interior angle of a square.

$$360° \div 4 = 90°$$

Each angle of a square has a measure of 90°.

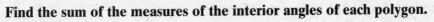

**Find the sum of the measures of the interior angles of each polygon.**

1. pentagon

   _____

2. hexagon

   _____

3. octagon

   _____

4. nonagon

   _____

5. decagon

   _____

6. heptagon

   _____

**Find the measure of each angle of the regular polygon. Round to the nearest tenth if necessary.**

7.

   **pentagon**

   _____

8.

   **hexagon**

   _____

9.

   **heptagon**

   _____

Name _____ Class _____ Date _____

# Practice 8-6

**Classify each polygon by the number of its sides.**

1.

2.

3.

4.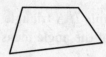

_____   _____          _____   _____

5. a polygon with 8 sides

_____

6. a polygon with 10 sides

_____

7. Find the measure of each angle of a regular hexagon.

_____

8. The measures of four angles of a pentagon are 143°, 118°, 56°, and 97°. Find the measure of the missing angle.

_____

9. What is the sum of the measures of the angles in a figure having 9 sides?

_____

10. What is the sum of the measures of the angles of a figure having 11 sides?

_____

11. Four of the angles of a hexagon measure 53°, 126°, 89°, and 117°. What is the sum of the measures of the other two angles?

_____

12. Four of the angles of a heptagon measure 109°, 158°, 117°, and 89°. What is the sum of the measures of the other three angles?

_____

13. Complete the chart for the total number of diagonals from all vertices in each polygon. The first three have been done for you.

| Polygon | Number of Sides | Number of Diagonals |
|---------|-----------------|---------------------|
| triangle | 3 | 0 |
| rectangle | 4 | 2 |
| pentagon | 5 | 5 |
| hexagon | | |
| heptagon | | |
| octagon | | |
| nonagon | | |
| decagon | | |

14. From the table you completed in Exercise 13, what pattern do you see? Explain.

_____

_____

# Reteaching 8-7

*Example 1:* Find the area of the parallelogram. Use the formula below.

Area = base × height

$A = bh$

$\quad = 5 \times 2$

$\quad = 10 \text{ cm}^2$

The area of a trapezoid is half the product of the height and the sum of the lengths of the bases.

$A = \frac{1}{2}h(b_1 + b_2)$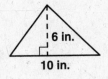

*Example 2:* Find the area of the triangle. You can cut a parallelogram into two congruent triangles. So, the area of a triangle is half the area of a parallelogram.

To find the area of a triangle, use this formula.

Area = $\frac{1}{2}$base × height

$A = \frac{1}{2}bh$

$\quad = \frac{1}{2} \times 5 \times 2$

$\quad = 5 \text{ cm}^2$

---

**Find the area of each parallelogram.**

1.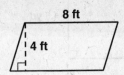

$A = $ _____

2.

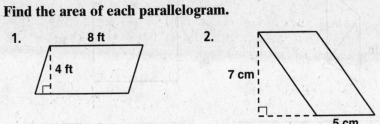

$A = $ _____

3.

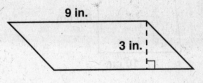

$A = $ _____

**Find the area of each triangle.**

4.

$A = $ _____

5.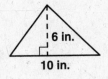

$A = $ _____

6.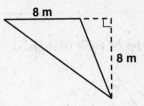

$A = $ _____

**Find the area of each trapezoid.**

7.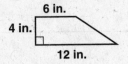

$A = $ _____

8.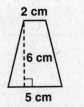

$A = $ _____

9.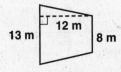

$A = $ _____

# Practice 8-7

**Find the area of each polygon.**

1.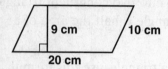
9 cm   10 cm
20 cm

_____

2.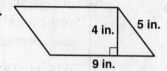
4 in.   5 in.
9 in.

_____

3.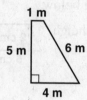
1 m
5 m   6 m
4 m

_____

4.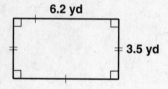
6.2 yd
3.5 yd

_____

5.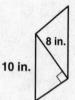
9 cm
6 cm
15 cm

_____

6.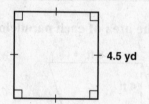
6.4 ft   5.8 ft
6.7 ft

_____

7.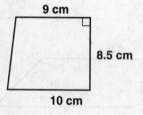
9 cm
8.5 cm
10 cm

_____

8.
8 in.
10 in.

_____

9.
4.5 yd

_____

10. The area of a parallelogram is 221 yd². Its height is 13 yd. What is the length of its corresponding base?

_____

11. The area of a parallelogram is 116 cm². Its base is 8 cm. What is the corresponding height?

_____

**Find the area of each triangle.**

12.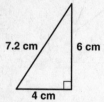
7.2 cm   6 cm
4 cm

_____

13.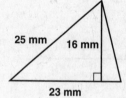
25 mm   16 mm
23 mm

_____

14.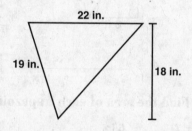
22 in.
19 in.   18 in.

_____

# Reteaching 8-8

The distance around a circle is called the *circumference*.

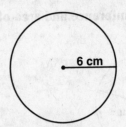

- You can use a formula to find the circumference ($C$) of a circle. *Pi* ($\pi$) is approximately equal to ($\approx$) 3.14.

  Circumference = $2 \times \pi \times$ radius
  $$C = 2\pi r$$

  Circumference = $2 \times \pi \times r$
  $$C = 2 \times \pi \times 6$$
  $$\approx 37.7 \text{ cm}$$

- If you know the diameter, use this formula:
  Circumference = $\pi \times$ diameter
  $$C = \pi d$$

To find the *area of a circle*, use this formula:

Area = $\pi \times$ radius$^2$
$$A = \pi r^2$$

Area = $\pi \times r^2$
$$A = \pi \times 6^2$$
$$\approx 113.1 \text{ cm}^2$$

The circumference of the circle is about 37.7 cm. The area of the circle is about 113.1 cm$^2$.

---

**Find the circumference and area of each circle. Round to the nearest tenth.**

1.

$C \approx$ _____ $A \approx$ _____

2.

$C \approx$ _____ $A \approx$ _____

3.

$C \approx$ _____ $A \approx$ _____

4.

$C \approx$ _____ $A \approx$ _____

5.

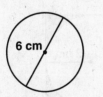

$C \approx$ _____ $A \approx$ _____

6.

$C \approx$ _____ $A \approx$ _____

# Practice 8-8

**Find the circumference and area of each circle. Round to the nearest hundredth.**

**1.**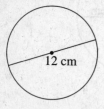

12 cm

_____

_____

**2.**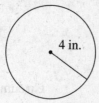

4 in.

_____

_____

**3.**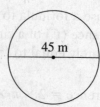

45 m

_____

_____

**4.**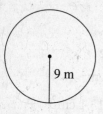

9 m

_____

_____

**5.**

43 ft

_____

_____

**6.**

126 km

_____

_____

**Find the circumference of a circle with the given diameter or radius. Use $\frac{22}{7}$ for $\pi$.**

**7.** $d = 70$ cm

_____

**8.** $r = 14$ cm

_____

**9.** $d = 35$ in.

_____

**Find the radius and the diameter of a circle with the given circumference. Round to the nearest hundredth.**

**10.** $C = 68$ cm

_____

_____

**11.** $C = 150$ m

_____

_____

**12.** $C = 218$ in.

_____

_____

**13.** Use the figure at the right. Find the area of the shaded region. Round your answer to the nearest hundredth.

_____

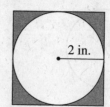

2 in.

# Reteaching 8-9

Congruent segments are segments that have the same length. You can use a *compass* and a straightedge to construct one segment congruent to another segment.

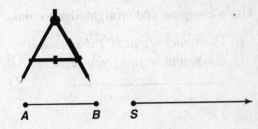

① Start with segment $\overline{AB}$. Draw a ray with endpoint $S$ that is longer than $\overline{AB}$.

② Place the compass tip on $A$. Draw an arc through $B$.

③ Use the *same* compass setting. Place the compass tip on $S$. Draw an arc intersecting the ray. Label this intersection $T$. You have constructed $\overline{ST}$, which should be congruent to $\overline{AB}$.

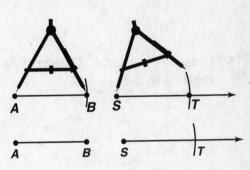

④ To check, measure $\overline{AB}$ and $\overline{ST}$ with a ruler. The segments should be the same length.

Segment $\overline{AB}$ is congruent to segment $\overline{ST}$.

$$\overline{AB} \cong \overline{ST}$$

Perpendicular bisectors and angle bisectors can be constructed in similar ways. Use the compass and the endpoints of a segment to draw two arcs that intersect above and below the segment. Connect the points of intersection to create the perpendicular bisector. To create an angle bisector, use the compass to draw two intersecting arcs from points on the legs of the angle that are equidistant from the vertex. Connect the intersection with the vertex of the angle.

---

**Use a compass and a straightedge for each construction.**

1. Draw segment $\overline{EF}$ that is 3 inches long. Then construct segment $\overline{GH}$ congruent to $\overline{EF}$.

2. Draw acute angle $B$. Construct the angle bisector of $\angle B$.

**Construct a perpendicular bisector to the given segment.**

3.

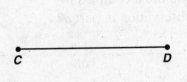

4.

# Practice 8-9

**Use a compass and straightedge to make each construction.**

1. Construct segment $\overline{YZ}$ so that it is congruent to the given segment $\overline{AB}$.

A          B

2. Construct $\angle PQR$ so that it is congruent to the given $\angle DEF$.

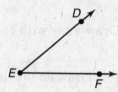

3. Draw an obtuse $\angle G$. Construct an angle congruent to $\angle G$.

4. Use a protractor to draw $\angle XYZ$ with $m\angle XYZ = 36°$. Then use a compass and straightedge to construct $\angle RST$ with the same measure.

5. Construct the perpendicular bisector of the given segment $\overline{JK}$.

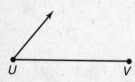

J          K

6. Construct the angle bisector of $\angle PRS$.

7. Use the figures below to complete triangle $TUV$. First, construct $\overline{TU}$ from the ray given with endpoint $U$. Make it congruent to $\overline{CD}$. Then draw $\overline{TV}$.

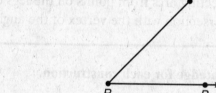

U          V          C          D

a. Judging by appearance, what might you say about the lengths $TU$ and $TV$?

_____

b. How could you use a compass to check your observation in part *a*?

_____

_____

_____

# Reteaching 9-1

These three-dimensional figures are space figures, or *solids*.

cylinder            cone              prism              pyramid

A *cylinder* has two congruent circular bases. $\overline{AB}$ is a radius.

A *cone* has one circular base. $\overline{CD}$ is a diameter.

A *prism* has two bases that are congruent and parallel. The lateral faces are parallelograms. A *pyramid* has one base. The lateral faces are triangles. The shape of a base is used to name the solid. A triangular prism and a square pyramid are shown above.

---

**For each figure, describe the base(s) and name the figure.**

1.

_____

_____

2.

_____

_____

3.

_____

_____

4.

_____

_____

5.

_____

_____

6.

_____

_____

**For the figure, name a pair of parallel lines and a pair of intersecting lines.**

7. _____

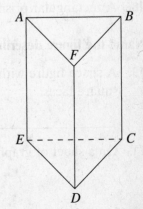

# Practice 9-1

**For each figure, describe the base(s) of the figure, and name the figure.**

1.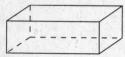

_____

_____

2.

_____

_____

3.

_____

_____

4.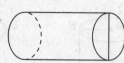

_____

_____

5.

_____

_____

6.

_____

_____

7.

_____

_____

8.

_____

_____

**Name each solid according to its description.**

9. bowling ball

_____

10. VCR

_____

11. soup can

_____

12. funnel

_____

**Complete.**

13. A _____ has exactly two circular bases.

14. A hexagonal prism has _____ faces.

15. A cube has _____ edges.

16. A pentagonal pyramid has _____ faces.

17. A pentagonal pyramid has _____ edges.

18. A rectangular prism has _____ vertices.

**Name the figure described.**

19. A space figure with six congruent square faces.

_____

20. A space figure with parallel bases that are congruent, parallel circles.

_____

21. On a sheet of graph paper, draw a rectangular prism.

# Reteaching 9-2

A *base plan* for the stack of cubes shows the
shape of the base and the number of cubes in
each stack. To make a base plan:

① Draw a square for each stack as seen from above.

② Write the number of cubes in each stack inside
each square.

③ Label the "Front" and "Right" sides.

An *isometric view* shows a corner view of a solid.
From this, three other views can be drawn. The *top
view* is suggested by the base plan. The *front view*
is what is seen from the front, and the *right view* is
what is seen from the right side.

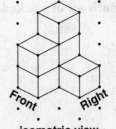

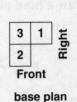

**isometric view**

**base plan**

**Top**          **Front**          **Right**

---

**Draw a base plan for each set of stacked cubes.**

**1.**

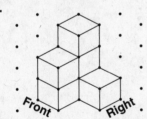

**2.**

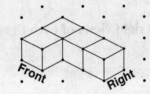

**3.**

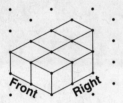

**4.**

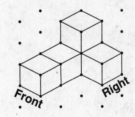

**Draw the top, front, and right views of each figure.**

**5.**

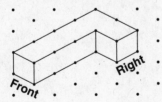

**6.**

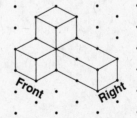

# Practice 9-2

**Drawing Views of Three-Dimensional Figures**

**Draw a base plan for each set of stacked cubes.**

**1.**

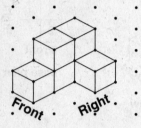

**2.**

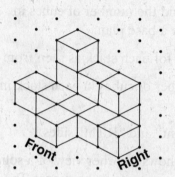

**Draw the top, front, and right views of each figure.**

**3.**

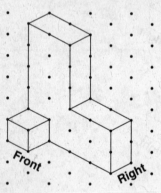

**4.**

# Reteaching 9-3

You can make *nets*, or flat patterns, of solids.
You can also identify a solid from its net.

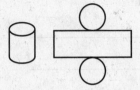

*Example 1:* The net of a cylinder shows a
rectangle and 2 circles. You can fold the
net to make the cylinder.

*Example 2:* The net of a cone shows a circle
and a part of a circle.

*Example 3:* The net of a triangular
pyramid shows 4 triangular surfaces. To
make the pyramid, fold up the outer triangles.

*Example 4:* The net of a triangular prism
shows 3 rectangles for the lateral faces of
the prism and 2 triangles for the bases.

---

**List the shapes that make up the net for each figure, and write the
number of times each shape is used.**

1. rectangular prism

_____

_____

2. cylinder

_____

_____

3. hexagonal prism

_____

_____

4. rectangular pyramid

_____

5. cube

_____

6. cone

_____

**Identify the solid that each net forms.**

7.

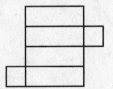

8.

9.

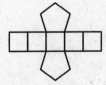

_____  _____  _____

# Practice 9-3

**List the shapes that make up the net for each figure, and write the number of times each shape is used.**

**1.** rectangular prism

_____

_____

**2.** pentagonal pyramid

_____

_____

**3.** cylinder

_____

_____

**4.** triangular pyramid

_____

_____

**5.** cone

_____

_____

**6.** hexagonal prism

_____

_____

**7.** Draw a net for a rectangular box that is 9 cm long, 5 cm wide, and 3 cm tall.

**8.** Draw a net for a cylinder whose height is 8 in. and whose radius is 3 in.

**Identify the solid that each net forms.**

**9.**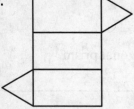

_____

**10.**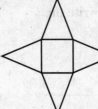

_____

**11.**

_____

**12.**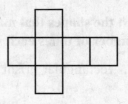

_____

**13.** **What three-dimensional figure can be made from this net?**

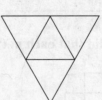

_____

# Reteaching 9-4

**Surface Areas of Prisms and Cylinders**

The *surface area* of a solid is the sum of the areas of its surfaces. S.A. stands for *surface area* and L.A. stand for *lateral area*.

*Example 1:* Find the surface area of the prism.

*Using a Net to Find Surface Area of a Prism*
Draw a net of the prism and find the area of each rectangle in the net.

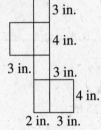

S.A. =
$(2 \cdot 3) + (2 \cdot 3) + (3 \cdot 4) + (3 \cdot 4) + (2 \cdot 4) + (2 \cdot 4)$
$= 6 + 6 + 12 + 12 + 8 + 8$
$= 52$ in.$^2$

*Using the Prism Surface Area Formula*
The lateral area of a prism is the product of the perimeter of the base and the height of the prism.

L.A. $= ph$
S.A. $=$ L.A. $+ 2B$
$\quad = ph + 2B$
$\quad = (2 + 2 + 3 + 3)4 + 2(2 \cdot 3)$
$\quad = 10(4) + 2(6)$
$\quad = 40 + 12 = 52$ in.$^2$

*Example 2:* Find the surface area of the cylinder.

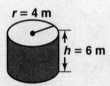

*Using a Net to Find Surface Area of a Cylinder*
Draw a net of the cylinder and find the area of each shape in the net.

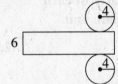

S.A. $= 16\pi + 16\pi + 48\pi$
$\quad = 80\pi$
$\quad \approx 251.33$

*Using the Cylinder Surface Area Formula*
S.A. $= 2\pi rh + 2\pi r^2$
$\quad = 2\pi(4)(6) + 2\pi(4^2)$
$\quad = 48\pi + 32\pi$
$\quad = 80\pi$
$\quad \approx 251.33$

---

**Find the lateral and surface area of each figure to the nearest whole unit.**

1.
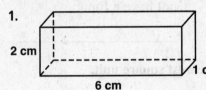

_____

2.
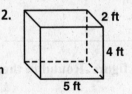

_____

3.
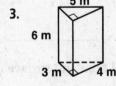

_____

4.
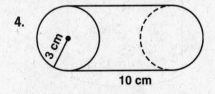

_____

5.
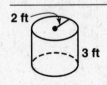

_____

6.
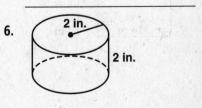

_____

Name _____ Class _____ Date _____

# Practice 9-4

**Surface Areas of Prisms and Cylinders**

Use a net or a formula to find the surface area of each figure to the nearest square unit.

1.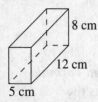
8 cm
12 cm
5 cm

_____

2.
8 m
15 m
6 m

_____

3.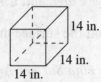
14 in.
14 in.
14 in.

_____

4.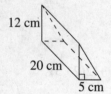
12 cm
20 cm
5 cm

_____

5.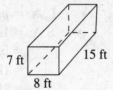
7 ft
15 ft
8 ft

_____

6.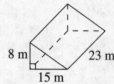
8 m
23 m
15 m

_____

7.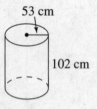
53 cm
102 cm

_____

8.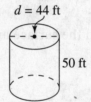
28 in.
7 in.

_____

9.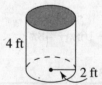
$d = 44$ ft
50 ft

_____

Rachel and Sam are going to paint the exposed surfaces of each figure. Find the area to be painted to the nearest square unit.

10.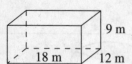
4 cm
15 cm
15 cm
2 cm

_____

11.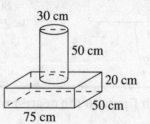
30 cm
50 cm
20 cm
50 cm
75 cm

_____

12.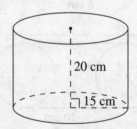
4 ft
2 ft
This cylinder does
not have a top.

_____

Find the lateral area and surface area of each figure. Round to the nearest square unit.

13.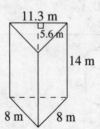
9 m
18 m
12 m

_____

14.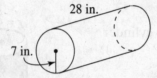
11.3 m
5.6 m
14 m
8 m
8 m

_____

15.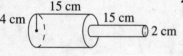
20 cm
15 cm

_____

# Reteaching 9-5

*Example 1:* Find the surface area of the prism.

The lateral area of a square pyramid is four times the area of one of the lateral faces.

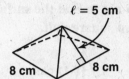

L.A. $= 4 \cdot \left(\frac{1}{2}b\ell\right) = 2b\ell$

The surface area of a square pyramid is the sum of the lateral area and the area of the base.

$$\begin{aligned}
\text{S.A.} &= \text{L.A.} + B \\
&= 2b\ell + b^2 \\
&= 2(8)(5) + 8^2 \\
&= 80 + 64 \\
&= 144 \text{ cm}^2
\end{aligned}$$

*Example 2:* Find the surface area of the cone.

The lateral area of a cone is one half the product of the circumference of the base and the slant height.

L.A. $= \frac{1}{2}(2\pi r)\ell = \pi r\ell$

$$\begin{aligned}
\text{S.A.} &= \text{L.A.} + B \\
&= \pi r\ell + \pi r^2 \\
&= \pi(3)(5) + \pi(3^2) \\
&= 15\pi + 9\pi \\
&= 24\pi \approx 75.4 \text{ m}^2
\end{aligned}$$

---

**Find the lateral and surface area of each square pyramid.**

1.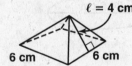

2.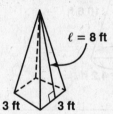

3.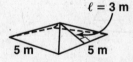

_____    _____    _____

**Find the surface area of each cone to the nearest whole unit.**

4.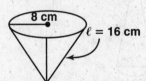

5.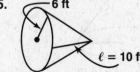

6.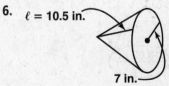

_____    _____    _____

# Practice 9-5

**Surface Areas of Pyramids and Cones**

**Use a net to find the surface area of each square pyramid to the nearest square unit.**

1.
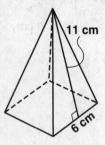
11 cm

6 cm

_____

2.
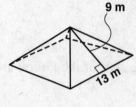
9 m

13 m

_____

3.
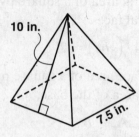
10 in.

7.5 in.

_____

**Find the lateral area of each pyramid to the nearest whole square unit.**

4.

14 m

2 m

_____

5.
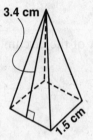
3.4 cm

1.5 cm

_____

6.
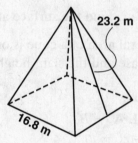
23.2 m

16.8 m

_____

**Find the surface area of each cone to the nearest square unit.**

7.

14 ft

8 ft

_____

8.
10.6 ft

4.2 ft

_____

9.
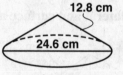
12.8 cm

24.6 cm

_____

**Find the lateral area of each cone to the nearest square unit.**

10.

23.4 m

18.02 m

_____

11.

20.04 m

12.14 m

_____

12.

17.3 in.

6.90 in.

_____

# Reteaching 9-6

To find the volume of a prism or a cylinder, multiply the base area
$B$ and the height $h$.

| | ① Find the base area $B$. | ② Multiply base area $B$ and height $h$. $V = Bh$ |
|---|---|---|
| 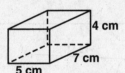 $h = 5$ yd $w = 4$ yd $\ell = 6$ yd | $B = \ell w$ $= 6 \cdot 4$ $= 24 \text{ yd}^2$ | $V = Bh$ $= 24 \cdot 5$ $= 120 \text{ yd}^3$ The volume is 120 yd³. |
| $h = 10$ yd $r = 3$ yd | $B = \pi r^2$ $= \pi \cdot 3^2$ $\approx 28.27 \text{ yd}^2$ | $V = Bh$ $\approx 28.27 \cdot 10$ $\approx 282.7 \text{ yd}^3$ The volume is about 283 yd³. |

**Find the base area and volume of each prism.**

1.
   4 cm
   7 cm
   5 cm

   $B = $ _____

   $V = $ _____

2.
   6 ft
   6 ft
   6 ft

   $B = $ _____

   $V = $ _____

3.
   8 m
   4 m
   6 m

   $B = $ _____

   $V = $ _____

**Find the base area of each cylinder to the nearest hundredth. Then find the volume of each cylinder to the nearest whole unit.**

4.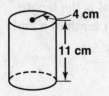
   4 cm
   11 cm

   $B \approx $ _____

   $V \approx $ _____

5.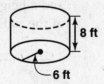
   8 ft
   6 ft

   $B \approx $ _____

   $V \approx $ _____

6.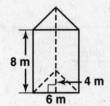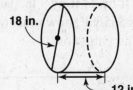
   18 in.
   12 in.

   $B \approx $ _____

   $V \approx $ _____

# Practice 9-6

**Find the volume of each solid to the nearest whole unit.**

**1.**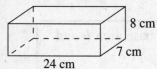
8 cm
7 cm
24 cm

_____

**2.**
27 in.
27 in.
27 in.

_____

**3.**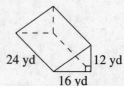
24 yd
12 yd
16 yd

_____

**4.**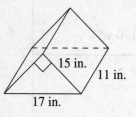
15 in.
11 in.
17 in.

_____

**5.**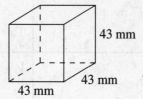
43 mm
43 mm
43 mm

_____

**6.**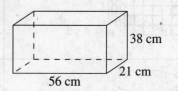
38 cm
21 cm
56 cm

_____

**7.**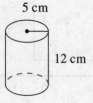
5 cm
12 cm

_____

**8.**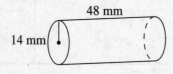
48 mm
14 mm

_____

**9.**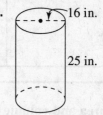
16 in.
25 in.

_____

**10.**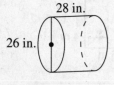
28 in.
26 in.

_____

**11.**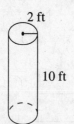
2 ft
10 ft

_____

**12.**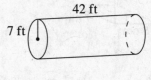
42 ft
7 ft

_____

**13.** Suppose you want to buy concrete for a 36 ft by 24 ft by 9 in. patio. If concrete costs \$55/yd$^3$, how much will the concrete for the patio cost?

_____

**14.** A cylinder has a volume of about 500 cm$^3$ and a height of 10 cm. What is the length of the radius to the nearest tenth of a cm?

_____

# Reteaching 9-7

**Volumes of Pyramids and Cones**

To find the volume of a pyramid or cone, multiply $\frac{1}{3}$, the base area $B$, and the height $h$.

| | ① Find the base area $B$. | ② Multiply $\frac{1}{3}$, the base area $B$, and the height $h$. $V = \frac{1}{3}Bh$ |
|---|---|---|
| 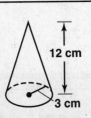 | $B = \ell w$ $= 6 \cdot 4$ $= 24 \text{ cm}^2$ | $V = \frac{1}{3}Bh$ $= \frac{1}{3}(24)(9)$ $= 72 \text{ cm}^3$ The volume is 72 cm³. |
|  | $B = \pi r^2$ $= \pi \cdot 3^2$ $\approx 28.27 \text{ cm}^2$ | $V = \frac{1}{3}Bh$ $\approx \frac{1}{3}(28.27)(12)$ $\approx 113.08 \text{ cm}^3$ The volume is about 113.08 cm³. |

**Find the volume of each figure to the nearest whole unit.**

**1.**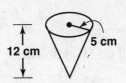

_____

**2.**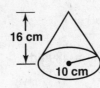

_____

**3.**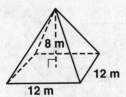

_____

**4.**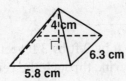

_____

**5.** Find the height of a cone with an approximate volume of 134 cm³ and a radius of 4 cm.

_____

# Practice 9-7

**Find the volume of each figure to the nearest cubic unit.**

**1.**
5 cm
6 cm
6 cm

**2.**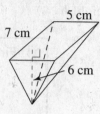
15.6 m
14.8 m

**3.**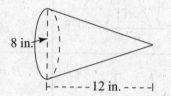
5 cm
7 cm
6 cm

_____

_____

_____

**4.**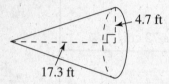
4.7 ft
17.3 ft

**5.**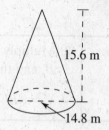
21 cm
35 cm
18 cm

**6.**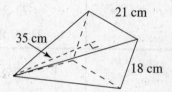
8 in.
12 in.

_____

_____

_____

**Find the missing dimension for each three-dimensional figure to the nearest tenth, given the volume and other dimensions.**

**7.** rectangular pyramid,
$l = 8$ m, $w = 4.6$ m, $V = 88$ m$^3$

**8.** cone, $r = 5$ in., $V = 487$ in.$^3$

_____

_____

**9.** square pyramid, $s = 14$ yd, $V = 489$ yd$^3$

**10.** square pyramid, $h = 8.9$ cm, $V = 56$ cm$^3$

_____

_____

**11.** cone, $h = 18$ cm, $V = 986$ cm$^3$

**12.** cone, $r = 5.5$ ft, $V = 592$ ft$^3$

_____

_____

**13.** Find the volume of a 4 ft by 2 ft by 3 ft rectangular prism with a cylindrical hole, radius 6 in., through the center.

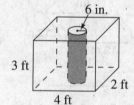
6 in.
3 ft
4 ft
2 ft

_____

**14.** Margarite has a cylindrical tin of popcorn that is 18 in. tall and has a radius of 4 in. She wants to use the tin for something else and needs to empty the popcorn into a box. The box is 8 in. long, 8 in. wide, and 14 in. tall. Will the popcorn fit in the box? Explain.

_____

_____

# Reteaching 9-8

**Problem Solving: Draw a Diagram and Make a Table**

A farmer has 100 ft of fencing. He wants to enclose the greatest possible area for his garden. He wants the fenced area to be rectangular. What dimensions should he use?

**Read and Understand**   The goal is to find the dimension of the fence that will give the largest area. The area has to be rectangular.

**Plan and Solve**   Draw a diagram to help you solve the problem and make a table to show possible dimensions of the fence and area.

```
100 ft of
fence
```

| Length (ft) | Width (ft) | Area (ft²) |
|---|---|---|
| 10 | 40 | 400 |
| 15 | 35 | 525 |
| 20 | 30 | 600 |

| Length(ft) | Width (ft) | Area (ft²) |
|---|---|---|
| 25 | 25 | 625 |
| 30 | 20 | 600 |
| 35 | 15 | 525 |

**Look Back and Check**   Can you find a greater area using 2-ft increments?

| Length (ft) | Width (ft) | Area (ft²) |
|---|---|---|
| 10 | 40 | 400 |
| 12 | 38 | 456 |
| 14 | 36 | 504 |
| 16 | 34 | 544 |

| Length(ft) | Width (ft) | Area (ft²) |
|---|---|---|
| 18 | 32 | 576 |
| 20 | 30 | 600 |
| 22 | 28 | 616 |
| 24 | 26 | 624 |

Making the fence 25 ft by 25 ft will result in the largest area.

---

**Make a drawing to help you solve each problem.**

1. Fred wants to protect his rectangular workbench by covering it with paper. The workbench is 24 in. by 36 in. He wants the paper to hang over the edges by 4 in. How big should the paper be? What would be its area?

2. The convention center uses cloths to cover display tables. The cloths must hang over the edges of the tables by 24 in. The tables are 30 in. by 72 in. How big are the cloths? What is the area of one cloth?

3. Meera is covering a bulletin board with fabric. The bulletin board is 36 in. by 48 in. She needs 6 in. overhang on each side to staple the fabric to the back of the board. How big should the piece of fabric be? What is the area of the fabric?

4. Ethan wants to put a plastic liner in the bed of his truck. The truck bed measures 42 in. by 64 in. He wants 8 in. extra on each side to go against the truck bed walls. How big should the liner be? What would be its area?

# Practice 9-8

**Problem Solving: Draw a Diagram and Make a Table**

**Choose a strategy or a combination of strategies to solve each problem.**

1.  You can cut square corners off an 11 in. by 14 in. piece of cardboard to get a pattern that you could fold into a box without a top.

    a.  What dimensions for the corners, to the nearest quarter-inch, will give the greatest volume?

    _____

    b.  What is the greatest volume of the box to the nearest tenth?

    _____

2.  Corinda has 400 ft of fencing to make a play area. She wants the fenced area to be rectangular. What dimensions should she use in order to enclose the maximum possible area?

    _____

3.  A restaurant dining room measures 100 ft by 150 ft. The height of the room is 9 ft. If the occupancy guidelines recommend at least 150 $ft^3$ per person, what is the maximum number of people that can be in the room?

    _____

4.  Maurice lives at point A. The library is at point B. How many different routes can Maurice take from home to the library if he only goes to the right and down, never retracing his route?

    _____

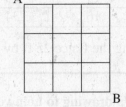

5.  The consecutive even integers from 2 to $n$ are 2, 4, 6, . . . , $n$. The square of the sum of the integers is 5,184. What is the value of $n$?

    _____

6.  A bicyclist has 120 mi to cover on a trip. One day she bicycles 40% of the distance. The next day she cycles 60% of the remaining distance. How much further does she have to cycle?

    _____

**Use the dartboard shown at the right.**

7.  Three darts are thrown at the target. If each dart lands on the target, how many *different* point totals are possible?

    _____

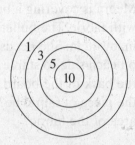

8.  If 3 darts are thrown at the target and each dart lands on a different zone, find the maximum number of points scored.

    _____

# Reteaching 9-9

Two solids are *similar solids* if they have the same shape and all of their corresponding lengths are proportional. A special relationship exists among the measures of similar solids:

- The ratios of the corresponding dimensions of similar solids is $\frac{a}{b}$.

- The ratio of their surface areas is $\frac{a^2}{b^2}$.

- The ratio of their volumes is $\frac{a^3}{b^3}$.

*Example:* Two similar cylindrical watering cans have diameters of 14 in. and 18 in. Find the volume of the larger watering can if the volume of the smaller watering can is 882 in.³.

①  Write the ratio of corresponding dimensions.

$\frac{14}{18} = \frac{7}{9}$, so the ratio of the volumes is $\frac{a^3}{b^3} = \frac{7^3}{9^3}$, or $\frac{343}{729}$.

②  Write a proportion: $\dfrac{\text{volume of small watering can}}{\text{volume of large watering can}} = \dfrac{343}{729}$

$\dfrac{882}{x} = \dfrac{343}{729}$          ← Substitute the known volume.

$343x = (882)(729)$     ← Cross multiply.

$343x = 642{,}978$       ← Divide each side by 343.

$\quad x = 1{,}874.57$        ← Simplify.

The volume of the larger watering can is about 1,875 in.³.

---

**For each pair of similar solids, find the value of the variable.**

1.

2.

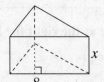 

_____     _____

3.  A triangular prism has a height of 18 cm, surface area of 463 cm², and volume of 279 cm³. Find the surface area and volume of a similar prism with a height of 12 cm. Round your answers to the nearest whole number.

_____

4.  A rectangular prism has a height of 24 inches, a surface area of 1,088 in.² and a volume of 2,112 in.³. Find the surface area and volume of a similar prism with a height of 36 in.

_____

# Practice 9-9

**Complete the table for each prism.**

| Original Size | | Doubled Dimensions | | |
| Dimensions (m) | S.A. ($m^2$) | Dimensions (m) | S.A. ($m^2$) | New S.A. ÷ Old S.A. |
|---|---|---|---|---|
| **1.** $2 \times 3 \times 4$ | | | | |
| **2.** $5 \times 5 \times 9$ | | | | |
| **3.** $7 \times 7 \times 7$ | | | | |
| **4.** $8 \times 12 \times 15$ | | | | |
| **5.** $15 \times 15 \times 20$ | | | | |
| **6.** $32 \times 32 \times 32$ | | | | |

**7.** What conclusion can you draw?

_____

_____

**8.** A rectangular prism is 8 cm by 10 cm by 15 cm. What are the
volume and surface area of the prism?

_____

**9.** In Exercise 8, if each dimension of the prism is halved, what are
the new volume and surface area?

_____

**Use the triangular prism shown at the right for Exercises 10 and 11.**

**10.** Find the volume and surface area.

_____

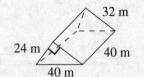

**11.** If each dimension of the prism is doubled, what are the new
volume and surface areas?

_____

**12.** A rectangular prism is 9 in. long, 15 in. wide,
and 21 in. high. The length is halved. What
happens to the volume?

_____

_____

**13.** A rectangular prism is 8 cm long, 24 cm
wide, and 43 cm high. The length is doubled,
and the width is tripled. What happens to
the volume?

_____

# Reteaching 10-1

The *frequency* of a data item is the number of times it appears. A *frequency table* provides intervals, then tallies each data item in its interval.

**Telephone Numbers (Last Four Digits)**

| | | | | | | | |
|---|---|---|---|---|---|---|---|
| 9782 | 8609 | 7880 | 9012 | 5620 | 1190 | 2324 | 2568 |
| 9877 | 4085 | 6856 | 7367 | 3642 | 6784 | 8015 | 7761 |
| 9001 | 4227 | 7452 | 9811 | 4326 | 6433 | 4228 | 8111 |

The last four digits of 24 phone numbers were chosen from a phone book.

Make a frequency table for the data.

① Choose an appropriate interval. All intervals must be the same size.

② Mark tallies and write totals for the data.

**Telephone Numbers**

| Last Four Digits | Tally | Frequency |
|---|---|---|
| 1000–1999 | \| | 1 |
| 2000–2999 | \|\| | 2 |
| 3000–3999 | \| | 1 |
| 4000–4999 | \|\|\|\| | 4 |
| 5000–5999 | \| | 1 |
| 6000–6999 | \|\|\| | 3 |
| 7000–7999 | \|\|\|\| | 4 |
| 8000–8999 | \|\|\| | 3 |
| 9000–9999 | ⅃Ⲏ | 5 |

You can use a frequency table to make a *histogram*.

In a histogram, there is no space between the bars.

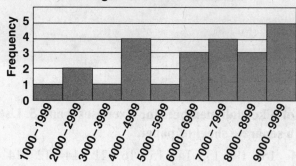

**Digits in Phone Numbers**

Frequency / Last Digits of Phone Numbers

---

**Use the following data for Exercises 1 and 2.**

Raisins in a small box:  33 32 30 40 29 35
36 33 42 28 41 39 30 29 35 40 33 34 31 28

1. Make a frequency table for the data.

2. Use your frequency table to make a histogram.

# Practice 10-1

**Use the Olympic medal data at the right for Exercises 1–3.**
**Use the space below or a separate sheet of paper.**

1. Make a frequency table. Do not use intervals.

| 2002 Winter Olympic Gold Medals | |
| --- | --- |
| **Country** | **Medals** |
| Germany | 12 |
| Norway | 11 |
| U.S.A. | 10 |
| Russia | 6 |
| Canada | 6 |
| France | 4 |
| Italy | 4 |
| Finland | 4 |
| Netherlands | 3 |
| Switzerland | 3 |
| Croatia | 3 |
| Austria | 2 |
| China | 2 |
| Korea | 2 |
| Australia | 2 |

2. Draw a line plot.

3. Draw a histogram.

**Use these ages of bike club members for Exercises 4 and 5. Use the**
**space below or a separate sheet of paper.**

19   16   10   14   15   19   13   14   15   16   21   14   12   14   16   13   13

4. Using intervals, display the data
   in a frequency table.

   Ex. 3

5. Use the frequency table to draw
   a histogram.

   Ex. 4

   Ex. 5

# Reteaching 10-2

Two important factors in determining whether a graph gives a correct impression of data are:

- how the scale is chosen and

- whether the entire scale is shown.

The data at the right can be shown in a bar graph.

| Countries with Most Universities (2000) | |
|---|---|
| India | 7,513 |
| United States | 3,559 |

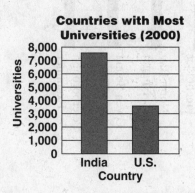

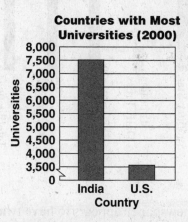

In the first graph, the scale is in multiples of 1,000. The entire scale from 0 through 8,000 is shown. The graph accurately compares the numbers of universities in the two countries.

In the second graph, the scale is in multiples of 500. There is a break in the vertical scale. The graph gives a misleading comparison between the two countries.

---

**Use the bar graphs above for Exercises 1–4.**

1. From which graph is it easier to tell that India has about twice the number of universities as the United States?

   _____

2. In the second graph, about how many times the number of U.S. universities does India *appear* to have?

   _____

3. Which graph makes it easier to estimate the number of universities in each country? Why?

   _____

   _____

   _____

4. Why does the second graph give a misleading impression of the data?

   _____

   _____

   _____

# Practice 10-2

**Use the graph below for Exercises 1–5.**

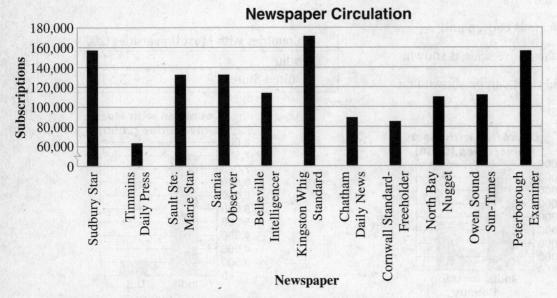

**Newspaper Circulation**

1. Which newspaper appears to have twice the circulation of
   *The Cornwall Standard-Freeholder?*                    _____

2. Which newspaper actually has about twice the circulation of
   *The Cornwall Standard-Freeholder?*                    _____

3. *Belleville Intelligencer* appears to have about how many times
   the circulation of *Chatham Daily News?*               _____

4. Explain why the graph gives a misleading visual impression of
   the data.

   _____

   _____

5. Redraw the graph to give an accurate impression of the data.

Name _____ Class _____ Date _____

# Reteaching 10-3

A *stem-and-leaf plot* is an easy way to show data arranged in order.

**8th Grade 100-M Dash**
**(Times to Nearest 0.1 s)**

| 13.1 | 16.2 | 15.5 | 15.2 | 13.5 |
|------|------|------|------|------|
| 15.3 | 14.8 | 14.4 | 17.5 | 12.2 |
| 14.1 | 16.1 | 16.9 | 15.3 | 16.8 |
| 16.0 | 15.3 | 12.0 | 18.2 | 14.6 |
| 13.2 | 18.3 | 16.6 | 15.3 | 18.8 |

① Choose *stems*. The times range from 12.0 to 18.8. Choose 12 to 18 as stems.

② List the tenths digits as *leaves*.

| 18 | 2 3 8 |
|----|-------|
| 17 | 5 |
| 16 | 0 1 2 6 8 9 |
| 15 | 2 3 3 3 3 5 |
| 14 | 1 4 6 8 |
| 13 | 1 2 5 |
| 12 | 0 2 |

③ Make a key to explain what each stem and leaf represents.

18 | 2 means 18.2

The *mode* is the most frequent number.
The mode is 15.3 seconds.

The *median* is the middle number or average of the middle two numbers. The median is 15.3 seconds.

---

1. Complete the stem-and-leaf plot for the data.

**8th Grade 200-M Dash**
**(Times to Nearest 0.1 s)**

| 32.5 | 32.1 | 38.5 | 31.7 | 34.7 |
|------|------|------|------|------|
| 29.3 | 35.2 | 34.4 | 30.2 | 35.3 |
| 34.7 | 31.9 | 36.0 | 32.2 | 36.7 |
| 32.2 | 31.4 | 34.7 | 29.5 | 36.9 |
| 36.4 | 33.4 | 38.6 | 34.7 | 37.3 |

**Times for the 200-M Dash**

| 38 | _____ |
|----|---------------|
| 37 | _____ |
| 36 | _____ |
| 35 | _____ |
| 34 | _____ |
| 33 | _____ |
| 32 | _____ |
| 31 | _____ |
| 30 | _____ |
| 29 | _____ |

**Use your stem-and-leaf plot for Exercises 2–5.**

2. The mode is _____.

3. The median is _____.

4. How many 8th grade students finished the race in less than 35 s?

   _____

5. How many 8th grade students finished the race in less than 33 s?

   _____

# Practice 10-3

The stem-and-leaf plot at the right shows the bowling scores for
20 bowlers. Use the plot for Exercises 1–3.

| 10 | 0 2 2 4 4 4 |
|----|-------------|
| 11 | 1 3 5 5 5 9 |
| 12 | 4 5 9 9 |
| 13 | 0 6 8 8 |

Key   13 | 8 means 138

1.  What numbers make up the stems?

_____

2.  What are the leaves for the stem 12?        3.  Find the median and mode.

_____        _____

**Make a stem-and-leaf plot for each set of data.  Then find the median
and mode.**

4.  8  19  27  36  35  24  6  15  16  24  38  23  20

_____

5.  8.6  9.1  7.4  6.3  8.2  9.0  7.5  7.9  6.3  8.1  7.1  8.2  7.0  9.6  9.9

_____

6.  436  521  470  586  692  634  417  675  526  719  817

_____

7.  17.9  20.4  18.6  19.5  17.6  18.5  17.4  18.5  19.4

_____

The back-to-back stem-and-leaf plot at the right shows the high and
low temperatures for a week in a certain city. Use this plot for
Exercises 8–10.

| Low | | High |
|-----|---|------|
| 8 7 | 5 | |
| 4 3 | 6 | 5 9 9 |
| 2 1 0 | 7 | 2 5 6 |
| | 8 | 0 |

63 ← 3 | 6 | 5 → 65

8.  Find the mean for the high temperatures.

_____

9.  Find the median for the low temperatures.

_____

10.  Find the mode for the high temperatures.

_____

11.  Make a back-to-back stem-and-leaf plot for the following data.
Then find the median and mode.

Set A:   75  82  79  80  75  76  83  74  75  86  80  71  75   _____

Set B:   71  73  75  80  79  80  74  80  74  79  76  80  81   _____

# Reteaching 10-4

**Box-and-Whisker Plots**

A *box-and-whisker plot* is a graph that summarizes a data set along a number line. Make a box-and-whisker plot for the data in the table at the right.

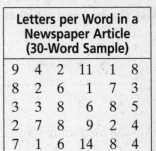

| Letters per Word in a Newspaper Article (30-Word Sample) | | | | | |
| --- | --- | --- | --- | --- | --- |
| 9 | 4 | 2 | 11 | 1 | 8 |
| 8 | 2 | 6 | 1 | 7 | 3 |
| 3 | 3 | 8 | 6 | 8 | 5 |
| 2 | 7 | 8 | 9 | 2 | 4 |
| 7 | 1 | 6 | 14 | 8 | 4 |

① Order the data

1 1 1 2 2 2 2 3 3 3 4 4 4 5 6 6 6 7 7 7 8 8 8 8 8 8 9 9 11 14

② Find the median. The median is 6.

③ Find the medians of the lower and upper halves of the data.

(lower) 1 1 1 2 2 2 2 **3** 3 3 4 4 4 5 6
(upper) 6 6 7 7 7 8 8 **8** 8 8 8 9 9 11 14

④ Mark the least and greatest values below a number line. Mark the three medians.

⑤ Draw a box connecting the lower and upper medians. This box shows where at least half the data lies. Draw a line through the box at the median of all the data.

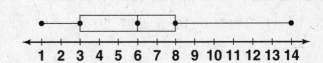

⑥ Draw whiskers from the box to the least and greatest values.

---

**Complete the steps to make a box-and-whisker plot for the data.**

1. Order the data.

_____

_____

2. Find the median.

_____

3. Find the median of the lower and upper halves.

_____

4. Draw the box-and-whisker plot.

| Letters per Word in a Magazine Article (30-Word Sample) | | | | |
| --- | --- | --- | --- | --- |
| 3 | 7 | 8 | 3 | 7 |
| 4 | 6 | 4 | 3 | 7 |
| 3 | 1 | 13 | 3 | 2 |
| 8 | 8 | 2 | 11 | 5 |
| 5 | 3 | 9 | 9 | 2 |
| 3 | 2 | 10 | 3 | 2 |

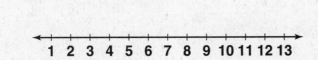

# Practice 10-4

**Use the box-and-whisker plot to find each value.**

**Height in Inches**

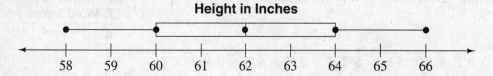

1. the median height _____
2. the lower quartile _____

3. the upper quartile _____
4. the greatest height _____

5. the shortest height _____
6. the range of heights _____

**Make a box-and-whisker plot for each set of data.**

**7.** 8  10  11  7  12  6  10  5  9  7  10

**8.** 20  21  25  18  25  15  27  26  24  23  20  20

| 9. Cargo Airlines in the U.S. (1991) | |
|---|---|
| **Airline** | **Freight ton-miles (1,000,000s)** |
| Federal Express | 3,622 |
| Northwest | 1,684 |
| United | 1,214 |
| American | 884 |
| Delta | 668 |
| Continental | 564 |
| Pan American | 377 |
| Trans World | 369 |
| United Parcel Service | 210 |

| 10. Immigration to the U.S. (1981–1990) | |
|---|---|
| **Country** | **Number (1,000s)** |
| Mexico | 1,656 |
| Philippines | 549 |
| China | 347 |
| Korea | 334 |
| Vietnam | 281 |
| Dominican Republic | 252 |
| India | 251 |
| El Salvador | 214 |
| Jamaica | 208 |
| United Kingdom | 159 |

# Reteaching 10-5

**Making Predictions from Scatter Plots**

*Example* Make a scatter plot and find a trend for the data below

① Choose a scale along each axis to represent the two sets of data.

② Locate the ordered pairs on the graph for the data.

③ Is there a trend? Do both sets of values increase? Does one decrease as the other increases? If neither occurs, there is no trend.

④ If there is a trend, draw a trend line that closely fits the data.

### Age and Height Survey

| Age (y) | Height (in.) | Age (y) | Height (in.) | Age (y) | Height (in.) |
|---------|--------------|---------|--------------|---------|--------------|
| 11 | 55 | 4 | 39 | 12 | 55 |
| 10 | 55 | 13 | 62 | 10 | 54 |
| 8 | 49 | 11 | 52 | 7 | 47 |
| 6 | 45 | 5 | 41 | 13 | 63 |
| 10 | 52 | 14 | 62 | 9 | 60 |
| 11 | 59 | 12 | 56 | 9 | 52 |
| 7 | 45 | 8 | 52 | 12 | 58 |
| 12 | 60 | 6 | 44 | 13 | 60 |
| 6 | 48 | 7 | 48 | 8 | 50 |
| 5 | 45 | 4 | 39 | 11 | 56 |

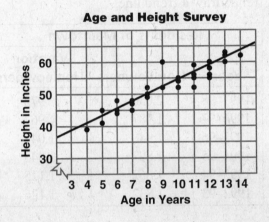

**Age and Height Survey**

---

**Use the data below for Exercises 1–5.**

| Weight (lb) | 78 | 63 | 67 | 52 | 81 | 92 | 60 | 34 | 83 | 47 | 73 | 98 | 45 | 31 | 95 | 71 | 76 | 41 |
|-------------|----|----|----|----|----|----|----|----|----|----|----|----|----|----|----|----|----|----|
| Height (in.) | 56 | 52 | 55 | 47 | 58 | 60 | 50 | 39 | 58 | 45 | 54 | 61 | 45 | 36 | 60 | 54 | 56 | 41 |

1. Draw the scatter plot and a trend line.

2. Use your graph to estimate the height of a person who weighs about 90 lb.

   _____

3. Use your graph to estimate the weight of a student 51 in. tall.

   _____

4. Is there a relationship between height and weight?

   _____

5. Write a sentence to explain your answer to Exercise 4.

   _____

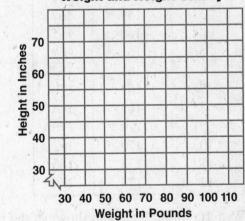

**Weight and Height Survey**

# Practice 10-5

**Tell whether a scatter plot made for each set of data would describe
a positive trend, a negative trend, or no trend.**

1. amount of education and
   annual salary

2. weight and speed in
   a foot race

3. test score and shoe size

   _____

   _____

   _____

4. Make a scatter plot showing the number of homeowners on one
   axis and vacation homeowners on the other axis. If there is a
   trend, draw a trend line.

| Residents of Maintown | | |
|---|---|---|
| Year | Homeowners | Vacation Homeowners |
| 1997–98 | 2,050 | 973 |
| 1996–97 | 1,987 | 967 |
| 1995–96 | 1,948 | 1,041 |
| 1994–95 | 1,897 | 1,043 |
| 1993–94 | 1,862 | 1,125 |
| 1992–93 | 1,832 | 1,126 |

5. Make a scatter plot for the data. If there is a trend, draw a trend
   line.

| Arm Span vs. Height | | |
|---|---|---|
| Person # | Arm Span | Height |
| 1 | 156 | 162 |
| 2 | 157 | 160 |
| 3 | 159 | 162 |
| 4 | 160 | 155 |
| 5 | 161 | 160 |
| 6 | 161 | 162 |
| 7 | 162 | 170 |
| 8 | 165 | 166 |
| 9 | 170 | 170 |
| 10 | 170 | 167 |
| 11 | 173 | 185 |
| 12 | 173 | 176 |

6. Wynetta found the graph shown at the right. The title of the
   graph was missing. What could the graph be describing?

   _____

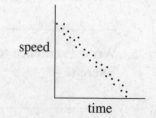

speed

time

# Reteaching 10-6

The class took a survey of their favorite breakfast foods. The results are shown in the table and the circle graph.

1. Find the total number of votes.

2. Find each part of the total as a fraction or percent.

3. Find the measure of each central angle in the circle graph by solving for $x$.

$$\frac{6}{36} = \frac{x}{360°} \; ; \; x = 60°$$

4. Draw, label, and title the graph.

**Favorite Breakfast Food**

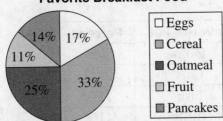

- ☐ Eggs
- ☐ Cereal
- ■ Oatmeal
- ☐ Fruit
- ■ Pancakes

| Breakfast | Votes | Fraction | % | Degrees |
|-----------|-------|----------|-----|---------|
| Eggs | 6 | $\frac{6}{36} = \frac{1}{6}$ | 17% | 60° |
| Cereal | 12 | $\frac{1}{3}$ | 33% | 120° |
| Oatmeal | 9 | $\frac{1}{4}$ | 25% | 90° |
| Fruit | 4 | $\frac{1}{9}$ | 11% | 40° |
| Pancakes | 5 | $\frac{5}{36}$ | 14% | 50° |
| **Total** | 36 | | 100% | 360° |

**Find the measure of the central angle that could represent each percent in a circle graph. Round your answer to the nearest degree.**

1. 37% _____

2. 61% _____

3. 26.5% _____

4. 7% _____

5. 19% _____

6. 85% _____

7. 46% _____

8. 54% _____

**Make a circle graph for each set of data.**

9. a monthly family budget

| Monthly Budget | |
|-------|--------|
| **Item** | **Amount** |
| Rent | $ 425 |
| Food | $ 150 |
| Clothes | $ 50 |
| Gas | $ 75 |
| Phone | $ 25 |
| Water | $ 35 |
| Other | $ 100 |

10. favorite sport to watch

| Favorite Sport to Watch | |
|-------|--------|
| **Sport** | **Votes** |
| Baseball | 255 |
| Football | 535 |
| Basketball | 593 |
| Soccer | 163 |
| Hockey | 176 |
| Wrestling | 261 |
| Other | 368 |

# Practice 10-6

**Use the circle graph for Exercises 1–2.**

1. From which group are about $\frac{1}{3}$ of used cars purchased?

   _____

2. If 49,778 people bought used cars one month, estimate how many bought them from a dealership.

   _____

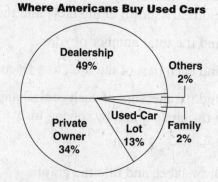

**Where Americans Buy Used Cars**

Dealership 49%
Others 2%
Used-Car Lot 13%
Family 2%
Private Owner 34%

**Make a circle graph for each set of data.**

3.

| Activity | Percent of Day |
|----------|----------------|
| Sleep | 25% |
| School | 25% |
| Job | 17% |
| Entertainment | 17% |
| Meals | 8% |
| Homework | 8% |

4.

| Favorite Pet | Percent |
|--------------|---------|
| Dogs | 30% |
| Cats | 25% |
| Fish | 12% |
| Birds | 11% |
| Other | 22% |

5.

| Type of Milk | Percent |
|--------------|---------|
| Skim | 27% |
| Lowfat | 37% |
| Whole | 36% |

6.

| Activity | Percent |
|----------|---------|
| Visiting w/Friends | 26% |
| Talk on Phone | 26% |
| Play Sports | 19% |
| Earn Money | 19% |
| Use Computers | 10% |

Name _____ Class _____ Date _____

# Reteaching 10-7

Bar graphs are useful for comparing sets of data.

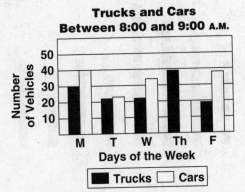

**Trucks and Cars Between 8:00 and 9:00 A.M.**

Line graphs and multiple line graphs show how data change over time. Line graphs help you see a trend.

**Sales**

Circle graphs help you see how a total is divided into parts. The parts may represent actual amounts or percents. If the parts represent percents, the entire circle is 100%.

**Sales Per State**

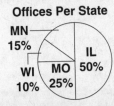

**Offices Per State**

---

**Decide which type of graph would be the most appropriate for the data: *circle graph*, *line graph*, *multiple line graph*, or *double bar graph*. Explain your choice.**

1. two classes' test scores over a school year

   _____

2. how a club spends its money

   _____

3. the numbers of boys and the numbers of girls who use the playground each day for one week

   _____

4. the percents of chemical elements in seawater

   _____

5. a company's profit

   _____

# Practice 10-7

**Use the graph to the right for Exercises 1 and 2.**

1. The bar graph shows the number of tickets a movie house sold each month last year. They want to look at last year's sales trend. Which type of graph would be more appropriate for the data?

   _____

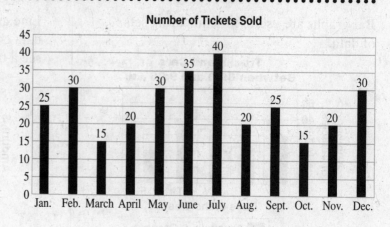

**Number of Tickets Sold**

2. Draw the graph.

**Decide which type of graph would be the most appropriate for the data. Explain your choice.**

3. sizes of U.S. farms from 1950 to 2000

   _____

4. lengths of rivers

   _____

5. height versus weight of students in a class

   _____

6. the way a family budgets its income

   _____

# Reteaching 10-8

*Example 1:* Carlos has classes in English, algebra, chemistry, track, and history. Otis has classes in business, English, history, tennis, and computer science. Which classes do both students attend?

**Read and Understand**   What do you know? *You know which classes each attends.*

**Plan and Solve**   You can use logical reasoning and a *Venn diagram.* Draw a rectangle. Draw circle *C* showing Carlos's classes. Draw circle *O* showing Otis's classes. The overlap shows the classes both boys attend.

**Look Back and Check**   Which classes do both attend? *Carlos and Otis both attend English and history classes.*

*Example 2:* Carlos asks 25 math/science students whether they are taking math or science. Twenty-two students take science classes. Fifteen take math classes. How many students take both math and science if each student takes at least 1 class?

**Read and Understand**   What do you know? *You know 25 students were surveyed; 22 take science and 15 take math.*

**Plan and Solve**   You can use logical reasoning and a Venn diagram. What number goes in the overlap? *12*

**Look Back and Check**   How can you check your answer? *There are 10 + 12 = 22 taking science, 12 + 3 = 15 taking math, and 10 + 12 + 3 = 25 students in all.*

---

**Solve each problem using logical reasoning.**

1. Phil's favorite sports are track, basketball, boxing, golf, and soccer. Jerry's favorite sports are boxing, baseball, football, bowling, and soccer. Which sports are favorites of both Phil and Jerry?

2. Barbara asks 18 friends who love to read whether they read fiction or non fiction. Twelve of her friends read fiction. Eleven of her friends read nonfiction. How many read both fiction and nonfiction?

3. Alice likes potatoes, sandwiches, fish, crackers, and steak. Rosie likes vegetables, rice, steak, chicken, and crackers. Which foods are liked by both Alice and Rosie?

4. Nine students like art only. Five students like music only. Twenty students were asked. How many liked both? Draw a Venn Diagram to solve.

Name _____  Class _____  Date _____

# Practice 10-8

Draw a Diagram and Use Logical Reasoning

**Solve each problem using logical reasoning to organize the information in a diagram.**

1. Place the factors of 32 and 24 in a Venn diagram. What are common factors of 32 and 24? What is the greatest common factor?

   _____

   | Factors |
   |---|
   | 32: 1, 2, 4, 8, 16, 32 |
   | 24: 1, 2, 3, 4, 6, 8, 12, 24 |

2. A favorite subject poll of 30 students shows that 18 like Math, 9 like History, and 10 like English. Three students like all three subjects, 3 like Math and History, 4 like Math and English, and 3 like only English. How many students did not like any class? _____

3. Twenty-six students were asked if they have a job or are in a club. Eighteen students have a job and 15 are in a club. Four students do neither. Place the information in a Venn Diagram. How many students have a job and are in a club? _____

4. A survey on favorite kinds of books shows that 9 people like mysteries, 10 like adventure stories, and 8 enjoy biographies. Three of the people read only mysteries and adventure stories, 4 read only adventure stories and biographies, 4 read only mysteries and 2 read all three kinds of books. How many people were surveyed? _____

**Choose a strategy or a combination of strategies to solve each problem.**

5. Maria plans to donate $3 in January, $4 in February, $6 in March, and $9 in April. If she continues this pattern, how much money will she donate in December? _____

6. Elena is building a fence around her rabbit hutch. She plans to put 8 posts along each side. The diameter of each post is 6 inches. How many posts will there be? _____

7. Alicia, Benito, Claudio, and Donna are musicians. One plays clarinet, one plays guitar, one is a pianist, and one is a singer. Alicia and Claudio saw the pianist perform. Benito and Claudio have heard the guitar player. The singer sang a song to Alicia and Donna. Benito plays the Clarinet. Who is the singer? _____

8. Laura is working on a jigsaw puzzle with 520 pieces. When she has placed four times as many pieces as she has already placed, she will have 184 pieces left. How many puzzle pieces has Laura placed? _____

Boilerplate All rights reserved. © Pearson Education, Inc., publishing as Pearson Prentice Hall.

# Reteaching 11-1

Andy has 3 pairs of pants: 1 gray, 1 blue, and 1 black. He has 2 shirts: 1 white and 1 red. If Andy picks 1 pair of pants and 1 shirt, how many different outfits does he have?

Andy can choose 1 of 3 pairs of pants and 1 of 2 shirts. A tree diagram can help you count his choices.

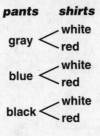

**pants    shirts**

gray &lt; white / red

blue &lt; white / red

black &lt; white / red

**3  ×  2  =  6 different outfits**

The total number of choices is the product of the number of choices for pants and the number of choices for shirts.

You can also use the *counting principle*.

$$n \quad \times \quad m \quad \text{gives} \quad n \times m$$

first choices      second choices      total choices

Andy has 6 different outfits.

---

**Find the total number of choices.**

1. Rich is trying to get from San Francisco to San Jose. He needs to stop in San Bruno on the way. There are 3 major roads or freeways from San Francisco to San Bruno and 3 major roads or freeways from San Bruno to San Jose. How many routes can Rich take?

   _____

2. Ralph wants to have soup and salad for lunch. There are 5 kinds of soup and 3 kinds of salad on the menu. He picks one of each. From how many possible combinations can he choose?

   _____

3. Carla has 4 hats and 4 scarves for winter weather. She picks one of each to wear. How many hat and scarf combinations are there?

   _____

4. Lorenzo is looking at 5 color markers and 4 types of paper. He picks one of each. How many choices of color and paper does he have?

   _____

5. Eric has 3 baseballs and 4 bats. From how many possible ball and bat combinations can he choose?

   _____

6. Ms. Wong is redecorating her office. She has a choice of 3 colors of paint, 4 kinds of curtains, and 4 colors of carpet. How many different ways are there to redecorate?

   _____

# Practice 11-1

**Draw a tree diagram to show all possibilities.**

1. Today, the school's cafeteria is offering a choice of pizza or spaghetti. You can get milk or juice to drink. For dessert you can get pudding or an apple. You must take one of each choice.

2. A clothing store sells shirts in three sizes: small, medium, and large. The shirts come with buttons or with snaps. The colors available are blue or beige.

**Use the counting principle for Exercises 3–8.**

3. A dinner menu at a restaurant offers 2 kinds of appetizers, 11 main courses, and 8 desserts. How many combinations of dinners are available?

   _____

4. A school assigns each student a 3-digit code number. How many possible 3-digit codes are there? What could cause the school to change to a 4-digit system?

   _____

   _____

5. A dress pattern offers two styles of skirts, three styles of sleeves, and four different collars. How many different types of dresses are available from one pattern?

   _____

6. In a class of 250 eighth graders, 14 are running for president, 12 are running for vice president, 9 are running for secretary, and 13 are running for treasurer. How many different results are possible for the class election?

   _____

7. A home alarm system has a 3-digit code that can be used to deactivate the system. If the homeowner forgets the code, how many different codes might the homeowner have to try?

   _____

8. A 4-letter password is required to enter a computer file. How many passwords are possible if no letter is repeated and nonsense words are allowed?

   _____

# Reteaching 11-2

The expression 5! is read "5 *factorial*." It means the product of all whole numbers from 5 to 1.

$5! = 5 \cdot 4 \cdot 3 \cdot 2 \cdot 1 = 120$

*Example 1:* Evaluate $\frac{5!}{3!}$.

Write the products, then simplify.

$\frac{5!}{3!} = \frac{5 \cdot 4 \cdot 3 \cdot 2 \cdot 1}{3 \cdot 2 \cdot 1} = 5 \cdot 4 = 20$

*Example 2:* How many 3-letter codes can be made from A, B, C, D, E, F, G, H with no repeating letters?

This is a *permutation* problem. Order is important. ABC is different from ACB.

- There are 8 choices for the first letter.

- There are 7 choices for the second letter.

- There are 6 choices for the third letter.

The number of codes possible = $8 \cdot 7 \cdot 6 = 336$.

You can write this as $_8P_3$, meaning the number of permutations of 8 objects chosen 3 at a time.

---

**Simplify each expression.**

1. 4! _____

2. 3! _____

3. $\frac{4!}{3!}$ _____

4. $\frac{10!}{8!}$ _____

5. $\frac{9!}{9!}$ _____

6. $5! \times 2!$ _____

**Simplify each expression.**

7. $_6P_3$ _____

8. $_5P_2$ _____

9. $_{12}P_3$ _____

10. $_4P_4$ _____

11. $_{15}P_2$ _____

12. $_6P_4$ _____

**Use the counting principle to find the number of permutations.**

13. In how many ways can you pick a football center and quarterback from 6 players who try out?

_____

14. For a meeting agenda, in how many ways can you schedule 3 speakers out of 10 people who would like to speak?

_____

# Practice 11-2

**Simplify each expression.**

**1.** 6!

**2.** 12!

**3.** 9!

**4.** $\frac{8!}{5!}$

**5.** $\frac{12!}{3!}$

_____  _____  _____  _____  _____

**6.** $_9P_5$

**7.** $_8P_2$

**8.** $_{10}P_8$

**9.** $_5P_5$

**10.** $_{15}P_6$

_____  _____  _____  _____  _____

**Use the counting principle to find the number of permutations.**

**11.** In how many ways can all the letters of the word WORK be arranged? _____

**12.** In how many ways can you arrange seven friends in a row for a photo? _____

**13.** A disk jockey can play eight songs in one time slot. In how many different orders can the eight songs be played?

_____

**14.** Melody has nine bowling trophies to arrange in a horizontal line on a shelf. How many arrangements are possible?

_____

**15.** At a track meet, 42 students entered the 100-m race. In how many ways can first, second, and third places be awarded?

_____

**16.** In how many ways can a president, a vice president, and a treasurer be chosen from a group of 15 people running for office?

_____

**17.** A car dealer has 38 used cars to sell. Each day two cars are chosen for advertising specials. One car appears in a television commercial and the other appears in a newspaper advertisement. In how many ways can the two cars be chosen?

_____

**18.** A bicycle rack outside a classroom has room for six bicycles. In the class, 10 students sometimes ride their bicycles to school. How many different arrangements of bicycles are possible for any given day?

_____

**19.** A certain type of luggage has room for three initials. How many different 3-letter arrangements of letters with no repetition of the same letter are possible?

_____

**20.** A roller coaster has room for 10 people. The people sit single file, one after the other. How many different arrangements are possible for 10 passengers on the roller coaster?

_____

# Reteaching 11-3

**Combustion**

Mr. Wisniewski wants to pick 2 students from Minh, Joan, Jim, Esperanza, and Tina to demonstrate an experiment. How many different pairs of students can he choose?

In this *combination* problem, the order of the choice of students does not matter. These are the possibilities:

Minh-Esperanza
Minh-Jim          Esperanza-Jim
Minh-Joan         Esperanza-Joan        Jim-Joan
Minh-Tina         Esperanza-Tina        Jim-Tina        Joan-Tina

There are 10 possible combinations.

The number of combinations of 5 students taken 2 at a time is $_5C_2$ where:

$$_5C_2 = \frac{1}{2!} \, _5P_2 = \frac{1}{2!} \cdot 5 \cdot 4 = 10$$

In general, the number of combinations of $n$ objects taken $r$ at a time is $_nC_r$ where:

$$_nC_r = \frac{1}{r!} \cdot _nP_r$$

**Simplify each expression.**

1. $_6C_3$ _____

2. $_5C_2$ _____

3. $_7C_5$ _____

4. $_4C_3$ _____

5. $_8C_2$ _____

6. $_6C_4$ _____

7. $_9C_4$ _____

8. $_5C_3$ _____

9. $_6C_5$ _____

10. $_7C_3$ _____

11. $_8C_3$ _____

12. $_9C_3$ _____

**Find the number of combinations.**

13. In how many ways can Susie choose 3 of 10 books to take with her on a trip?

_____

14. In how many ways can Rosa select 2 movies to rent out of 6 that she likes?

_____

15. In how many ways can Bill pick 2 of his 7 trophies to show his grandfather?

_____

16. In how many ways can Mr. Wu choose 5 tulip bulbs out of 15 to plant in a flower bed?

_____

17. In how many ways can a town name 5 citizens out of 10 to serve on a committee?

_____

18. In how many ways can Mrs. Harris pick 3 flowers from 8 for a bouquet?

_____

# Practice 11-3

**Simplify each expression.**

**1.** $_9C_1$ _____

**2.** $_8C_4$ _____

**3.** $_{11}C_4$ _____

**4.** $_{11}C_7$ _____

**5.** $_4C_4$ _____

**6.** $_9C_3$ _____

**7.** $_{12}C_6$ _____

**8.** $_8C_2$ _____

**9.** 3 videos from 10 _____

**10.** 2 letters from LOVE _____

**11.** 4 books from 8 _____

**12.** 5 people from 7 _____

**Solve.**

**13.** Ten students from a class have volunteered to be on a committee to organize a dance. In how many ways can six be chosen for the committee?

_____

**14.** Twenty-three people try out for extra parts in a play. In how many ways can eight people be chosen to be extras?

_____

**15.** A team of nine players is to be chosen from 15 available players. In how many ways can this be done?

_____

**16.** In a talent show, five semi-finalists are chosen from 46 entries. In how many ways can the semi-finalists be chosen?

_____

**17.** At a party there are 12 people present. The host requests that each person present shakes hands exactly once with every other person. How many handshakes are necessary?

_____

**18.** In math class there are 24 students. The teacher picks 4 students to serve on the bulletin board committee. How many different committees of 4 are possible?

_____

**19.** Five friends, Billi, Joe, Eduardo, Mari, and Xavier, want one photograph taken of each possible pair of friends. Use B, J, E, M, and X, and list all of the pairs that need to be photographed.

_____

**20.** A team of 3 people is chosen from 8 available players. Describe the number of possible teams using combination notation.

_____

# Reteaching 11-4

You can collect data through observations or experiments and use the data to state the *experimental probability*.

Alan has a coin. He tosses the coin 100 times and gets 60 heads and 40 tails. The experimental probability of getting heads is:

$$P(\text{heads}) = \frac{\text{number of heads}}{\text{number of trials}} = \frac{60}{100} = 0.6$$

Then Sarita calculated the *theoretical probability* of getting heads on one toss of the coin.

$$P(\text{heads}) = \frac{\text{favorable outcomes}}{\text{number of possible outcomes}} = \frac{1}{2} = 0.5$$

Alan thinks that his coin is unfair since the experimental probability is different from the theoretical probability.

Sarita suggests that they run the experiment again. This time they toss 53 heads and 47 tails. This suggests that the coin is more fair than Alan thinks. To form a more convincing conclusion, they should run the test several more times.

---

**Suppose you have a bag with 75 marbles: 15 red, 5 white, 25 green, 20 black, and 10 blue. You draw a marble, note its color, and then put it back. You do this 75 times with these results: 12 red, 9 white, 27 green, 17 black, and 10 blue. Find each probability as a fraction in simplest form.**

| | **1.** $P(\text{red})$ | **2.** $P(\text{white})$ | **3.** $P(\text{green})$ | **4.** $P(\text{black})$ | **5.** $P(\text{blue})$ |
|---|---|---|---|---|---|
| **Experimental Probability** | | | | | |
| **Theoretical Probability** | | | | | |

**Suppose you surveyed the students in your class on their favorite juice flavors. Their choices were 6 apple, 10 orange, 1 grapefruit, and 3 mango. Find each probability as a fraction in simplest form.**

**6.** $P(\text{apple})$       **7.** $P(\text{orange})$       **8.** $P(\text{grapefruit})$       **9.** $P(\text{not mango})$

_____       _____       _____       _____

# Practice 11-4

**Theoretical and Experimental Probability**

A dart is thrown at the game board shown. Notice that the diameters are at right angles and the slices that are congruent. Find each probability.

1. P(A) _____    2. P(B) _____    3. P(C) _____

4. P(not A) _____    5. P(not B) _____    6. P(not C) _____

**The odds in favor of winning a game are 5 to 9.**

7. Find the probability of winning the game. _____

8. Find the probability of *not* winning the game. _____

A box of marbles contains 10 red, 12 blue, 15 yellow, and 8 green marbles. A marble is drawn at random. Find each probability.

9. P(red) _____    10. P(blue) _____    11. P(yellow) _____    12. P(green) _____

13. What are the odds in favor of picking a blue marble?

_____

14. What are the odds in favor of picking a green marble?

_____

15. What is the probability of picking a marble that is not yellow?

_____

16. What is the probability of picking a marble that is not red?

_____

**Solve.**

17. a. You buy a ticket for the weekly drawing by a community charity. Last week you bought one ticket. Find the probability and odds of winning if 1,200 tickets were bought that week.

_____

b. Find the probability and odds of you winning if you bought three tickets and there were 1,200 tickets bought that week.

_____

18. A bakery's bread display case contains wheat and rye bread. If you randomly pick a slice of bread, P(wheat) = 0.45. Find P(rye). If there are 200 slices of bread, how many slices of wheat bread are in the display case?

_____

# Reteaching 11-5

There are 3 chips in a bag. You draw 2 chips from the bag.

*Experiment 1:* Draw one chip, put it back. Draw a chip again.

Draw 2 *is not* affected by draw 1.

Two events are *independent* when the outcome of the second *is not* affected by the outcome of the first.

If $A$ and $B$ are independent events,
$$P(A, \text{then } B) = P(A) \times P(B)$$

Suppose 2 chips in the bag are red and 1 chip is blue. You draw 1 chip and then put it back before drawing a second chip. Find the probability that the chip color in both draws is red.

$$\begin{aligned} P(\text{red, then red}) &= P(\text{red}) \times P(\text{red}) \\ &= \frac{2}{3} \times \frac{2}{3} \\ &= \frac{4}{9} \end{aligned}$$

*Experiment 2:* Draw one chip. Then, draw another without replacing the first.

Draw 2 *is* affected by draw 1.

Two events are *dependent* when the outcome of the second *is* affected by the outcome of the first.

If $A$ and $B$ are independent events,
$$P(A, \text{then } B) = P(A) \times P(B \text{ after } A).$$

Suppose 2 chips in the bag are red and 1 chip is blue. You draw 1 chip and then another without putting the first chip back. Find the probability that both chips are red.

$$\begin{aligned} P(\text{red, then red}) \\ &= P(\text{red}) \times P(\text{red after red}) \\ &= \frac{2}{3} \times \frac{1}{2} = \frac{2}{6} = \frac{1}{3} \end{aligned}$$

---

**A store has 3 cans of green paint, 3 cans of blue paint, and 2 cans of yellow paint. You randomly choose one can of paint and then replace it. Then you choose a second can of paint. Find each probability.**

**1.** $P(\text{green, then yellow})$       **2.** $P(\text{green, then blue})$       **3.** $P(\text{both yellow})$

_____       _____       _____

**A jar has 3 pennies, 4 nickels, and 2 dimes. You pick one coin and then pick another without replacing the first coin. Find each probability.**

**4.** $P(\text{nickel, then dime})$       **5.** $P(\text{penny, then nickel})$       **6.** $P(\text{dime, then penny})$

_____       _____       _____

**State whether the events are dependent or independent.**

**7.** Flipping a coin twice

_____

**8.** Choosing a hammer and a paint color in a hardware store

_____

**9.** Selecting a can of corn and a container of juice in a supermarket

_____

**10.** Picking a board from a pile, nailing it on a fence, then picking another board from the pile

_____

# Practice 11-5

**A drawer contains 3 black and 2 white socks. A sock is drawn at random and then replaced. Find each probability.**

1. $P$(2 blacks)       2. $P$(black and white)       3. $P$(white and black)       4. $P$(2 whites)

_____ _____ _____ _____

**Each letter from the word MASSACHUSETTS is written on a separate slip of paper. The 13 slips of paper are placed in a sack and two slips are drawn at random. The first pick is not replaced.**

5. Find the probability that the first letter is M and the second letter is S. _____

6. Find the probability that the first letter is S and the second letter is A. _____

7. Find the probability that the first letter is S and the second letter is also S. _____

**Solve.**

8. On a TV game show, you can win a car by drawing a 1 and a 15 from a stack of cards numbered 1–15. The first card is not replaced. What is your probability of winning?

9. You roll a number cube eight times, and each time you roll a 4. What is the theoretical probability that on the ninth roll, you will roll a 6? Is rolling a 6 dependent or independent of rolling a 4 eight times?

_____

10. Two letters of the alphabet are chosen randomly without replacement. Find each probability.

   a. $P$(both vowels) _____

   b. $P$(both consonants) _____

11. There are 4 brown shoes and 10 black shoes on the floor. Your puppy carries away two shoes and puts one shoe in the trash can and one shoe in the laundry basket.

   a. Complete the tree diagram to show the probability of each outcome.

   b. What is the probability that there will be a brown shoe in both the trash and the laundry basket?

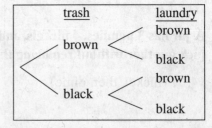

   _____

12. Use the data at the right to find $P$(right-handed female and left-handed male) if two people are chosen at random.

_____

|  | Male | Female |
|---|---|---|
| Right-handed | 86 | 83 |
| Left-handed | 14 | 17 |
| Total | 100 | 100 |

# Reteaching 11-6   Problem Solving: Make an Organized List and Simulate a Problem

You can use simulation to estimate solutions to probability problems.

A juice company puts one of the five letters, L, E, M, O, and N, inside the bottle cap. The letters are equally distributed among the caps. If you collect all five letters, you get a bottle of juice at half price. Estimate how many bottles you need to buy to collect all five letters.

| | |
|---|---|
| **Read and Understand** | What do you want to find? *You want to find how many bottles of juice you need to buy to collect all five letters.* |
| **Plan and Solve** | Instead of actually buying bottles of juice, develop a simulation. You can use a five-part spinner. Spin until you get all five letters. Keep track of your results.<br><br>Show the results of the simulation in a list. You spun the spinner 7 times before you got all five letters. So you estimate that you would have to buy 7 bottles of juice to collect all five letters. |
| **Look Back and Check** | Would you get the same result if you repeat the simulation? |

**Spins**

**M L M O E L N**

---

**Solve each problem by making an organized list or by simulating the problem. Describe your method.**

1. There is one of ten team cards inside a box of cereal. The teams are equally distributed among the boxes. Estimate how many boxes of cereal you need to purchase to collect all ten teams.

   _____

   _____

   _____

2. There is one of five shapes on the inner wrapper of each granola bar. The symbols are equally distributed among the wrappers. Estimate how many bars you need to buy to collect all five shapes and win a free bar.

   _____

   _____

   _____

3. A gas station gives away one of eight drinking glasses each time you buy a tank of gas. There is an equal chance of getting any one of the glasses. Estimate how many tanks you will have to buy to get all eight glasses.

   _____

   _____

   _____

4. A store prints one of 12 different symbols on each receipt. Collect all 12 and you get a 10% discount on your next purchase. Symbols are equally placed among the receipts. Estimate how many receipts you would have to get to collect all 12 symbols.

   _____

   _____

   _____

# Practice 11-6

**Problem Solving: Make an Organized List and Simulate a Problem**

**Solve by making an organized list or by simulating the problem.**

1. The probability of a newborn puppy being either a male or female is $\frac{1}{2}$. What is the probability that a litter of 4 puppies contains 3 females?

   _____

2. In a mixed-badminton tournament, each team consists of one boy and one girl. Three boys and three girls signed up for the tournament. How many different badminton games can be played with different mixed-doubles teams?

   _____

**The Coast Guard reports that the probability for calm water each day for the next few days is 50%. You begin a three-day sailing trip.**

3. Simulate the situation to find the probability of three days of calm water in a row.

   _____

4. Simulate the situation to find the probability of only two days of calm water out of the three.

   _____

5. Simulate the situation to find the probability of only one day of calm water out of the three.

   _____

6. Simulate the situation to find the probability of no calm water for any of the three days.

   _____

**A soccer player scores a goal on about 1 out of every 6 shots.**

7. Explain how you could use a number cube to simulate the player's scoring average.

   _____

8. Use your simulation to find the probability of the player making 4 out of 5 of her next attempts.

   _____

# Reteaching 11-7

In a survey, the entire group is called the *population*.
A *sample* is a small part of the population.

For a sample to be fair, it should be *random*. In a random sample, each member of the population has an equal chance of being selected.

- Samples can be either systematic or stratified.

  In a *systematic sample*, members are selected using randomness.

  In a *stratified sample*, members are grouped by similar characteristics.

- Survey questions should be fair, not *biased*. They should not make one answer appear better than another.

  *Biased question:* Did you hate that movie as much as I did?

  *Fair question:* What did you think of that movie?

---

**Suppose you want to find out how students feel about new school colors. Tell whether each survey plan describes a good sample. Justify your answer.**

1. You interview students while they are in art class.

   _____

   _____

   _____

2. You randomly select students from each homeroom in the school.

   _____

   _____

   _____

**Describe each sample as systematic or stratified.**

3. You ask 25 people coming out of 3 different types of movies if they enjoy the movie.

   _____

4. You pick 5 names from a hat and ask those people their favorite food.

   _____

**Explain why each question is biased.**

5. Don't you agree that Mrs. Meredith expects too much of her students?

   _____

   _____

6. Were you able to follow that boring movie?

   _____

   _____

# Practice 11-7

1. What population does the sample represent?

    _____

    _____

**In a mall, 2,146 shoppers (age 16 and older) were asked, "How often do you eat at a restaurant in the mall?" Here is how they responded.**

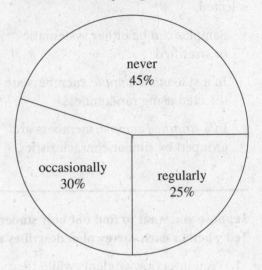

2. How many people responded in each of the categories?

    _____

    _____

3. What is the sample size?

    _____

4. Can you tell if the sample is random?

    _____

5. What type of sampling is used?

    _____

**Explain why the survey questions in Exercises 6 and 7 are biased.**

6. Would you rather buy the TV dinner with a picture of a luscious, gourmet meal on it, or one in a plain package?

    _____

    _____

7. Do you want your kids to receive a faulty education by having their school day shortened?

    _____

    _____

8. A researcher wants to find out what brand of tomato sauce is most popular with people who work full-time. He samples shoppers at a supermarket between 10 A.M. and 2 P.M. Is this a good sample? Explain.

    _____

    _____

9. You decide to run for student council. What factors are important to consider if you decide to survey your fellow students?

    _____

    _____

    _____

# Reteaching 12-1

A *sequence* is a set of numbers that follows a pattern.

In an *arithmetic sequence,* each term is found by *adding* a fixed number to the previous term. The number that you add is called the *common difference.*

In a *geometric sequence,* each term is found by *multiplying* the previous term by a fixed number. The number that you multiply by is called the *common ratio.*

*Example 1:* Find the next three terms in the arithmetic sequence: $8, 5, 2, -1, -4, \ldots$

- The common difference is $5 - 8 = -3$.

- Add $-3$ for the next three terms.

  $-4 + (-3) = -7$
  $-7 + (-3) = -10$
  $-10 + (-3) = -13$

The next three terms are $-7, -10,$ and $-13$.

*Example 2:* Find the next three terms in the geometric sequence: $2, 6, 18, 54, \ldots$

- The common ratio is $\frac{18}{6} = 3$.

- Multiply by 3 for the next three terms.

  $54 \times 3 = 162$
  $162 \times 3 = 486$
  $486 \times 3 = 1{,}458$

The next three terms are $162, 468,$ and $1{,}458$.

The sequence: $1, 4, 9, 16, \ldots$ is neither arithmetic nor geometric.

Its pattern is $1^2, 2^2, 3^2, 4^2, \ldots$

Its next three terms are $5^2, 6^2, 7^2,$ or $25, 36, 49$.

---

**Find the common difference or ratio in each sequence.**

**1.** $2, 6, 10, 14, \ldots$

**2.** $30, 20, 10, 0, \ldots$

**3.** $-12, -4, 4, 12, \ldots$

_____

_____

_____

**4.** $6, 12, 24, 48, \ldots$

**5.** $1, \frac{1}{3}, \frac{1}{9}, \frac{1}{27}$

**6.** $250, 25, 2.5, 0.25, \ldots$

_____

_____

_____

**Identify each sequence as *arithmetic, geometric,* or *neither.* Find the next three terms of the sequence.**

**7.** $4, 2, 1, \frac{1}{2} \ldots$

**8.** $0.2, 0.4, 0.6, 0.8, \ldots$

_____

_____

**9.** $1, \frac{1}{4}, \frac{1}{9}, \frac{1}{16}$

**10.** $70, 50, 30, 10, \ldots$

_____

_____

**11.** $1, 2, 1, 2, 1, 2, \ldots$

**12.** $4, 8, 16, 32, \ldots$

_____

_____

# Practice 12-1

**Write the rule for each sequence and find the next three terms.**

**1.** 3, 8, 13, 18, ____ , ____ , ____

_____

**2.** 7, 14, 28, 56, ____ , ____ , ____

_____

**3.** 32, 8, 2, $\frac{1}{2}$, ____ , ____ , ____

_____

**4.** 14, 11, 8, 5, ____ , ____ , ____

_____

**5.** 35, 23, 11, −1, _____ , _____ , _____

_____

**6.** 3,000, 300, 30, 3, _____ , _____ , _____

_____

**Find the next three terms in each sequence. Identify each as arithmetic, geometric, or neither. For each arithmetic or geometric sequence, find the common difference or ratio.**

**7.** 7.1, 7.5, 7.9, 8.3, ____ , ____ , ____

_____

**8.** 5, 6, 8, 11, 15, 20, ____ , ____ , ____

_____

**9.** 8,000; 4,000; 2,000; 1,000; ____ ; ____ ; ____

_____

**10.** 92, 89, 86, 83, ____ , ____ , ____

_____

**11.** −1, 2, −4, 8, ____ , ____ , ____

_____

**12.** 2.3, 2.03, 2.003, 2.0003, ____ , ____ , ____

_____

**13.** 1, 3, 6, 8, 16, 18, 36, ____ , ____ , ____

_____

**14.** 140, 133, 126, 119, ____ , ____ , ____

_____

**15.** 3, 9, 27, 81, ____ , ____ , ____

_____

**16.** 540, 270, 90, 22.5, ____ , ____ , ____

_____

**Tell whether each situation produces an *arithmetic sequence*, *geometric sequence*, or *neither*.**

**17.** The temperature rises at the rate of 0.75°F per hour. _____

**18.** A person loses 2 lb each month. _____

**19.** A toadstool doubles in size each week. _____

**20.** A person receives a 6% raise each year. _____

**Find the first four terms of the sequence represented by each expression.**

**21.** $4 \cdot 3^{n+1}$

_____

**22.** $4 + 3(n-2)$

_____

**23.** $n^2(n-1)$

_____

# Reteaching 12-2

A *function* describes the relationship between two variables called the *input* and the *output*. In a function, each input value has only one output value.

Function:

$$y = 2x + 4$$

$\uparrow \quad \uparrow$

*output variable y*    *input variable x*

You can list input/output pairs in a table.

$y = 2x + 4$

| Input *x* | Output *y* |
|-----------|------------|
| −10 | −16 |
| −5 | −6 |
| 0 | 4 |
| 1 | 6 |

To find output *y*, substitute values for input *x* into the function equation.

For $x = -10$:  $y = 2(-10) + 4$
$\qquad\qquad\qquad y = -16$

You can also show input/output pairs using *function notation*.

Function rule:

$$f(x) = 2x + 4$$
$$f(-10) = 2(-10) + 4 = -16$$

$\qquad \uparrow \qquad\qquad\qquad\qquad \uparrow$

*input* $\qquad\qquad\qquad$ *output*

Find $f(0)$.

$$f(0) = 2(0) + 4$$
$$f(0) = 4$$

---

**Complete the table of input/output pairs for each function.**

**1.** $y = 3x$

| Input *x* | Output *y* |
|-----------|------------|
| 5 | |
| 7 | |
| 9 | |
| 11 | |

**2.** $d = 20r$

| Input *r* | Output *d* |
|-----------|------------|
| 1 | |
| 2 | |
| 3 | |
| | 160 |

**3.** $y = 25 - 2x$

| Input *x* | Output *y* |
|-----------|------------|
| 0 | |
| 1 | |
| | 21 |
| | 19 |

**Use the function rule $f(x) = 3x + 1$. Find each output.**

**4.** $f(0)$

$= 3(\underline{\phantom{xxx}}) + 1$

$= \underline{\phantom{xxxx}}$

**5.** $f(1)$

$= 3(\underline{\phantom{xxx}}) + 1$

$= \underline{\phantom{xxxx}}$

**6.** $f(2)$

$= 3(\underline{\phantom{xxx}}) + 1$

$= \underline{\phantom{xxxx}}$

**7.** $f(-2)$

$= 3(\underline{\phantom{xxx}}) + 1$

$= \underline{\phantom{xxxx}}$

**8.** $f(5)$

**9.** $f(-6)$

**10.** $f(10)$

**11.** $f(5.5)$

# Practice 12-2

**Complete the table of input/output pairs for each function.**

**1.** $y = 3x$

| Input x | Output y |
|---------|----------|
| 4 | |
| 8 | |
| 12 | |
| 16 | |

**2.** $z = 15n$

| Input n | Output z |
|---------|----------|
| 1 | |
| 2 | |
| 3 | |
| | 60 |

**3.** $d = 30 - s$

| Input s | Output d |
|---------|----------|
| 0 | |
| 5 | |
| | 20 |
| | 15 |

**4.** $h = 120 \div g$

| Input g | Output h |
|---------|----------|
| 2 | |
| 6 | |
| | 10 |
| 15 | |

**5.** $r = 2t - 1$

| Input t | Output r |
|---------|----------|
| 3 | |
| 9 | |
| 20 | |
| | 99 |

**6.** $p = 2v - 12$

| Input v | Output p |
|---------|----------|
| | 6 |
| | 40 |
| 43 | |
| 75 | |

**Does each situation represent a function? Explain.**

**7.** Input:     the distance that needs to be biked

    Output:  the time it takes if you bike at 5 mi/h

_____

**8.** Input:     the time of day you go to the grocery store

    Output:  the cost of the groceries

_____

**9.** Input:     the number of copies of a book

    Output:  the total cost of the books

_____

**10.** Input:     a T-shirt color

    Output:  the T-shirt cost

_____

**Use the function rule $f(x) = 5x + 1$. Find each output.**

**11.** $f(3)$

**12.** $f(-6)$

**13.** $f(8)$

**14.** $f(-2)$

_____  _____  _____  _____

**15.** $f(1.5)$

**16.** $f(25)$

**17.** $f(30)$

**18.** $f(100)$

_____  _____  _____  _____

**Use the function rule $f(x) = 4n^2 - 1$. Find each output.**

**19.** $f(0)$

**20.** $f(1)$

**21.** $f(-1)$

**22.** $f(2)$

_____  _____  _____  _____

**23.** $f(-2)$

**24.** $f(3)$

**25.** $f(2.5)$

**26.** $f(5)$

_____  _____  _____  _____

# Reteaching 12-3

You can graph a function in the coordinate plane. To plot points for the graph, use *input* as *x*-values (*x*-axis) and *output* as *y*-values (*y*-axis).

*output as y-values*      *input as x-values*

↓          ↓

$$y = 2x + 4$$

This function has the form of a linear equation and is called a *linear function*. To draw its graph, use

slope and *y*-intercept:

$$y = 2x + 4$$
$$\text{slope} = 2$$
$$y\text{-intercept} = 4$$

*or*

a table of input/output pairs.

| x | y |
|---|---|
| 0 | 4 |
| 1 | 6 |
| 2 | 8 |

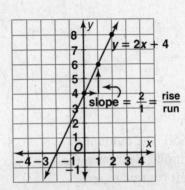

---

**Graph each linear function.**

**1.** $y = 3x$

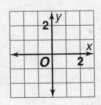

**2.** $y = 2x - 2$

**3.** $y = \frac{1}{2}x + 1$

**4.** $y = 2 - x$

# Practice 12-3

**Graphing Linear Functions**

**Make a table of input/output pairs for each function. Then graph the function. Show only the portion that makes sense for each situation.**

**1.** On a trip Alex averages 300 mi/day. The distance he covers (output) is a function of the number of days (input).

| Input | | | | |
|---|---|---|---|---|
| Output | | | | |

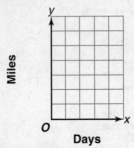

**2.** Suppose you earn $7 per hour. The number of hours you work (input) determines your pay (output).

| Input | | | | |
|---|---|---|---|---|
| Output | | | | |

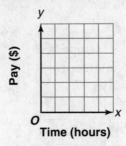

**3.** Suppose you have $50. The amount of money you spend (input) decreases the amount you have left (output).

| Input | | | | |
|---|---|---|---|---|
| Output | | | | |

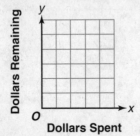

**4.** You have $10.00. Each week you save $2.50. The number of weeks you save (input) increases your savings (output).

| Input | | | | |
|---|---|---|---|---|
| Output | | | | |

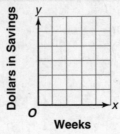

**Graph each linear function.**

**5.** $f(x) = -x + 4$

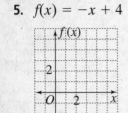

**6.** $f(x) = \frac{2}{3}x + 1$

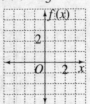

**7.** $f(x) = -2x + 1$

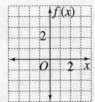

**8.** $y = -\frac{1}{2}x + 3$

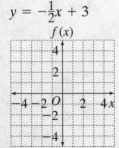

**9.** $y = -2 - 3x$

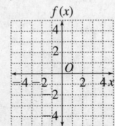

**10.** $y = 5 - 0.2x$

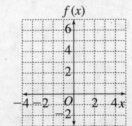

# Reteaching 12-4

Sometimes you can write a function rule to describe a situation.

Cookies at a bazaar sell for $2 each. The booth costs $25 to rent for the day. The profit depends on how many cookies are sold.

Words:          Profit = 2 × (number of cookies sold) − $25

Function rule:   $y = 2x - 25$

The output $y$ is the profit.

The input $x$ is the number of cookies sold.

You can use the graph of a linear function to write its function rule. First, you need to find the slope and the $y$-intercept.

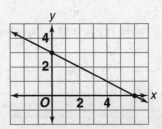

① From the graph, the slope ($m$) is $-\frac{1}{2}$.

② The point $(0, 3)$ is on the graph so the $y$-intercept ($b$) is 3.

③ Substitute in the slope-intercept form.

$$y = mx + b$$

$$y = -\frac{1}{2}x + 3$$

The function rule is $y = -\frac{1}{2}x + 3$.

---

**Write a function rule for each situation. Identify the input and output variables.**

1. A person burns 350 calories for every hour of bicycling. The number of calories burned is a function of the number of hours spent bicycling.

2. Janice earns $150 a week plus a commission of $3 for every magazine she sells. Her total pay depends on how many magazines she sells.

_____        _____

_____        _____

**Identify the slope and $y$-intercept of each graph. Then write a linear function rule.**

3.
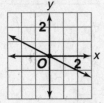

4.
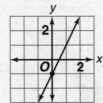

5.
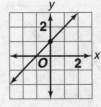

_____        _____        _____

_____        _____        _____

# Practice 12-4

**Write a linear function rule for each situation. Identify the input and output variables.**

1. Amy sells tote bags at a craft fair for a day. She pays $50 to rent a booth. The materials and labor cost on each tote bag is $3.50. Her expenses for the day depend on how many tote bags she sells.

   _____

2. Ms. Watson receives a base pay of $150, plus a commission of $45 on each appliance that she sells. Her total pay depends on how many appliances she sells.

   _____

**Does the data in each table represent a linear function? If so, write the function rule.**

3.

| Input | 0 | 1 | 2 | 3 | 4 |
|-------|---|---|---|----|----|
| Output | 2 | 5 | 8 | 11 | 14 |

   _____

4.

| Input | 0 | 1 | 2 | 3 | 4 |
|-------|---|---|---|---|---|
| Output | 0 | 2 | 5 | 2 | 0 |

   _____

5.

| Input | −2 | 0 | 4 | 6 | 8 |
|-------|----|---|---|---|---|
| Output | −1 | −3 | −7 | −9 | −11 |

6.

| Input | −3 | −2 | −1 | 0 | 1 |
|-------|----|----|----|---|---|
| Output | −1 | 1 | 2 | 2 | 2 |

**Use the slope and *y*-intercept to write a linear function rule for each graph.**

7.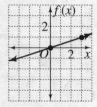

   _____

8.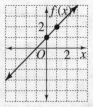

   _____

9.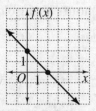

   _____

10.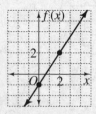

   _____

11.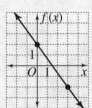

   _____

12.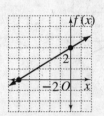

   _____

# Reteaching 12-5

The graph at the right shows the outside temperature during 16 hours of one day.

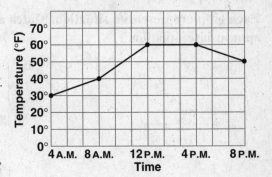

- You can see how the temperature changed throughout the day. *The temperature rose 10°F from 4 A.M. to 8 A.M. The temperature remained at 60°F for 4 hours, from 12 P.M. to 4 P.M.*

- You can also compare the temperatures throughout the day. *The temperature at 8 P.M. was 20° higher than it was at 4 A.M.*

The graph at the right shows a train moving between stations. *The train moves slowly while leaving the station. Then it picks up speed until it reaches a cruising speed. It slows down as it approaches the next station and gradually comes to a stop.*

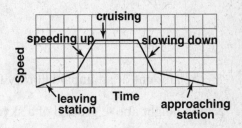

- Since the graph is *sketched* to show relationships, the axes do not need number scales. But the axes and the parts of the graph should have labels to show what they represent.

**The graph at the right shows the altitude of an airplane during a flight. Use the graph for Exercises 1–3.**

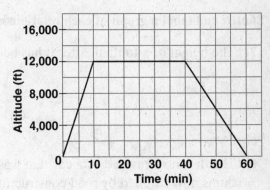

1. What was the airplane's altitude for most of the flight?

   _____

2. How long did it take the airplane to reach an altitude of 12,000 ft?

   _____

3. The third segment in the graph is not as steep as the first segment. What does this mean?

   _____

   _____

**Sketch and label a graph of the relationship.**

4. You enter the freeway in your car, constantly accelerating until you are on the freeway. Then you turn the cruise control on and drive at a constant speed. When you reach your exit you slow down as you exit the freeway until you stop at the stop light.

# Practice 12-5

**Each graph represents a situation. Match a graph with the appropriate situation.**

a.

Time

b.

Time

c.

Time

d.

Time

e.

Time

f.

Time

1. the amount of an unpaid library fine. _____

2. the height above ground of a skydiver during a dive. _____

3. one's adrenaline flow when receiving a fright. _____

4. the temperature of the air during a 24-h period beginning at 9:00 A.M. _____

5. oven temperature for baking cookies. _____

6. elevator ride up with stops. _____

**Sketch and label a graph of each relationship.**

7. The height of a football after it has been kicked

8. The distance traveled by a car that was driving 50 mi/h, but is now stopped by road construction

9. The function table at the right shows the distance in feet that an object falls over time.

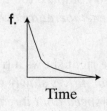

| Time (s) | Distance (ft) |
|----------|---------------|
| 1        | 16            |
| 2        | 64            |
| 3        | 144           |
| 4        | 256           |

# Reteaching 12-6

When a function rule is based on squaring the input variable, it is a *quadratic function*. Study the table.

The graph of a quadratic function is a ∪-shaped curve called a *parabola*. You can make a table of values to help you draw the graph.

*Example 1:* Graph $y = 2x^2 - 3$

| x | $2x^2 - 3 = y$ |
|----|----|
| −2 | $2(-2)^2 - 3 = 5$ |
| −1 | $2(-1)^2 - 3 = -1$ |
| 0 | $2(0)^2 - 3 = -3$ |
| 1 | $2(1)^2 - 3 = -1$ |
| 2 | $2(2)^2 - 3 = 5$ |

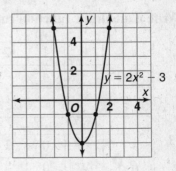

A nonlinear function has a graph that is not straight.

To graph a nonlinear function

① Make a table of values.

② Plot the points from the table.

③ Draw the graph to contain the points following the pattern suggested by the points.

*Example 2:* Graph $y = \frac{16}{x} + 1$ for positive values of *x*.

| x | $\frac{16}{x} + 1 = y$ |
|----|----|
| 1 | $\frac{16}{1} + 1 = 16 + 1 = 17$ |
| 2 | $\frac{16}{2} + 1 = 8 + 1 = 9$ |
| 4 | $\frac{16}{4} + 1 = 4 + 1 = 5$ |
| 8 | $\frac{16}{8} + 1 = 2 + 1 = 3$ |
| 16 | $\frac{16}{16} + 1 = 1 + 1 = 2$ |

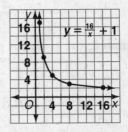

**Write a quadratic function rule for the data in each table.**

**1.**

| x | 0 | 1 | 2 | 3 | 4 |
|----|----|----|----|----|----|
| y | 4 | 5 | 8 | 13 | 20 |

_____

**2.**

| x | 0 | 1 | 2 | 3 | 4 |
|----|----|----|----|----|----|
| y | −1 | 0 | 3 | 8 | 15 |

_____

**Complete the table for each function. Then graph the function.**

**3.** $y = 2x^2 - 1$

| x | $2x^2 - 1 = y$ |
|----|----|
| −2 | |
| −1 | |
| 0 | |
| 1 | |
| 2 | |

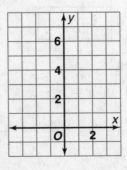

**4.** $y = 3^x - 5$

| x | $3^x - 5 = y$ |
|----|----|
| 1 | |
| 2 | |
| 3 | |

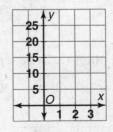

# Practice 12-6

**Write a quadratic function rule for the data in each table.**

**1.**

| x | 0 | 1 | 2 | 3 | 4 |
|---|---|---|---|---|---|
| f(x) | 3 | 4 | 7 | 12 | 19 |

**2.**

| x | −2 | −1 | 0 | 1 | 2 |
|---|---|---|---|---|---|
| f(x) | −8 | −2 | 0 | −2 | −8 |

**3.**

| x | −1 | 0 | 1 | 2 | 3 |
|---|---|---|---|---|---|
| f(x) | 4 | 0 | 4 | 16 | 36 |

**4.**

| x | −10 | −5 | 0 | 5 | 10 |
|---|---|---|---|---|---|
| f(x) | 95 | 20 | −5 | 20 | 95 |

**Complete the table for each function. Then graph the function.**

**5.** $f(x) = x^2 + 1$

| x | $x^2 + 1 = f(x)$ |
|---|---|
| −3 | |
| −2 | |
| −1 | |
| 0 | |
| 1 | |
| 2 | |
| 3 | |

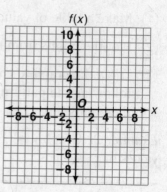

**6.** $f(x) = 4 - x^2$

| x | $4 - x^2 = f(x)$ |
|---|---|
| −3 | |
| −2 | |
| −1 | |
| 0 | |
| 1 | |
| 2 | |
| 3 | |

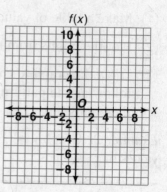

**7.** $f(x) = \frac{20}{x}$

| x | f(x) |
|---|---|
| 2 | |
| 4 | |
| 5 | |
| 10 | |

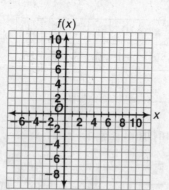

**8.** $f(x) = 2^x - 1$

| x | f(x) |
|---|---|
| −1 | |
| 0 | |
| 1 | |
| 2 | |
| 3 | |

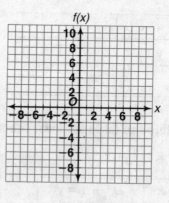

**Does the point (2, 2) lie on the graph of each function?**

**9.** $f(x) = 2x - 2$

**10.** $f(x) = \left(\frac{1}{2}\right)^x$

**11.** $f(x) = x^2 - x$

**12.** $f(x) = \frac{4}{x}$

# Reteaching 12-7

You can write equations to solve many types of problems.

**Read and Understand**     A bacteria culture starts with 5 cells. The
number of cells doubles every day. Write a
function rule that relates the number of
bacteria cells in the culture to the amount of
time that has passed. Use the rule to find the
number of cells there are in the culture after
12 days.

What are you asked to do?     *Write a function rule that relates bacteria cells
to the amount of time that has passed.*

| Day | Cells |
|-----|-------|
| 1   | 5     |
| 2   | 10    |
| 3   | 20    |
| 4   | 40    |

**Plan and Solve**     Start by making a table that shows the first few
days and the number of cells per day.

Notice that each output is equal to 5 times 2 raised to the power of the
input. So, the number of cells is 5 times 2 raised to the number of days.
Let $d$ = the number of days that have passed. Let $y$ = the number of
bacteria cells.

Function:     $y = 5 \cdot 2^d$

Evaluate the function rule to find how many cells there are after 12 days.

$$y = 5 \cdot 2^{12}$$
$$= 5 \cdot 4,096$$
$$= 20,480$$

**Look Back and Check**     How could you check your answer? *You can
solve a simpler problem to check the function
rule. Extend the table for 5 and 6 days and then
evaluate the rule for these times.*

---

**Solve each problem by writing a function rule.**

1. Suppose you save $30 this year. You plan to double the amount
   you save each year. Write a function rule that relates the amount
   you save in a given year to the number of years that have passed.
   Use the rule to find out how much you will save after the sixth
   year and after the eighth year.

   _____

2. A population of 10 rabbits is released into a wildlife refuge. The
   population triples each year. Write a function rule that relates the
   population of the rabbits to the number of years that have
   passed. Use the rule to find out how many rabbits will be in the
   refuge after 5 years.

   _____

# Practice 12-7

**Problem Solving: Write an Equation**

**Use any strategy to solve each problem. Show your work.**

1. A population of 30 mice is released into a wildlife region. The population triples each year. Write a function rule that relates the number of mice to the amount of time that has passed. Use the rule to find the number of mice after 4 years and 8 years.

   _____

2. You bought a used car for $6,000. The value of the car will decrease 12% per year. So each year the car is 88% of the previous year's value. Write a function rule that relates the value of the car to the years that have passed. Use the rule to find the value of the car after 6 years.

   _____

3. The sum of two integers is −44. Their difference is 8. What are the two integers?

   _____

4. Margot earns $225 per week plus a commission of 2% on each appliance that she sells. Write a function rule that relates Margot's pay to the number of appliances that she sells. Use the rule to find her pay for a week in which she has sales of $15,234.

   _____

5. The cost of an international long distance phone call is $6.25 for the first minute and $3.75 for each additional minute. What was the total length of a call that cost $28.75?

   _____

6. A garden supply shop sells bags of topsoil. The bags come in six sizes: 16, 17, 23, 24, 39, and 40 pounds. The shop will not open or split bags. A greenhouse asks for 100 pounds of topsoil. Can the order be filled with bags in the sizes available? If not, how close can the supply shop come to filling the order?

   _____

# Reteaching 12-8

Algebra tiles:

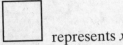 represents $x^2$,   represents $x$,   represents 1,

represents $-x^2$,   represents $-x$,   represents $-1$.

You can use the algebra tiles to model variable expressions.

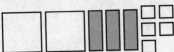 is a model for $2x^2 - 3x + 5$.

The expression $2x^2 - 3x + 5$ is a *polynomial*.
To simplify a polynomial, combine like terms.

*Example:* Simplify $2x^2 - 3x + 5 + 2x$.

$$2x^2 - 3x + 5 + 2x$$
$$= 2x^2 - 3x + 2x + 5$$
↑
*Use the Commutative Property*
$$= 2x^2 - x + 5$$

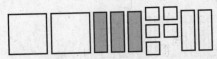

Group tiles of the same size together.
Remove zero pairs.

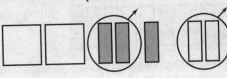

---

**Write a variable expression for each model.**

1.

_____

2.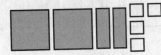

_____

3.

_____

4.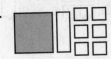

_____

**Simplify each polynomial.**

5. $x^2 - 2x^2 - 5x - 1 + 4$

6. $3x^2 + 2x^2 + 4x - 5x - 1$

7. $x^2 + x^2 - x - 1 + 5$

8. $3x^2 - x - x^2 + 6x + 2$

9. $4x^2 - 2x + 6x - 2$

10. $x^2 - 3x + 2x^2 - x$

# Practice 12-8

**Exploring Polynomials**

**In Exercises 1–5:**

 represents $x^2$, ⬜ represents $x$, ☐ represents 1,

⬛ represents $-x^2$, ▮ represents $-x$, ▪ represents $-1$.

**Write a variable expression for each model.**

1.

_____

2.

_____

3.

_____

**Write and simplify the polynomials represented by each model.**

4.

_____

5.

_____

**Simplify each polynomial.**

6. $2x^2 - x^2 + 7x - 2x + 5$

_____

7. $3x^2 + 2x - 8x + 6$

_____

8. $x^2 - 4x^2 + x + 5x - 8 + 3$

_____

9. $x^2 + 6x + x^2 - 4x + 1 - 5$

_____

10. $3x^2 + 2x + 3x + 3 - 1$

_____

11. $x^2 + 3x^2 + 3x - 9 + 2x$

_____

# Reteaching 12-9

To add polynomials, combine like terms. Add the *coefficients* in the like terms.

*Example 1:* Add $(3x^2 - 5x - 1)$ and $(x^2 - 6x + 3)$.

$3x^2 - 5x - 1 + x^2 - 6x + 3$      ← Write the sum.

$\quad = (3x^2 + x^2) + (-5x - 6x) + (-1 + 3)$   ← Group like terms.

$\quad = (3 + 1)x^2 + (-5 - 6)x + (-1 + 3)$   ← Use the Distributive Property.

$\quad = 4x^2 - 11x + 2$      ← Add and subtract.

To subtract a polynomial, rewrite the second polynomial to be the opposite and add to the first polynomial.

*Example 2:* Subtract $(2x^2 + x - 3)$ from $(x^2 - 3x + 1)$.

$(x^2 - 3x + 1) - (2x^2 + x - 3)$

$\quad = (x^2 - 3x + 1) + (-2x^2 - x + 3)$   ← Add the opposite of each term in the second polynomial.

$\quad = (x^2 - 2x^2) + (-3x - x) + (1 + 3)$   ← Group like terms.

$\quad = (1 - 2)x^2 + (-3 - 1)x + (1 + 3)$   ← Use the Distributive Property.

$\quad = -x^2 - 4x + 4$      ← Add and subtract.

---

**Add.**

**1.** $(x^2 + 4x) + (2x^2 - 6x)$

_____

**2.** $(3x^2 - x - 1) + (2x^2 + 2x - 1)$

_____

**3.** $(y^2 - y - 1) + (y^2 + y + 3)$

_____

**4.** $(2y^2 - y) + (y^2 + 3)$

_____

**5.** $(2k^2 + 1) + (k^2 - 2k + 5)$

_____

**6.** $(4n^2 + n - 2) + (n^2 - 3n)$

_____

**Subtract.**

**7.** $(2x^2 + 3x) - (x^2 + x)$

_____

**8.** $(3l^2 - 2l + 1) - (2l^2 + l - 3)$

_____

**9.** $(x^2 + 1) - (2x^2 + x - 1)$

_____

**10.** $(m^2 - 2m + 6) - (4m^2 - 3)$

_____

**11.** $(z^2 - 4z) - (3z^2 + 2z + 1)$

_____

**12.** $(p^2 + 6p + 5) - (3p^2 - 2p)$

_____

Name _____ Class _____ Date _____

# Practice 12-9

**Name the coefficients in each polynomial.**

**1.** $x^2 - 3x + 5$

_____

**2.** $b^2 - 4b + 3$

_____

**3.** $-2a^2 + 4a - 6$

_____

**4.** $x^3 - 2x^2 + 4x$

_____

**5.** $14y^3 + 4y + 0$

_____

**6.** $-11s^2 - 9s + 2$

_____

**Add.**

**7.** $(5x - 4) + (6x + 2)$

_____

**8.** $(3x^2 - 6x) + (x^2 + 2x)$

_____

**9.** $(7x^2 + 3x - 5) + (-4x^2 - x + 4)$

_____

**10.** $(x^2 - 2x) + (4x^2 + 7)$

_____

**11.** $(2x^2 + 8) + (3x^2 - 9)$

_____

**12.** $(7x^2 + 3x - 5) + (x^2 - 6x + 4)$

_____

**13.** $(5x^2 - 3x + 3) + (4x - 5)$

_____

**14.** $(3x^2 - 4x) + (2x^2 + x - 6)$

_____

**Find the perimeter of each figure.**

**15.**

**16.**

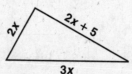

**17.**

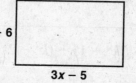

_____     _____     _____

**Subtract.**

**18.** $(4x^2 + 1) - (x^2 + 3)$

_____

**19.** $(2x^2 + 2x) - (8x + 7)$

_____

**20.** $(3x^2 + 7x - 5) - (x^2 - 4x - 1)$

_____

**21.** $(x^2 - 2x + 7) - (3x^2 - 9x + 2)$

_____

**22.** $(6x^2 + 8x + 1) - (4x^2 - 8x + 7)$

_____

**23.** $(4x^2 - 6x + 3) - (2x^2 - 7x - 9)$

_____

Name _____ Class _____ Date _____

# Reteaching 12-10

The tile model suggests how to find the area of a rectangle with length $3x + 1$ and width $2x$.

The area of the rectangle is $6x^2 + 2x$.

$\ell \cdot w = (3x + 1) \cdot 2x = 6x^2 + 2x$

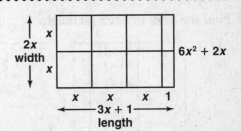

A polynomial with one term is called a *monomial*. To multiply monomials, multiply the coefficients and use the properties of exponents.

*Example 1:* Multiply $(-5x^2)(2x)$.

$(-5x^2)(2x)$

$\quad = -10 \cdot x^2 \cdot x \leftarrow$ Multiply coefficients.

$\quad = -10x^3 \qquad \leftarrow$ Add exponents.

A polynomial with two terms is called a *binomial*. Use the distributive property to find the product of a monomial and a binomial.

*Example 2:* Multiply $4x$ by $(2x + 3)$.

$4x(2x + 3)$

$\quad = 4x(2x) + 4x(3) \leftarrow$ Use the Distributive Property.

$\quad = 8x^2 + 12x \qquad \leftarrow$ Multiply monomials.

---

**Find the area of each rectangle.**

**1.**

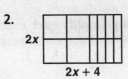

$2x + 1$

$3x$

_____

**2.**

$2x$

$2x + 4$

_____

**Simplify each expression.**

**3.** $y^2 \cdot 2y$

_____

**4.** $3x^2 \cdot 5x$

_____

**5.** $(-2n^3)(2n)$

_____

**6.** $(2x^2)(6x^2)$

_____

**7.** $(8j^2)(-4j^3)$

_____

**8.** $(-x^3)(-3x)$

_____

**Use the Distributive Property to simplify each expression.**

**9.** $z(z + 2)$

_____

**10.** $x(3x - 1)$

_____

**11.** $2b(b + 5)$

_____

**12.** $-5x(x - 4)$

_____

**13.** $-2k(k^2 + 4)$

_____

**14.** $3x^2(2x - 2)$

_____

# Practice 12-10

**Multiplying Polynomials**

**Find the area of each rectangle.**

**1.**

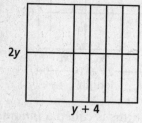

**2.**

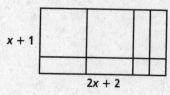

**3.**

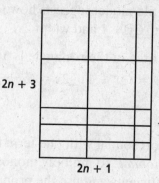

_____  _____  _____

**Simplify each expression.**

**4.** $x^2 \cdot x^2$

**5.** $7x \cdot 2x$

**6.** $(-3t)t$

**7.** $(4x^2)(-2x)$

_____  _____  _____  _____

**8.** $5m^2 \cdot 2m^2$

**9.** $(-x)(7x^2)$

**10.** $(3x^2)(-2x^3)$

**11.** $(-z)(-8z^2)$

_____  _____  _____  _____

**Use the Distributive Property to simplify each expression.**

**12.** $x(x + 2)$

**13.** $3b(b - 5)$

**14.** $2x^2(x + 9)$

_____  _____  _____

**15.** $2(a^2 + 8a + 1)$

**16.** $2x^2(4x + 1)$

**17.** $3l(l^2 + 4l - 6)$

_____  _____  _____

**Find the area of each figure.**

**18.**

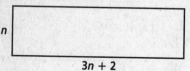

**19.**

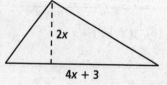

**20.**

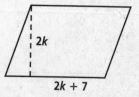

_____  _____  _____

**21.** Multiply $4x$ by $-x^2 + 2x - 9$.

_____

**22.** Multiply $-6x$ by $-2x^2 - 3x + 1$.

_____